# Washington
## IN THE PACIFIC NORTHWEST

**Michael K. Green**
**Laurie Winn Carlson**

*with* **Susan Allen Myers**

GIBBS·SMITH
P
PUBLISHER

SALT LAKE CITY

## ABOUT THE AUTHORS

**Michael K. Green, Ph.D.** was born in Spokane and has spent the past thirty-four years teaching the history of the Pacific Northwest. As professor of history at Eastern Washington University, he helped prepare college students to teach in the public schools. Dr. Green earned a Ph.D. at the University of Idaho.

**Laurie Winn Carlson** earned an M.Ed. from Arizona State University, an M.A. in history from Eastern Washington University, and is currently working on a Ph.D. She has taught students at all grade levels and published fourteen nonfiction books, for which she has received many national awards.

**Susan Allen Myers** is an author and editor and works with historians, reading specialists, authors, editors, and artists to publish quality history textbooks for elementary and secondary students. She has produced fifteen state history textbooks for schools across the country.

## CONTRIBUTORS AND REVIEWERS

**Gary Kleinknecht** is chairman of the board of directors of East Benton County Historical Society, chairman of the Social Science Department and teacher at Kamiakin High School in Kennewick, Washington, and director of education programs for the Ice Age Floods Institute.

**Kraig A. Schwartz, Ph.D.** teaches U.S. history and the history of the Pacific Northwest at Seattle Central Community College. His special area of interest is late nineteenth and early twentieth century social history.

10 09 08 07 06 05 04 03        10 9 8 7 6 5 4

Published by
Gibbs Smith, Publisher
P.O. Box 667
Layton, Utah 84041
800–748–5439
www.gibbs-smith.com/textbooks

Managing Editor: Susan Allen Myers
Associate Editors: Aimee L. Stoddard, Courtney J. Thomas

Book Designer: J. Scott Knudsen

Front Cover Photo: The Olympic Rain Forest is one of Washington's unique features. Photograph by Tom Till

Back Cover Photos: Some of Seattle's hills are leveled by powerful streams of water in the early 1900s. Young girls in Davenport celebrate the Fourth of July.

Printed and bound in China

ISBN 0-87905-988-5

THIS BOOK IS DEDICATED TO:

*Rebecca and Victoria Panwala*
*Brian Brueggeman*
*Tyler Carlson*

# Contents

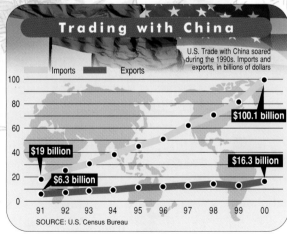

**Trading with China**

Imports    Exports

U.S. Trade with China soared during the 1990s. Imports and exports, in billions of dollars

$19 billion

$6.3 billion

$100.1 billion

$16.3 billion

91  92  93  94  95  96  97  98  99  00

SOURCE: U.S. Census Bureau

## ▷▷ PLACES TO LOCATE

Pacific Rim
Canada
British Columbia
Washington
Oregon
Idaho
Five Regions:
  Coastal Range
  Puget Sound Lowlands
  Cascade Range
  Columbia Plateau
  Rocky Mountain
Bitterroot Mountains
Olympic Mountains
Pacific Ocean
Columbia River
Snake River
Grand Coulee Dam
Seattle
Tacoma
Spokane
Tri-Cities

## ▷▷ WORDS TO UNDERSTAND

arid
commercial
confluence
finite
formidable
geography
headwaters
hinterland
human characteristics
hydroelectric
physical features
temperate
tributaries

## Washington's State Symbols:

**Flower:** Coast Rhododendron    **Bird:** Willow Goldfinch or Wild Canary    **Tree:** Western Hemlock

# The Far Corner: Washington's Geography

Mt. Rainier, the Seattle skyline, and house-boats on Lake Union illustrate how people interact with their natural environment.
*Photo by Chuck Pefley*

**Fish:** Steelhead

**Fruit:** Apple

**Insect:** Green Darner Dragonfly

## Geography and History

The study of the natural features of the earth is called ***geography***. Geography is also the study of where and how people live on the earth. Washington's coastline, rivers, mountains, deserts, forests, and plateaus have always influenced where people live and what they do for a living. Our geography even influences what people do when they seek recreation or solitude in nature.

The interaction between people and their environment is one of the most useful ways to study history. Consider how ***formidable*** nature's obstacles were for the people who traveled by boat, foot, and later by wagon. It must have been terrifying to cross wide fast rivers and clear a path through steep mountain passes with rocky cliffs falling hundreds of feet below. It was common for pioneers to view the environment as an obstacle that needed to be subdued.

Trees are planted on a hillside near the Calawah River. Replanting is one of the ways lumber companies and government agencies are preserving the environment.
*Photo by Sunny Walter*

## Physical and Human Characteristics

All locations have ***physical features*** that make them different from other places on earth. Physical features are natural to the environment and include mountains, rivers, soil, and climate, as well as plant and animal life. Washington has a striking diversity of physical features. If you travel around the state, you will see rocky beaches, beautiful islands, miles of forests, mountains, volcanoes, deep river gorges, deserts, and rich farmland.

A place is also defined by changes made by people. We call these ***human characteristics.*** What we have built and how we have altered our physical environment in other ways help to define the place we call Washington. Large cities, freeways, dams, bridges, and acres of apple trees seem natural to us, but they have not always been here.

### Preserving the Environment

There was so much land and so many forests on the frontier that settlers thought natural resources were limitless. Americans saw in the West a supply of resources they thought would last forever. A careless, wasteful attitude toward the environment was

People change the land by building roads, railroads, and dams. This is Box Canyon Dam on the Pend Oreille River. *Photo by Sunny Walter*

### WHAT DO YOU THINK?

**Only in the late twentieth century did most Americans come to recognize that our resources are *finite* and that the environment is more fragile than we had realized. Think about modern development. Think about the vital importance of protecting our environment. What can be done to satisfy both needs?**

common. Too many trees were cut down. Too many wild animals were killed. Too many salmon were taken from the water.

Later, rivers were dammed to supply water for irrigation and power to run electric generators. Railroads and highways were built through the mountains. Large parts of the Puget Sound region have actually been paved over by the many buildings, parking lots, and roads of large cities. Water and air pollution have become serious health concerns.

Today, companies act more responsibly when they cut down forests, build roads, and fish commercially. Laws have been passed that protect our water, land, plant and animal life, and the air we breathe. People are careful not to litter, and they try to conserve our natural resources. We have subdued the environment, but are we responsible enough to live in harmony with it?

One way the people of eastern Washington have changed their dry natural environment is by irrigation. Ditches carry water from man-made reservoirs to farmers' fields. The farms on the right would not be possible without irrigation.

Factories make the things we all want. They can also pollute the air and water if strict guidelines are not followed. *Photo by Shirlee Simon-Glaze*

## Location

The location of a place is like an address. Washington is located between the 46th and 49th parallels north latitude. It is between 117 degrees and 125 degrees west longitude. You can follow these lines around the world.

Some of Washington's boundaries are natural features of the land. Others were decided by people.

• British Columbia, a Canadian province, is north of Washington.

**PHYSICAL AND POLITICAL WASHINGTON**

CANADA

124°

122°

B

49°

Blaine

Lynden

Ferndale

North Cascades NP

Vancouver Island

Bellingham

L. Whatcom

Baker

SAN JUAN ISLANDS

L. Shann

Friday Harbor

Sedro-Woolley

STRAIT OF JUAN DE FUCA

Anacortes

Mount Vernon

Oak Harbor

La Conner

Coupeville

Arlington

Darrin

Ozette L.

Port Angeles

Port Townsend

Sol Duc R.

Sequim

Langley

Marysville

L. Crescent

48°

Forks

Mukilteo

Everett

Edmonds

Inde

Poulsbo

Lynnwood

Olympic NP

Olympic NP

Seattle

Washington

Skykomis

Quinault River

Bellevue

Sammamish L.

Bremerton

Retsil

Issaquah

L. Cushman

Normandy Park

Renton

Gig Harbor

Kent

Shelton

Fort Lewis

Tacoma

Enumclaw

Olympia

Lacey

Mount Rainier NP

Aberdeen

Tenino

Eatonville

Westport

Alder L.

Oakville

Centralia

Raymond

Chehalis

South Bend

Pe Ell

Mayfield L.

Riffe L.

Rimroc

Winlock

Mossyrock

Vader

Long Beach

Ilwaco

Castle Rock

Kelso

Pacific

Longview

46°

Ocean

L. Merwin

Swift Res.

Yale L.

Woodland

Battle Ground

COLUMBIA RIV

Vancouver

124°

123°

122°

- The Pacific Ocean forms the western boundary.
- Idaho and Oregon are on the other sides. Which river forms our southern border?

## A Hinterland

Washington is located on the "far corner" of the United States. For much of its history,

Washington's remote location has resulted in a ***hinterland*** status. Hinterland is a term used by geographers to describe a region that is far from other settled areas. Hinterland regions are usually the last to be explored and populated. They usually export raw materials and import many manufactured goods.

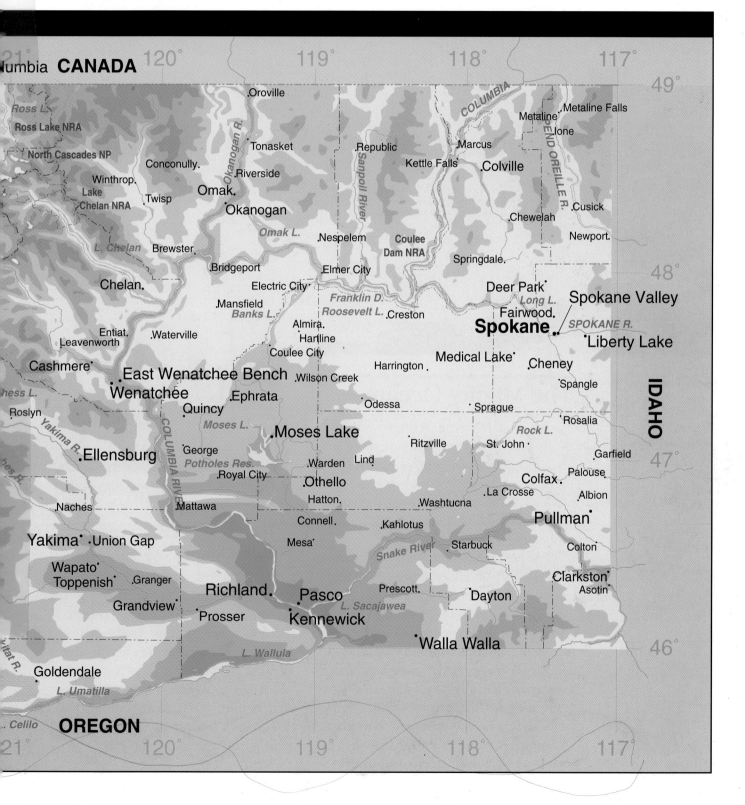

Gulls hover over the water after a storm on the Olympic Peninsula.
*Photo by Sunny Walter*

# The Mighty Ocean

Our state's western border is the Pacific Ocean. Washington has only 157 miles of ocean coastline, but there are over 3,000 miles of shoreline along the Strait of Juan de Fuca, the numerous bays and inlets of Puget Sound, and around the islands.

Washington has more deep-water harbors than either California or Oregon. Shipping goods in and out of our harbors links Washington to the rest of the world. The Pacific Ocean and Puget Sound are the source of the state's **commercial** fishing industry. Fishing provides less than one percent of the state's income, but it is still significant. Salmon accounts for about one-third of the fishing income, followed by oysters, crabs, and shrimp. Other fish caught in ocean waters are halibut, flounder, tuna, and cod.

A freighter is outbound from Grays Harbor.
*Photo by Robert Esposito*

## A Mild Climate

More important than the beautiful scenery it provides, the ocean has an important influence on our land and climate. Westerly winds from the Pacific give Washington a **temperate** climate. This is because the temperature of large bodies of water does not change as quickly as the temperature of the air. The warmer water of the ocean warms up the air next to it. Winds pick up the warmer air and carry it across the land.

Compare the wet rain forest along the coast to the dryness of the land east of the mountains. What are the two main landforms that cause the differences in climate?

*Photo of rain forest by Tom Till. Photo of sagebrush on the plateau by Mike Green*

## The Rain Shadow Effect

**H**igh mountain ranges greatly affect the climate of a place. Here is what happens. Far out over the Pacific Ocean, winds pick up moisture from evaporating ocean water. The moist air blows over the coast and continues east. When the air reaches the mountains, it must rise to get over them. As air rises, it cools. Cool air cannot hold as much moisture as warm air does, so the moisture falls to the earth as rain or snow.

This means that the land along the coast and on the west side of the Cascade Mountains is rainy. Some parts of western Washington receive over 100 inches of rain per year. It rains almost every day. Washington's west side is often called the "wet side."

By the time the winds go up over the mountains and reach the east side of the Cascades, the air has very little moisture left. The dry winds continue east. This is why the eastern regions of the state are so dry. Some *arid* regions in Washington receive less than six inches of rain each year.

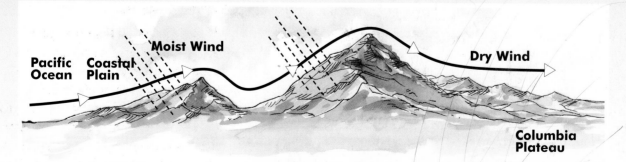

**Pacific Ocean** | **Coastal Plain** | **Moist Wind** | **Dry Wind** | **Columbia Plateau**

# Regions

Regions are places that share common features. There are land regions, political regions, and commercial regions. You live in several different regions at the same time. You might live in a city, a county, a voting district, a school sports region, and the Pacific Northwest.

## The Pacific Rim—a Trading Region

The Pacific Rim is a huge trading region that includes all the countries that border the Pacific Ocean. Each country around the rim makes products that other countries want to buy. For example, the people of the United States buy clothing made in China and the Philippines. We buy cars, televisions, and electronic equipment made in Japan. Washington exports aircraft, wheat, fruit, and computer software to China, Japan, Korea, and many other countries on the Pacific Rim.

Goods in large metal cases are constantly being shipped across the Pacific. The ships move in and out of port cities in Washington, Oregon, and California. Ships from the East Coast and Europe come here too, passing first through the Panama Canal.

**THE PACIFIC RIM**

ASIA

NORTH AMERICA

SOUTH AMERICA

AUSTRALIA

In our port cities, goods are loaded onto trucks and trains and moved to other places in the United States and Canada.

## The Pacific Northwest

The Pacific Northwest is a region of states that share similar landforms and early pioneer history. Washington, Oregon, and Idaho have tall snowy mountains and rushing rivers. Evergreen forests, dry grasslands, and farming valleys are part of the whole region. The region is divided from the rest of the United States by the Rocky Mountains.

As you read through the chapters of this book, you will notice that our early history is the same as the early history of the other states in the Pacific Northwest. Indians moved freely across the land. Then fur trappers, missionaries, and pioneer settlers came to what was called the Oregon Country. It included today's Idaho, Washington, and Oregon.

**THE PACIFIC NORTHWEST**

WASHINGTON

OREGON

IDAHO

## Landforms

Landforms are features of the earth's surface. They are the result of powerful forces moving inside and outside the earth's surface. Some of these forces result in volcanoes and earthquakes. Others move oceans and even continents. Landforms are also the result of wind and water wearing away the earth's surface.

## LANDFORMS

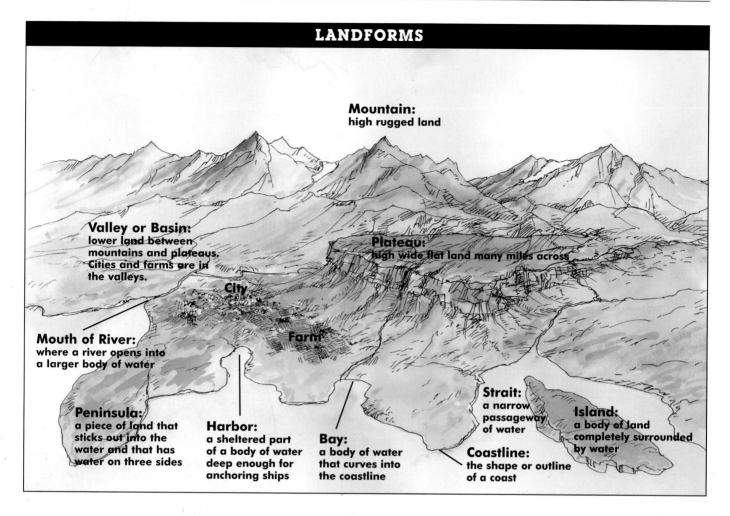

**Mountain:** high rugged land

**Valley or Basin:** lower land between mountains and plateaus. Cities and farms are in the valleys.

**Plateau:** high wide flat land many miles across

City

Farm

**Mouth of River:** where a river opens into a larger body of water

**Peninsula:** a piece of land that sticks out into the water and that has water on three sides

**Harbor:** a sheltered part of a body of water deep enough for anchoring ships

**Bay:** a body of water that curves into the coastline

**Strait:** a narrow passageway of water

**Coastline:** the shape or outline of a coast

**Island:** a body of land completely surrounded by water

## Washington's Five Land Regions

Washington can be divided into five land regions. Each region has at least one main type of landform, but may contain more. Major landforms are **mountains** and hills, **plateaus** (high, wide, flat areas hundreds of miles across), and **lowlands** that stretch to the ocean. **Basins** (wide bowl-shaped areas also called valleys) are surrounded by mountains or plateaus. Rivers, oceans, and lakes are also called landforms because they are natural features of the earth.

Each of our state's land regions is unique. Starting at the western coast and moving across the state, the land regions are:

- Coastal Range
- Puget Sound Lowlands
- Cascade Range
- Columbia Plateau
- Rocky Mountain

### WASHINGTON'S LAND REGIONS

Coastal Range

Puget Sound Lowlands

Cascade Range

Rocky Mountain

Columbia Plateau

Coastal
Range

The Olympics are
jagged mountains
with snowcapped
peaks year round.
*Photo by Eugene Kiver*

A gray whale comes
right up to a tour
boat near Westport.
*Photo by Sunny Walter*

## The Coastal Range Region

On the Olympic Peninsula there is a rain forest that supports such a profusion of plant life that naturalist Roger Tory Peterson proclaimed it "the greatest weight of living matter, per acre, in the world." This narrow region offers the beauty of the Pacific Coast, the rainforest you can see on page 9, the snowcapped Olympic Mountains, and the thick forests. Olympic National Park is part of this region.

There is little industry in the region since most lumber mills have closed and commercial fishing is in decline. The small towns rely on tourism.

There are five Indian reservations on the coast and one along the strait.

## The Puget Sound Lowlands

Large cities such as Seattle, Tacoma, Bellevue, Bremerton, Bellingham, Everett, and Olympia, the state capital, make this region the population center of the state. Seattle is the heart of the region. Home to Microsoft, one of the world's largest corporations, this region boasts one of the highest per capita income levels in the country. Traffic congestion is considered one of the worst in the country. This is a bustling, crowded, exciting, prosperous region.

Deep-water seaports on Puget Sound and other ports on the Columbia River are important for the shipping industry. The bays, harbors, and San Juan Islands are popular recreation and vacation places.

Not everyone in the lowlands lives in cities, of course. One of the state's richest farming areas is the Skagit River Valley. Tulips and daffodils are the most famous crop. Peas, carrots, cauliflower, broccoli, and other crops are grown for their seeds or are canned or frozen. The Cowlitz and Chehalis River Valleys are also farming regions. Dairy cattle and chickens are raised for profit.

Puget
Sound
Lowlands

Miles of daffodils and tulips are grown in the Skagit Valley near Mt. Vernon. Selling the flowers and bulbs brings income to the people there. *Photo by Chuck Pefley*

Seattle shines at sunset. *Photo by Chuck Pefley*

Tacoma and Commencement Bay on Puget Sound are seen from the air. Seattle is in the distance. *Photo by Chuck Pefley*

A ferryboat glides between islands on the Strait of Juan de Fuca. *Photo by Chuck Pefley*

## The Cascade Range Region

The Cascade Mountain range, with its high volcanic peaks and many glaciers, is considered Washington's most prominent geographic feature. These rugged mountains cut across the state, dividing the land sharply. They are a barrier to commerce and travel.

The mountains are sometimes called the "Cascade Curtain." This term recognizes the very different interests of the large seaport and manufacturing cities in the west and

the less-populated agricultural regions in the east.

The mountains also contribute to the startling differences in climate and rainfall between the eastern and western sections of the state. The land to the west of the mountains is rainy. Hemlocks, firs, and cedar forests grow in the damp climate. The forests of the western slopes are thick with mosses, ferns, and bushes growing beneath the trees. The eastern mountain slopes get

Glacier Peak towers in the North Cascades.

Cascade Range

much less rain, so sparse ponderosa pine forests flourish there.

Five famous mountains are part of this region—Mt. St. Helens, Mt. Rainier, Mt. Adams, Mt. Baker, and Glacier Peak. Lake Chelan is also part of the region.

Two national parks, the North Cascades and Mt. Rainier, bring thousands of visitors to view the breathtaking beauty of the mountains. You will read more about Mt. St. Helens in Chapter 2.

## Mountain Travel

The Cascades are not the great obstacle to travel they were in past years, though two of the five mountain passes are closed in the winter. Early wagon roads across the mountains were a dangerous adventure. Railroad access came only late in the 1800s. Now the four-lane Interstate 90 traverses the mountains through Snoqualmie Pass. When winter snows pile up and the threat of avalanches is great, however, Snoqualmie Pass can be closed for days at a time. Travelers just have to wait.

*Photo by Barbara MacNulty*

Travel over Snoqualmie Pass was quite different in 1919 than in 2000. The trip from Seattle to Spokane took three days in 1919. It takes four or five hours today. *Photo by Mike Green*

Snoqualmie Pass

## The Columbia Plateau

On the other side of the Cascades is the Columbia Plateau region. The high flat plateau covers most of eastern Washington and parts of Oregon and Idaho. It includes some of the driest land in the Pacific Northwest. Natural vegetation ranges from grassland to desert sagebrush.

The region includes the wheat growing area of the Palouse and the huge Columbia Basin Irrigation Project made possible by Grand Coulee Dam. These irrigated lands grow a large variety of crops, including apples, cherries, grapes, corn, and alfalfa.

Spokane is the metropolitan center of the Columbia Plateau. Spokane is the commercial, financial, and medical center of a large region covering parts of surrounding states and southern British Columbia. Other cities on the plateau are Yakima, Moses Lake, Wenatchee, Walla Walla, Pullman, and the Tri-Cities (Richland, Pasco, and Kennewick).

### WHAT DO YOU THINK?

**Why do you think the cities on the Puget Sound Lowlands attract more people than places on the Columbia Plateau? What factors of geography affect where people start cities, where industry thrives, and where farming is successful?**

The climate and soil of the Columbia Plateau prove ideal for growing grapes. Washington's wine industry has flourished in recent years. *Photo by Otto Stevens*

Moving water has cut deep canyons and river gorges through the rock at Palouse Falls. *Photo by Barbara Murray*

Columbia Plateau

Wheat and peas as far as the eye can see are harvested in the Palouse Hills. *Photo by Otto Stevens*

Spokane is seen from the North Hill across to South Hill. *Photo by Chuck Pefley*

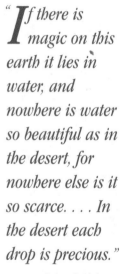

"*If there is magic on this earth it lies in water, and nowhere is water so beautiful as in the desert, for nowhere else is it so scarce. . . . In the desert each drop is precious.*"

—Edward Abbey

Washington State University lies in the beautiful town of Pullman. *Photo by Chuck Pefley*

# THE COLUMBIA RIVER

The Columbia River flows to the Pacific Ocean, forming the border between Washington and Oregon.

*Photo by Chuck Pefley*

Our southern border is formed by the "Great River of the West," as it was called by early explorers. The river has its **headwaters** at Columbia Lake, high in British Columbia, Canada. The river enters Washington flowing south, then sweeps around the "Big Bend" to its **confluence** with the Snake River. Carrying the water of both rivers, the Columbia turns west. Cutting through the Cascades in the spectacular Columbia Gorge, the river continues to flow to the sea.

When summer arrives and mountain snow melts, what happens to all the water? Much of it flows in thousands of tiny streams into larger streams, then into rivers. These **tributaries** eventually become part of the mighty Columbia River, and the water

flows into the Pacific Ocean. In this way, the Columbia River drains water from the mountains like the drain in a sink.

The river's course across the state helps to explain much of Washington's history. Early explorers hoped it would provide a waterway all the way across the continent. Indian tribes and early fur trappers relied on it for transportation in their large canoes and as a source of food. The river became the source of a thriving commercial salmon industry. Railroads followed its route through the Cascades, while steamboats braved its wild waters.

The river's huge volume of water, together with its very steep fall in elevation, makes it the most powerful river in North America in terms of **hydroelectric** energy. Major dams on the river produce more electricity than any other state. By the late 1900s, the Columbia had been so altered by dams it was called an "engineered" river. The wild river was tamed. Roosevelt Reservoir behind Grand Coulee Dam and Banks Lake behind Dry Falls Dam are man-made lakes that are welcomed as recreation places in dry regions.

Grand Coulee Dam provides electricity and flood control for the Columbia Plateau.

Power lines carry electricity from the dams to the cities.
*Photo by Barbara Murray*

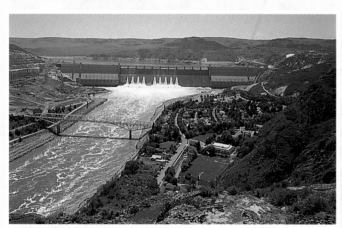

## WASHINGTON'S MAJOR RIVERS

Kayaking is great sport on the rapids of the Elwha River. *Photo by Sunny Walter*

"Round 'em up!" Ranchers take cattle from higher pastures to the lower valleys for the winter.
*Photo by Jim Oltersdorf*

Rocky Mountain

| National Parks | |
| --- | --- |
| **National Park** | **Date Created** |
| Mt. Rainier | 1899 |
| Olympic | 1938 |
| North Cascades | 1963 |
| Klondike Gold Rush (downtown Seattle) | 1976 |

## The Rocky Mountain Region

This region in the corner of the state is sometimes called the Okanogan Highlands. The steep hills are foothills of the great Rocky Mountains.

To make a living in this region, people rely on farming, mining lead and zinc, ranching, and lumbering. A few small towns depend on tourism. Native Americans live on three reservations.

## A Generous Uncle Sam

In early United States history, two factors greatly influenced every aspect of this region's settlement and economic development:

One was the vastness of the land—thousands and thousands of miles of open spaces far from settled areas in the East.

The other was that the United States government either bought land from other countries, got it by Indian treaties, or won it in war. Then the government gave away, free or at very low cost, large pieces of land to pioneer homesteaders, cattlemen, timber companies, miners, and the railroad.

# Washington's National Parks

National parks are government-protected places that are unique in some way. They are set aside so everyone can enjoy nature. Changes to the land, such as roads and buildings, are kept to a minimum. The parks are a refuge for natural plants and animals.

Washington has three national parks and several national historic parks:

**Olympic National Park** has a constant wet climate. On the ocean beaches of the park, you can search for interesting rocks and shells and climb on huge driftwood logs that have been carried ashore by the ocean. Just beyond the beaches, a rain forest, thick and green and full of many kinds of plants, is unique in North America. Only trails penetrate this mountain wilderness.

**Mt. Rainier National Park** was the first national park in Washington and one of the first in the United States. A giant volcano is covered with glaciers. Lower slopes are decorated with dense forests and flowering meadows. Skilled mountain climbers find this highest peak in the state—and one of the highest in North America—a challenge. For other nature lovers, miles of high mountain roads offer splendid views.

San Juan Island

North Cascades

Klondike Gold Rush

Mount Rainier

Olympic

**North Cascades National Park** is a breathtakingly beautiful place to visit. Jagged glaciated peaks loom above an alpine region of meadows, forests, fast-running streams, and spectacular waterfalls. The park is rich in wildlife.

**Klondike Gold Rush National Historic Park** is located in downtown Seattle. The park tells the city's historic role as the beginning site for trips to the Alaskan gold fields in the mid-1800s.

**San Juan Island National Historic Park** is the site of British and American military campsites when the United States and Great Britain both claimed the islands.

**Whitman Mission National Historic Site** is where Marcus and Narcissa Whitman started an Indian mission and were later massacred. The Whitmans provided education and religious instruction to the native people and assistance to pioneers on the Oregon Trail.

# Canada, Our Northern Neighbor

An important feature of Washington's geography is its border with Canada's British Columbia. Relationships between the people in both countries are friendly. People can move freely between the two countries without a passport. Vancouver Island and Victoria are favorite vacation places for U.S. tourists.

There are, however, complicated trade issues about fishing rights, lumber sales, and pollution problems in shared waters. Since the Columbia River flows through Canada and the United States, both countries are concerned about the use of water for irrigation, shipping, fishing, and the electricity generated at the dams on the river. These issues involve negotiations between both national governments.

*Photo by Chuck Pefley*

## CHAPTER 1 REVIEW

1. Define geography and describe how geography and history are related.

2. Define and give examples of physical and human characteristics of a place.

3. Why did pioneers often regard the environment as an adversary?

4. What are Washington's most serious environmental problems?

5. What can people do today to preserve the natural environment?

6. Name the country, states, and bodies of water that form Washington's boundaries.

7. List at least two important ways that the Pacific Ocean affects the land and people of Washington.

8. What are the three most common types of landforms in Washington? What bodies of water are also considered landforms?

9. What type of region is the Pacific Rim? How does Washington's place on the Pacific Rim give us an advantage in a global economy?

10. List our state's five land regions.

11. Which two land regions have the highest population?

12. Which land region is mostly at sea level, but also has a rainforest and mountains?

13. Which land region is the driest?

14. Name three large cities in the Puget Sound Lowlands.

15. Name three land features or cities in the Columbia Plateau.

16. The Columbia River has its headwaters in

_____ _____.

17. Name a large tributary of the Columbia River.

18. List at least three ways the Columbia and the dams on the river help the people of Washington.

Fire and Ice

## PEOPLE TO KNOW

J. Harlen Bretz

## PLACES TO LOCATE

Asia
North America
Pacific Northwest
Columbia Plateau
Palouse Hills
Cascades
Olympic Mountains
Okanogan Mountains
San Juan Islands
Mt. St. Helens
Mt. Rainier
Grand Coulee
Dry Falls
Puget Sound
Columbia River
Toutle River

## WORDS TO UNDERSTAND

abrasive
aquifer
basalt
cataracts
continental drift
coulee
decompose
deluge
dormant
erratics
fault lines
fissure
geologic time
geologist
igneous rock
lahars
loess
molten
sedimentary
tectonics

## A Timeline of Washington's Geologic History

*MYA means millions of years ago

| TIMELINE 600 mya* | 500 mya | 400 mya |
|---|---|---|

**Precambrian Era**
(85% of the earth's time period)

**Paleozoic Era** (570–240) MYA
Pangaea supercontinent divides.
Shallow seas cover most of North America.
Trilobites, amphibians, and reptiles live in the seas.
Coal is formed.

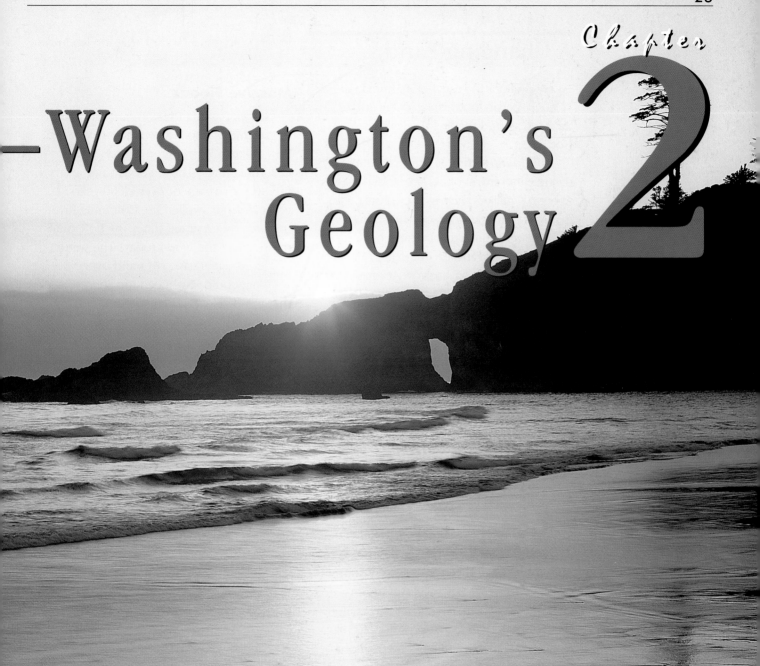

# Washington's Geology

Geologic forces drastically changed our coastline. Millions of years ago, the coast was in the Spokane region. Second Beach in Olympic National Park is elegant at sunset. *Photo by Tom Till*

| 300 mya | 200 mya | 100 mya | PRESENT |
|---|---|---|---|

**Mesozoic Era** (240–65) MYA
Sedimentary rock is formed.
Rocky Mountains begin to take shape.
Okanogan micro-continent joins North America.

**Cenozoic Era** (65 MYA to present)
North Cascades micro-continent docks against the mainland.
Volcanic activity forms the Cascade Range.
Lava flow forms the Columbian Plateau.
Ice Age glaciers blanket northern Washington.
Glaciers carve valleys. Melting ice forms lakes.
Pacific Coast changes as ice melts.
Grand Coulee and Dry Falls were eroded by floods.
Olympic Mountains are formed.
Humans hunt mammoths in the Pacific Northwest.

# A Changing Land

Millions of years before human life began, powerful geologic forces started shaping the Pacific Northwest.

*Continental drift* is a term used to describe movement of the largest land masses. About 200 million years ago, scientists think that Africa, Europe, and North and South America were joined together in a huge super-continent called Pangaea. Then the continents drifted apart, creating a narrow Atlantic Ocean. The Atlantic Ocean widened, causing North America to move west. The Atlantic has continued to widen one to three inches a year.

### ANCIENT PANGAEA

*A* Micro-continent is a very small continent.

## A Jigsaw Puzzle

The shape of North America also changed. Eastern Washington used to be part of the coast of the North American continent. Spokane would have been on that seashore long ago. The rest of our land was still underwater.

Land areas along the old coast changed as a result of a collision between the continent and the floor of the Pacific Ocean. A piece of the old coastal plain was crushed into a long belt of folded *sedimentary* rock. A portion of this belt extending from Washington into British Columbia is called the Kootenay Arc.

The next pieces of the puzzle to be added were the Okanogan and North Cascades micro-continents.

*Tectonic* forces caused the micro-continents to "dock" against the main continent. Many of the fossil remains found in the North Cascades resemble those of a similar age found in Southeast Asia. The North Cascades' granite rock is different than the volcanic rock of the rest of the Cascade Range. This leads geologists to believe that the landmass was once a separate continent joined to Asia.

## Massive Floods

Starting about 15,000 years ago, a series of enormous floods swept across what is now eastern Washington and down the Columbia River. These floods came every fifty to sixty years for over 2,000 years. A great *deluge* swelled the Columbia River until it contained ten times the flow of all the rivers in the world today! The water eroded the landcape over and over.

What could have been the source of all that water? How did it affect our current landscape? What geologic changes are still occurring today?

## Fossils Are Clues to the Past

Fossils tell us what kinds of animals and plants once lived in a region. Sometimes the imprints are found in rocks. Sometimes thousands of shells are found in layers of rock. Sometimes entire skeletons of ancient animals and people are unearthed.

Shells and bones from ancient sea life tell us that oceans once covered our land. Fossils of ferns and other plants in central Washington indicate that a large tropical rainforest once flourished there.

## Fossil Fuels

Coal was formed by the combination of prehistoric plants, heat, and pressure over millions of years. In the wet climate of prehistoric times, ferns and other plants lived and died. Just like today, they *decomposed,* layer upon layer. In

*Geologists study rocks, land formations, and fossils to learn the history of the land.*

## GEOLOGIC JIGSAW

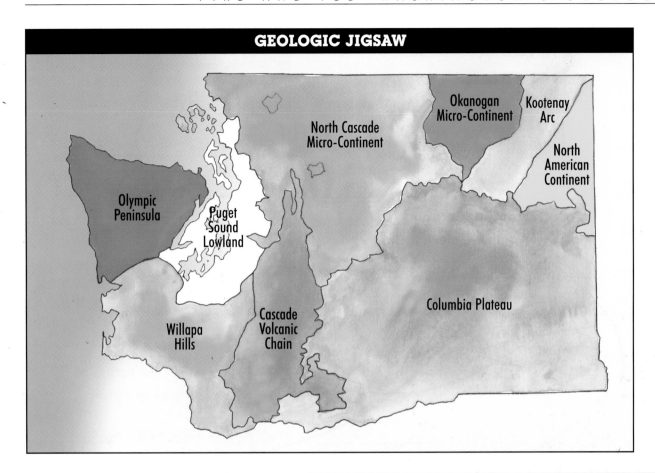

time, rock and earth covered the plants. Later, when mountains were thrust upward, the rock sometimes contained layers of coal. Other deposits were still under the ground.

Today, coal is burned to provide the heat that boils the water that makes the steam that runs the generators that produce electricity. There are fairly large coal deposits in King, Kittitas, and Lewis counties.

## Plate Tectonics

**T**ectonic forces are strong forces in the earth that cause landmasses to move. They also cause the earth to fold and crack.

The earth's crust may be made up of around twenty moving plates. These plates carry both the earth's continents and pieces of the ocean floor. In some places plates spread apart, and in other places they collided with, or scraped against, each other.

## Earthquake!

**T**ectonic forces left *fault lines*—fractures in the earth's crust—in the Puget Sound region and off the Pacific Coast. A shift in one of the landmasses causes earthquakes every few years.

About a thousand years ago, there was a major earthquake where Seattle is now. More recent large shakes occurred in 1949, 1965, and 2001. The potential for a "big one" is always there.

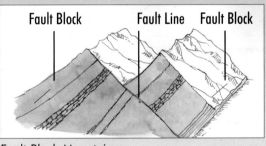

Fault-Block Mountains

Folded Mountains

# Forming Our Mountains

**M**ountain ranges were uplifted, tilted, and folded in various ways. You can see the folded and tilted layers of rock as you explore mountain canyons. The uplifting is partly the result of the tectonic forces that pushed huge ridges of land against each other. Where the two landmasses met, land ridges were forced upward.

After the mountains were formed, erosion by moving wind, water, and ice started immediately. That is why older mountains are more rounded, and younger mountains are more jagged.

The Rocky Mountains are the oldest mountains in the West. Both the Cascades and the Olympic Mountains are much younger. Because so much of our land was still underwater when the mountains were forming, the Olympic Mountains, the youngest in the state, were once off-shore islands.

**MOUNTAIN CHAINS OF THE PACIFIC NORTHWEST**

Olympic Mtns.

Cascade Mtns.

Rocky Mtns.

The sun rises over the Olympic Range near Mt. Olympus, as it has for millions of years. The Olympic Mountains are some of the newest in the world. *Photo by Tom Till*

Mt. Angelos in the Olympics shows the dramatic upthrusting of what were once horizontal sedimentary rock layers. Now they stand on end!
*Photo by Eugene Kiver*

When the Okanogan micro-continent slid into the mainland, sedimentary rock layers tilted upward. *Photo by Eugene Kiver*

## Mountains of Fire

M ountains were also formed by volcanic action. After the upthrusting, folding, and faulting, volcanic activity occurred in both the Cascade and Olympic Mountains. They are part of a great Ring of Fire that includes volcanoes in Indonesia, the Philippines, Japan, Alaska, and the west coast of North and South America. How were these tall mountains formed?

Steam and gases expanded inside the earth until the pressure was too great for the earth to withstand. Then ***molten*** (liquid) rock called lava rose to the surface of the earth's crust in a violent explosion. The lava flowed down the mountainside, building it higher and higher.

The Cascades include Washington's five "sleeping giants." Mt. Baker, Glacier Peak, Mt. Rainier, Mt. Adams, and Mt. St. Helens are ***dormant*** now. That means they are not active. No one knows when they will "wake up" and again cover the land around them with lava, mud, and ash.

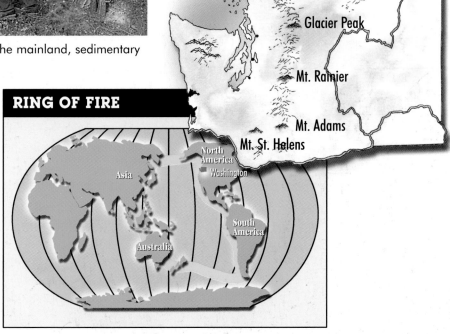

### LINKING THE PAST TO THE PRESENT

**If you live in a region that might be affected by volcanic eruption, floods, earthquakes, or other geologic activity, call your state emergency preparedness office to see if there are plans to deal with a catastrophe. Is your family prepared for an emergency?**

RING OF FIRE

# THE LESSONS OF MT. ST. HELENS

It was May 18, 1980. Mt. St. Helens awoke with an eruption equal to 21,000 atomic bombs the size of those dropped on Japan at the end of World War II. This mountain was the youngest of the Cascade volcanoes and had been fairly active over the past 300 years. It was so active, in fact, that Indians had been afraid of the mountain and seldom traveled on the highest places.

the river, closing it to ocean-going vessels.

A towering cloud of ash and gas from the erupting volcano rose 12 miles into the air, where winds carried it across the continent. Ash choked automobile air filters, causing vehicles to stall. In Spokane, 200 miles to the east, visibility was reduced to 10 feet and the airport was forced to close.

In the immediate blast area, ice and snow were melted quickly. Tens of thousands of stately Douglas firs 6 feet in diameter and 200 feet tall were laid flat over an area of 250 square miles. The earth beneath them was blown away to bedrock. All the wild land animals, fish, and birds were killed.

The damage from the eruption was caused by gas, ash, and flowing mud. *Photo by Don Wilson*

Mt. St. Helens loomed tall before the eruption. *Photo by Karen Jacobsen*

Mt. St. Helens

*No lava flowed from the mountain during the eruption.*

A few months earlier, in late March, tremors deep in the mountain signaled that an eruption was likely. By early May, a large bulge began to form on the mountain's north side. A week later, a large patch of the mountain turned into a churning brown liquid mass and began to slide downward. Then came an enormous explosion and a chain reaction of catastrophic events.

The collapsing mountain filled the north fork of the Toutle River with debris 600 feet deep. **Lahars**, huge mud flows containing boulders and uprooted trees, filled the river all the way to its junction with the Cowlitz River. That river carried the load down to the Columbia River, where the mud clogged up

## Deadly Consequences

Fifty-seven people lost their lives in the eruption. Probably the first to die was David Johnston, a geologist who had permission to set up his monitoring equipment six miles north of the mountain. Johnston and his colleagues had greatly underestimated the wide range and force of the eruption. He had time for one brief radio message. "Vancouver, Vancouver, this is it!" were his last words. His jeep, trailer, and his body were never found.

Why did people risk their lives by staying so close to the mountain? The story of eighty-four-year-old Harry R. Truman provides one explanation. Truman had operated a resort on Spirit Lake since 1926. When he was urged to leave, Truman stubbornly refused. He had a lot of money invested in his lodge. He had sixteen cats that depended on him. This was his home, filled with memories of his wife who had died. As he put it, "If the mountain did do something, I'd rather go right here with it." Truman was buried under several hundred feet of volcanic debris.

## The Mountain Today

Nature destroys, but it also heals. Plants and animals are slowly reclaiming the scarred landscape, and the mountain has become a place to study volcanoes, earthquakes, and changes to the environment.

The top of Mt. St. Helens was blown away, leaving only a huge rock crater. Spirit Lake is now filled with debris.
*Photo by Lori Smith*

Visitors to the three Mt. St. Helens National Monument visitor centers typically ask two questions. The first: "Will the mountain explode again?" The answer is "Yes." The second: "When?" The answer is "We do not know."

In *geologic time*, the eruption was an ordinary event, typical of the forces that have always shaped our physical environment. It serves as a powerful reminder that geologic forces continue to work.

## Our Most Dangerous Volcano

Geologists today are concerned about Mt. Rainier, Washington's largest dormant volcano. Mt. Rainier, a towering pile of loose rocks and a cubic mile of glacier ice, looms over the Puget Sound region near Seattle and Tacoma.

Rainier's capacity for destruction is truly frightening. Geologists consider the mountain to be dangerously unstable. If Rainier collapses in an earthquake or the volcano erupts, an avalanche of red-hot lava and ash will sweep down the mountain. Huge lahars of mud and ice will travel swiftly down river valleys. Thousands of people will have less than an hour to flee the destruction. Geologists predict a one-in-seven chance of that happening in the lifetime of anyone living in the potential path of destruction.

*One comes more intimately in touch with the mountains when he travels the trails. . . . Here where vegetation makes its last stand amid a world of ice and snow, with the lower world stretching away to the horizon, nature unfolds in all her beauty.*

—Asahel Curtis, naturalist

Mt. Rainier

Mt. Rainier's enormous ice cap looms beautiful and threatening. *Photo by Asahel Curtis*

# Forming the Columbia Plateau

**V**olcanic activity formed more than mountains. Lava also helped form the relatively flat Columbia Plateau. It is one of the largest and most spectacular volcanic regions in the world. Repeated eruptions from long ***fissures*** (cracks in the earth's crust) covered the plateau with lava that sometimes spread out more than 100 miles from its source.

## Rich Soil of the Palouse

After the lava flows ended, another feature changed the landscape. Rich soil was formed by deposits of glacial ***loess***. Loess is a mixture of fine volcanic ash and dust carried by wind before being deposited on the ground in another place. Soil up to 150 feet deep gradually covered large regions of rock. Today, this is the Palouse wheat-growing region in eastern Washington.

### Basalt

**B**asalt is ***igneous rock***, formed of hardened lava. Overlapping basalt layers of the plateau are up to over 4,000 feet deep, leaving geologists to speculate about what might be buried beneath them.

Palouse Hills

Columbia Plateau

Basalt takes many forms when it cools. This form, in columns, was more easily eroded. *Photo by Mike Green*

Loess soil on Steptoe Butte forms the rich farmland of the Palouse Hills region. *Photo by Bill McKinney*

The falls on the river in downtown Spokane are the result of a smaller basalt flow that originated on the city's South Hill and moved down across the river. *Photo by Barbara Murray*

# Ice Age Washington

A long time after the major lava flows ceased, the air got much colder. Snow fell much of the year. Snow and ice accumulated, and the polar ice cap moved southward. The continental ice sheet moved into what is now Canada and the northern areas of what is now the United States. The cooling and warming happened over and over again. We call the last glacial period the Ice Age. It happened about one million to ten thousand years ago.

*A mile is 5,280 feet. Glaciers were over a mile thick in some places.*

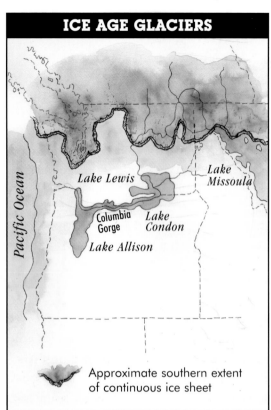

## ICE AGE GLACIERS

Approximate southern extent of continuous ice sheet

Huge boulders that were carried long distances by glaciers or glacial melt flood water are called **erratics**. This one is located a few miles southwest of the Tri-Cities and probably came from northern Idaho.
*Photo by Gary Kleinknecht*

The moving glaciers shaped the Puget Sound lowlands, filling in some areas of the landscape and carving out others. The ice sheet was 5,000 feet thick over the place where the city of Bellingham is today. It was 4,000 feet thick over the place where Seattle is today, and 1,800 feet over the Tacoma region. The Ice Age glaciers ended south of present-day Olympia.

## The Great Floods

Glacial action also produced the great floods described at the start of this chapter. The ice sheet blocked the Clark Fork River near the present Idaho-Montana border, forming an ice dam half a mile high. The water backed up and formed a prehistoric lake. Lake Missoula was larger than any lake in the western United States today. It was about half as large as Lake Michigan. When the rising water from glacial melt became deep enough, the force of the water tore over and through the ice dam, unleashing an immense flood. Ice, debris, and water rushed out at speeds of up to fifty miles per hour.

The progression of the glacier then created a new dam and formed a new lake that produced yet another flood. This process was repeated every 50 years or so for 2,000 years. The site of today's city of Spokane was repeatedly covered by water over 500 feet deep. Today, Spokane draws its water from a huge **aquifer** created by the great floods.

Filled with rocks and chunks of ice as **abrasive** agents, the floods spread out across the Columbia Plateau, leaving a sculptured landscape where there had been a mostly level landscape before the floods.

## Grand Coulee

Large sections of eastern Washington were sculpted by ice and flood water. The ice plugged the Columbia River and forced the water out of its regular channel. Water flowed across the Columbia Plateau, eroding the rock of the Grand Coulee. A *coulee* is a dry streambed.

Today, the Grand Coulee is one of the state's most spectacular geologic features. It is between one and six miles wide and fifty miles long. Halfway down the channel is Dry Falls, site of the largest prehistoric waterfall the world has ever known. During Ice Age melting, water spread out over three miles, thundering over the 400-foot-high falls.

Geologists now think that at the very peak of the huge floods, Dry Falls and the five smaller *cataracts* (large waterfalls) to the east were actually submerged for a time. As the glaciers melted and the ice dams broke up, the waters retreated, leaving the coulee region high and dry. This process was repeated many times.

Millions of years ago, the falls were the largest in the world. Tons of water cascaded over the basalt cliffs. Dry Falls, like its name implies, has no water flowing over its basalt cliffs anymore.
*Photo by Dale Stradling*

Dry Falls

*Washington* PORTRAIT

# J. HARLEN BRETZ

The story of the great floods is a geological detective story. America's leading geologists could not agree that the floods existed. There was one geologist, however, who spent most of his life trying to convince his colleagues that the floods had actually happened. From the early 1920s through the 1960s, J. Harlen Bretz argued the case of the Spokane Flood. His peers scoffed at his ideas, but he persevered. How else, he said, could you explain the breadth and depth of the water-scoured coulees, the enormous gravel bars topped with giant ripple marks, and the huge abandoned cataracts and dry water falls?

Slowly, the Bretz theory came to be accepted by his fellow geologists. By then, Bretz was nearly ninety years old. Satellite photographs now show the full extent of the flood-ravaged land that Bretz laboriously explored on foot. Today, in recognition of his accomplishment, most geologists call the great floods the Bretz Floods.

With a touch of humor, Bretz captioned the above photo of himself: "Five great men in one picture—four of them didn't show."

### Ice Age Animals

Washington's most spectacular prehistoric animal remains are those of the Columbian Mammoth. The large animals had long shaggy hair and long curved tusks. They lived in many places in North America during and after the Ice Age.

Skeletal remains of at least six mammoths were taken from a swamp in Spokane County in the 1870s. In 1886, bones from several of the mammoths were combined into one giant skeleton. In 1893, the mammoth skeleton was exhibited at the Chicago World's Fair. Since 1914, the mammoth has been on display at the Field Museum in Chicago.

### Buried Bones

Dinosaurs lived before the Ice Age. Their bones have been found in many places of North America, but they are curiously missing in the Washington region. Geologists think that dinosaurs might have lived on the Columbia Plateau, but that very thick layers of igneous rock buried their remains.

*In 1998, Mrs. Sara Aebly's second grade class at Windsor Elementary School near Spokane got the state legislature to make the Columbian Mammoth the state's official fossil.*

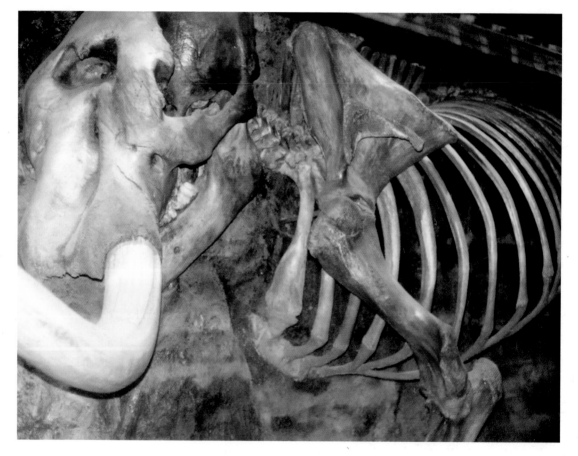

Long after the dinosaurs became extinct, giant mammoths, sloths, saber tooth tigers, camels, and giant bison lived in many regions of North America and in the Pacific Northwest.

## Glaciers and the First People

Glaciers shaped the physical environment of Washington in spectacular fashion. During the Ice Age, so much water was frozen into ice that the level of the ocean went down hundreds of feet. In Europe, Britain and France were connected by land. The land along our Pacific Coast extended at least 25 miles, and in places more than 100 miles, farther out to sea than it does today.

Many scholars believe the Ice Age glaciers made it possible for groups of people to make their way out of Asia into the Americas. So much of the ocean water was frozen that a land bridge up to a thousand miles wide was exposed, linking Alaska and Siberia. We will discuss this more in Chapter Three.

## ACTIVITY

### Oral History Interview

You can learn a lot by talking to a person who has witnessed an important event. The eruption of Mount St. Helens was one of these events. There may be other important events relating to natural disasters or changes in the environment where you live.

Conduct an oral history interview with these guidelines:

1. Select a person to talk to and then make an appointment for the interview.

2. Research your project. Go to the library and use the Internet to read magazines or newspaper articles, or even books, on your subject. You might research a volcanic eruption, a flood, a mudslide, a drought, or other event.

3. As you research, develop a questionnaire. This will be an outline of topics you wish to cover during your interview. Use words such as "explain, discuss, describe." Avoid yes and no questions. Include a question about what effect the event had on the person.

4. Conduct the interview. Record the full name of the person, the date and place of the interview, and your name. As you ask questions, record them with a tape recorder or video camera, or take notes. Encourage the person to fill in interesting details of the story and to describe how he or she felt.

5. Finally, write what was said in the interview, leaving in the most important or most interesting things the person said. Include as many direct quotes as you can.

## CHAPTER 2 REVIEW

1. What kinds of information can we learn from fossils?
2. Describe continental drift. What effect does tectonic force have on landmasses?
3. Name four ways that mountains are formed.
4. The Ring of Fire includes what kinds of mountains?
5. What are lahars?
6. Name at least three ways the land was changed by the eruption of Mt. St. Helens.
7. Which mountain do scientists label as our most dangerous volcano?
8. Describe how lava helped form the Columbia Plateau.
9. What makes up the soil of the Palouse Hills region and how was it deposited?
10. Describe the process that produced the Bretz Floods.
11. How did the Bretz Floods change the Columbia Plateau?
12. What is Washington's most famous Ice Age animal?

# American

**Makah petroglyphs are carved into the rock at Cape Alava, Ozette region, Olympic National Park.**
*Photo by Tom Till*

**TIMELINE** **30,000** B.C.　　　　**20,000** B.C.　　　　**10,000** B.C.　　　　**0**

**30,000–8,000** B.C.
Paleo-Indians enter the Pacific Northwest.

**10,000–8,000** B.C.
Salmon return to the Columbia River
as the Ice Age ends.

**4,500–2,000** B.C.
Plateau and Coastal Cultures emerge.

**2,000–200** B.C.
"Indian Golden Age" of population expansion

# Chapter 3

# Indians of the Pacific Northwest

| 1700 | 1750 | 1800 | | 1950 | 1960 | 1970 | 1980 | 1990 | 2000 |
|------|------|------|---|------|------|------|------|------|------|

**1700–1810** Protohistoric period
(time of great change)

Smallpox
epidemics devastate
Indian tribes. **1760–1800**

**1800**
Ash falls from Mt. St. Helens.
Prophet Dance appears.

**1786–1810**
Most tribes experience
white contact.

**1950s**
Marmes Rockshelter
site is discovered.

**1966**
Ozette site is
discovered.

**1977**
Sequim
mastodon
site is
discovered.

**1987**
East
Wenatchee
Clovis site is
discovered.

**1996**
Kennewick
Man is
discovered.

# The First Americans

A recent discovery occupies a unique place in the story of when and how humans came to the New World. Discoveries in the last decade have given new possibilities to the question of how the first people came to the Americas. The long-held theory of one large migration of Asian people across a land bridge that linked Siberia with Alaska about 12,000 years ago is now being challenged.

*An anthropologist studies the origin, distribution, physical features, and culture of human beings.*

## Kennewick Man

In July 1996, college students watching a hydroplane race on the Columbia River near Kennewick found a human skull in the river. Thinking it might be that of a murder victim, they called the police. The skull was turned over to the local **coroner**, a man whose job was to look into any unnatural death. The coroner asked for the assistance of James Chatters, a **forensic anthropologist**. A forensic anthropologist determines the cause of death of ancient humans.

Returning to the river, Chatters found most of the skeleton. The remains were remarkably complete, with only a few bones missing. Apparently the bones had washed out of a bank during recent flooding.

Chatters' examination revealed "a very large number of **Caucasoid** features." Caucasoid features are non-Indian and non-Asian. He determined that the skeleton was male, between forty and forty-five years old at the time of his death. The man was tall—about five feet nine inches—much taller than prehistoric Indian people in the region. Chatters' first assumption was that the man had been an early pioneer or fur trapper.

While cleaning the pelvis, the anthropologist found a gray object imbedded in the bone, which had partly healed around it. It was part of a spear point that resembled those in use from 4,500 to 9,000 years ago.

Chatters sent a bone fragment to a radio-carbon laboratory. The results were startling. Kennewick Man, as Chatters called him, was between 9,300 and 9,500 years old, making him one of the oldest and most complete skeletons ever found in North America.

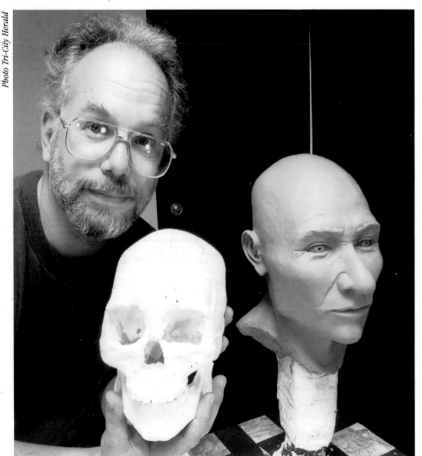

Photo Tri-City Herald

Tom McClelland of Richland shows the skull casting of Kennewick Man. McClelland and Jim Chatters used the casting to recreate the facial features of the 9,400-year-old discovery.

Kennewick

## Battle of the Bones

Indian tribes in the area soon claimed Kennewick Man's remains. Calling him the "Ancient One," they demanded that the skeleton be **repatriated** (returned to the place of origin) for immediate reburial in a secret place. Under provisions of the Native American Graves Protection and Repatriation Act passed in 1990, the federal government was required to rule on the origins of the remains. If they were found to be American Indian, they would be turned over to the appropriate tribe (if that could be determined).

Kennewick Man's discovery stirred scientists across the country. They were concerned because in recent years **Paleo-Indian** skeletons found elsewhere in the West had been returned to Indian tribes for reburial before detailed studies could be done. In fact, the remains of one young woman reburied by Indian people in Idaho were determined to be 12,800 years old! She and other Paleo-Indian skeletons shared Kennewick Man's non-Indian Caucasoid features. A group of scientists sued for the right to study Kennewick Man's remains, and won. "It's a victory for science," said one anthropologist.

Christopher Francisco, a member of the Navajo tribe, flies an American flag upside down outside of the U.S. Courthouse in Portland during the Kennewick Man hearing. He is protesting the indecision over whether to turn over the skeleton to Indian tribes for burial. *Associated Press*

## Mystery of the Bones

Many scholars believe that the earliest migrations to the New World started in Asia, then traveled across Siberia to the Americas over the Bering Land Bridge. They also believe there was a series of migrations over many thousands of years.

There is also growing evidence that people may have traveled down the Pacific Coast using boats or walked along the coastal plain. Over hundreds of years, groups reached the tip of South America. Other scholars argue that some groups of people came directly from Europe, Aisa, and some Pacific islands in boats.

## WHAT DO YOU THINK?

**Kennewick Man publicized a long-standing conflict between Indians and scientists over control of human remains. Indian people believe that digging bones up from the earth and studying them is a** *desecration* **of their ancestors.**

**On the other hand, anthropologists and archaeologists insist the remains hold the key to explaining the origin of human beings in the Americas.**

**What do you think should be done with ancient skeletons?**

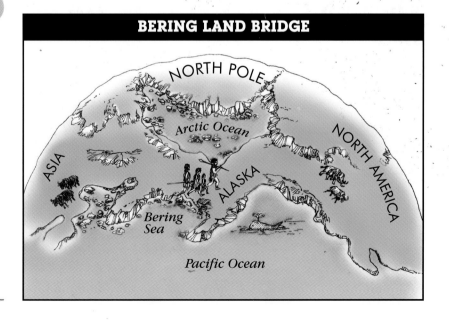

**BERING LAND BRIDGE**

NORTH POLE

Arctic Ocean

ASIA

ALASKA

NORTH AMERICA

Bering Sea

*Pacific Ocean*

# Paleo-Indians

Native peoples entered the Pacific Northwest sometime before the end of the last Ice Age—about 10,000 to 12,000 years ago. We call these people Paleo because they were here first. Paleo means ancient. The people were hunting the large animals that ranged through the region. In 1987, a ***cache*** of "Clovis" spear points was found in an apple orchard in East Wenatchee. The Wenatchee Clovis site has been dated to about 11,000 years ago.

This discovery links our area to the Clovis, New Mexico site. There, in 1937, the Clovis-style spear point was found along with mammoth bones. The Clovis people were big game hunters who moved across North America hunting Ice Age animals such as mammoths, giant bison, and giant sloths.

In 1977, a 12,000-year-old mastodon skeleton was found near Sequim. It had a spear point embedded in a rib.

### Adaptation and Survival

After the Paleo-Indians, groups called Archaic Indians lived here. They had developed better tools, including a spear thrower called an *atlatl*. The large mastodons were gone by then, and the *atlatl* helped the hunters kill the smaller, faster deer for food. There may have been several groups of Paleo and Archaic in the Northwest. Based on limited archaeological evidence, their populations were sparse and widely scattered.

Kennewick Man and his people were probably part of a small population, perhaps numbering only in the hundreds to a few thousand, who roamed in small bands across the Columbia Plateau.

Life for these people was harsh. They struggled constantly with the forces of nature—climate, volcanic eruptions, and catastrophic floods. About 4,500 years ago, the climate grew milder. Indian populations increased.

By about 2,000 years ago, two clearly defined culture groups—Coastal and Plateau peoples—had emerged. Like today, the people were divided by the high Cascade Mountains. They adapted to life on different land and in varying climates.

*From 2,000 years ago until the coming of the white people, the American Indians enjoyed a "Golden Age" of progress and population growth.*

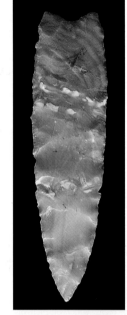

This flint projectile point was made by the Clovis people about 11,000 to 12,000 years ago.

## Marmes Man

Dr. Richard Daugherty, a geologist from Washington State University, led a group of students to the Marmes Rockshelter on the Palouse River. As the group explored the area, they found human bones. The bones were determined to be those of people who had lived in the region during the final stages of the Ice Age. After many years of excavation, the Marmes Rockshelter was flooded by the reservoir waters of a dam on the Snake River.

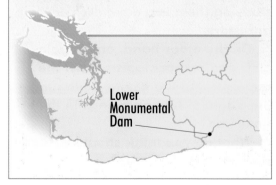

Lower Monumental Dam

Sequim

Wenatchee

# Digging for Artifacts

Archaeologists are scientists who study artifacts to learn about people who lived long ago. In 2000, a new Paleo-Indian site was discovered downstream from Vantage Bridge on the Columbia River. The date of the settlement is thought to be about 10,250 years ago.

The staff of Eastern Washington University's Archaeological and Historical Services Department work under a hot June sun. They unearthed a number of stone tools and many stone flakes from tool making. *Photo by Mike Green*

A staff member photographs the artifacts. *Photo by Mike Green*

Scientists use ancient volcanic ash falls to date sites. This exposed surface shows the Glacier Peak ash fall from an eruption 11,200 years ago. On the extreme left is the Mount St. Helen's Ash Fall of 13,000 years ago. *Photo by Mike Green*

# Historic American Indians

Historic peoples are those about whom we have writings, paintings, or photographs produced at the time the Indians were living. For example, Lewis and Clark wrote many accounts in their diaries about the native peoples they met. Many other explorers and trappers also wrote about native peoples. And, of course, archaeologists continually study the lifestyle of the people who lived many years after the Paleo-Indians.

When white settlers came to the Pacific Northwest, there were many groups of Indian peoples living all over the land. Their lifestyles were alike in many ways, but different in other ways. Some spoke related languages, and some spoke entirely different languages.

Groups were divided by geographic landforms such as mountains and large rivers. This affected native culture.

## HISTORIC NATIVE AMERICAN GROUPS

Nooksack
Lummi
Samish
Swinorish          Salish
Makah    Clallam    Suiattle
Ozette
Hoh      Suquamish
         Duwamish   Muckleshoot
Quileute
Humptulip           Puyallup
Satsop   Nisqually  Chehalis
Lower    Kwalniokwa
Chehalis          Cowlitz
Chinook
                   Cascade

Lakes
Methow    Nespelem
          Colville
Chelan    San Poil
Entiat                   Spokane
Wenatchi
Kittitas
Meshal    Columbia      Palouse
          Yakama
Taidnapah
Klickitat        Walla Walla  Nez Perce
Wishram

**Coastal Tribes**          **Plateau Tribes**

# The Coastal People

During the 2,000 years before contact with white explorers, Indians of the Northwest Coast—an area extending from northern California to southwestern Alaska—created a remarkably unique and rich culture. The Pacific Ocean nurtured this culture. Its waters teemed with fish, shellfish, and sea mammals. Its moisture-laden winds fostered an abundance of plant life, including the giant red cedar—the Indians' source of shelter, clothing and transportation. The mild marine climate made life easier than life in other places. Large semi-permanent villages were found at the mouths of virtually every river.

Most of all, the ocean's resources gave the Coastal Indians the extraordinary gift of leisure time in the winter months. The winter months could be spent on recreation and on artistic projects. Winter was also the time for elaborate ceremonies, a basic feature of coastal social life.

## Salish

The largest group of Indians on the coast was the Salish-speaking people. The mild climate and plentiful food from the sea made life easy. The coastal Salish thrived living next to the ocean. They occupied all of Puget Sound, much of the Olympic Peninsula, and most of western Washington.

## Chinook

Along the Columbia River upstream to The Dalles lived various divisions of the Chinook. They spoke Penutian, an ancient language. The Chinooks were the great middlemen in a vast network of Indian trade. They traded slaves from California to Vancouver Island for canoes and prized ***dentalium shells.*** The shells were long and narrow and were strung on long rope necklaces that were worn by both men and women. They were used in trade as we use money.

To facilitate their wide-ranging commerce, the Chinook developed a trade language known as "Chinook Jargon." This was a simple spoken language understood by dozens of tribes over a vast stretch of western North America.

## Makah

On the very northwest corner of the Olympic Peninsula at Cape Flattery lived the Makah. They were a division of the Nootka, a tribe that occupied much of the west coast of Vancouver Island.

The Makah, Nootka, and a few neighboring tribes were the only coastal peoples to pursue the largest of all sea mammals—the gray whales that regularly migrated along the coast. They hunted the whales in large cedar canoes so well built and decorated that they became prized trade items.

The photo of a Makah mask was taken on the Makah Reservation. The mask was made by Frank Smith. *Photo by Tom Till*

### The Ozette Dig

In 1966, at a place called Ozette, archaeologists uncovered a Makah village that had been engulfed by a huge mudslide 500 years ago. Thousands of artifacts documented an indisputable fact—the Makah were once a proud and prosperous people completely dedicated to whaling. In one large cedar house were found containers of whale oil, harpoons, and numerous examples of artwork celebrating the whale hunt.

Ozette Dig

## A Marine Economy

Fishing was the foundation of the coastal economy. Five species of salmon ascended the rivers to **spawn.** The people caught them as they swam upriver. Men also trolled for salmon in the ocean, using baited hooks on kelp lines. Halibut and cod were also caught on baited hooks. The Chinook used similar techniques to catch large sturgeon from the lower Columbia River.

After a hard day fishing, the people preserved the catch for later use by smoking and air-drying it. Then they placed the fish in baskets lined with fish skins.

The ocean also provided edible shellfish. Many kinds of clams, mussels, oysters, and crabs were harvested. Old village sites along the coast are still marked by large mounds of discarded shells.

Seals, sea lions, and porpoises were also hunted by nearly all coastal tribes. Whaling, however, was the most spectacular form of sea hunting. This was a dangerous activity. The equipment—from the canoe to the harpoon, lines, and inflated sealskin floats used to keep the animal from sinking—was always in perfect readiness. The harpooner and his crew practiced constantly and carried out ceremonial rituals to prepare for the hunt.

*The salmon were speared, caught in nets or weirs, or scooped up in large baskets beneath waterfalls.* **Weirs were fences put across streams to stop fish from getting away.**

Salmon were caught in nets or speared.

## Salmon Life Cycle

Year after year, in the spring or fall, salmon leave the ocean to start their difficult journey up a stream to the exact same place where they hatched from salmon eggs three to five years earlier. Covering over ten miles a day, they fight their way upstream against the current. They brave swift rapids and rushing falls, jumping as much as ten feet up the falls, facing the danger of fishermen, birds, and modern dams.

Bruised and starved, survivors reach the still freshwaters of the spawning ground. A female fish lays as many as 10,000 eggs about the size of peas in the stream beds. After the male covers the eggs with a milky substance, both adult fish float tail first downstream. In a few days they are dead, and unfit for human food.

After several months, the eggs hatch and tiny fish start to grow. Within a year, they, too, start downstream on their journey to the salty sea. Only a small percentage ever make their destination—the others are caught and eaten by wild animals, birds, or larger fish.

The damming of many streams in the Pacific Northwest has seriously affected the salmon runs. "Fish ladders"— artificial sloping waterfalls—have been made so the salmon can continue their journey.

This community home of the Nooksack had been much larger at one time. Families had separate apartments, or sections, of the large house.

## Homes of Cedar

The Coastal Indians used wood as their basic building material. Red cedar was the most important wood. Red cedar was easily split into wide straight planks for building houses and ceremonial lodges.

Longhouses were built by overlapping cedar planks to make exterior walls. Cedar shavings or planks covered the dirt floors. Several related families lived together in one longhouse that faced the sea.

## Family Groups

The basic social unit was the extended family—a local group of relatives. These groups united for defense or for ceremonial purposes. There were no true tribal divisions among Coastal Indians.

## Social Status

Wealth determined social status. A wealthy family might own more canoes, tools, weapons, animal skins, and dentalium and clam shell ropes. Wealthy people also had slaves. The leaders of a group were nearly always wealthy. As a person got more possessions, he moved up in social status.

No single chief ruled the group. Councils met and made decisions together. There were chiefs, nobles, commoners, and slaves in the communities.

Slaves were usually women and children who were stolen from other groups. Slaves lived in the house with the rest of the family and did the hardest work. Sometimes they were sold to other groups.

A Chinook longhouse was home to several related families. A hole in the center of the roof let out smoke from the cooking fire. The people made cattail and cedar mats that formed movable interior walls.

## The Potlatch

Nothing showed the **materialism** of Coastal Culture more than the potlatch. A **potlatch** was a huge celebration hosted by a family for a special event. There were marriage, birth, and death potlatches. A large feast for the entire village and the presenting of gifts were basic features. The people of the highest social status received the most expensive gifts first. Those of the lowest social status got smaller gifts.

### LINKING THE PAST TO THE PRESENT

In what ways do people today use wealth as a way of measuring a person's worth? Do we look down on the poor? Do they have the same opportunities for a good education, a good job, and do they get the same respect as people with more money?

Wool blankets were given as gifts at a potlatch in the early 1900s.

## A Spiritual People

Spirituality was an important part of everyday life. Belief in a Supreme Being was common. Some groups believed in one god whose power was present in all things in nature. Other people believed in many gods.

*Animism* is a modern word for the belief that both living and non-living things in nature have spirits, either good or evil. American Indians lived close to nature. They felt that they knew its secrets. The ground under their feet was more than just grass, rock, and dirt. The sun was more than a ball of fire. They believed that the sun, moon, stars, rain, wind, plants, rocks, and animals had spirits. The spirits could grant favors or punish. They must always be treated with reverence.

Shamans were men who were revered because of their special healing and spiritual gifts. They had special ceremonies and dances to heal the sick. A shaman could also use his power to harm an enemy, and so could be blamed for someone's death.

## Art

Nothing distinguishes the Coastal Culture as impressively as its art. Wood carving in *relief* was highly developed and the result of centuries of skill. Using tools of shell, bone, and beaver teeth, artists interpreted the animal species with great skill and imagination.

The people were also excellent basket weavers. They wove beautiful baskets from grasses, reeds, cattails, and thin strips of cedar bark. Baskets were used for carrying and storing food and other items.

### Salmon-People

**B**eliefs relating to the *immortality* of salmon were widespread. The salmon appeared year after year, offering themselves to the Indians. The people believed that the salmon were a race of supernatural beings that lived in human form in a large house under the sea. Once a year the Salmon-People assumed their salmon form to sacrifice themselves to their brothers on land. After death, a fish's spirit returned to the house under the sea.

Returning salmon bones to the water was essential. If bones were discarded on land, the "Salmon-Person" might lack a leg or some other body part upon *resurrection*. This would make him angry and he and his people would not return to a river where they had been treated so rudely. All Coastal tribes had lengthy lists of prohibitions and rules for dealing with the Salmon-People so that good relations could be maintained.

Young Doctor made elaborate wood carvings. Notice the carved people sitting in the canoe.

# The Plateau People

Large groups of people lived east of the Cascade Mountains long before white settlers arrived. The land and climate of the plateau shaped the lives of the people who lived there just as the marine environment influenced the lives of the Coastal Indians. The plateau's hot dry summers and cold snowy winters required seasonal moves and changes in clothing and shelter.

The plateau's most prominent feature, the Columbia River system, was a major transportation route and was also the Indians' most important source of food.

## Two groups

Plateau tribes were divided into two main language groups. The Salish-speaking tribes of the northern plateau included the Spokane, Kalispel, Coeur d' Alene, Colville, Okanagon, Columbia, and Wenatchee. Most of the tribes of the southern plateau spoke a different language. These groups included the Nez Perce, Yakama, Palouse, Klickitat, Kittitas, Umatilla, and Wanapum.

Because they lived between the Pacific Coast and the Great Plains, Plateau Peoples were influenced by the cultures of both. Many Plateau tribes adopted a limited version of the coastal potlatch, while contact with plains tribes brought widespread use of the tepee.

Coastal Indians lived in the same place all year, while the Plains Indians east of the Rocky Mountains were nomadic. The semi-nomadic Plateau Indians fit between these extremes. They lived in winter villages for years, but often spent months at a time on long food-gathering trips. At these times, they lived in tepees that could be taken apart and moved to a new place.

## Pit Houses

Permanent homes on the eastern edge of the Cascade Range were widely used until the early 1800s. They were called pit houses.

The person who wanted to build the house asked all his neighbors to help. Twenty or more came, so that the building was sometimes completed in a single day.

A bark rope twenty to forty feet long was laid on the ground. Another rope was laid across it to determine the center. Each end and the middle were marked with small stakes. A man marked a circle on the ground with a stick.

Then the women began to dig the soil with digging sticks or scrapers with sharp, flat blades. The loose earth was put into large baskets and carried from the widening hole.

Thick poles of green timber were measured with bark ropes. Trees were cut, barked, and hauled with stout bark rope. These poles would be the roof supports. Thin poles for the roof were also cut, tied into bundles, and carried to the site by men and women.

Upright braces were placed about two feet deep in the ground around the circle and formed the roof. An opening was left at the top. The structure was then covered with thinner poles or, in other places or later years, with woven grass mats. The slanted roof was covered with pine needles or dry grass, and then covered with earth.

A large notched log was placed down through a hole in the top of the house and was used as a ladder. Fires were built on stone slabs in the center of the house.

**Tule** houses replaced pit houses after the early 1800s. Tall tule rushes were cut, dried, and laid flat side by side. The ends were tied to form mats. Tule mats were laced to a log framework, overlapped to provide more protection from wind and rain.

Small baskets about eight inches high were attached to a woman's belt and used to gather camas bulbs.

## The Seasonal Round

To get food, the people traveled between known sites on a yearly basis. The same family groups were found at their regular fields or fishing sites at the same time each year.

During the spring and summer, women and children dug for camas bulbs. Later in the summer, groups of people moved into the mountains to pick huckleberries, while others returned to the fishing sites to prepare for the salmon run.

Fishing was men's work. The most popular fishing sites, such as The Dalles or Kettle Falls, became large intertribal meeting places, where trading, socializing, and work intermingled. While the men fished, the women cleaned the salmon, then laid them out on wooden racks to dry.

Fall was the time for hunting. Hunting methods varied, but a favorite technique was the "surround." A large number of hunters formed a circle in the woods, leaving the prey no route to escape. Men hunted larger game, including elk and buffalo, and smaller animals such as rabbits, mountain goats, sheep, and birds.

Following the hunts, usually by late November, the tribes returned to their winter camps. This was a quiet time. Stories were told and retold. Ceremonies and dances were held. Men made weapons and

Camas lilies grew wild all over the dry plateau lands. The bulbs were an important food. A camas root looks like a small white onion. The camas was baked in large underground pits, formed into cakes, and then dried in the sun.
*Photo by Mike Green*

tools and, if the weather allowed, went hunting. Women made and repaired clothing. The supply of camas cakes, dried salmon, and venison would have to last until the start of the next seasonal round when the cycle could begin again.

## Gender Roles and Equality

Plateau Indian groups lived with a strict system of gender roles. Most tasks were either men's work or women's work. Women gathered the roots and berries, dried the meat and fish, prepared the animal skins, made the family's clothing, and cared for the young children. Men fished and hunted, made tools and weapons, built the houses, and, if necessary, went to war. Children and teenaged girls generally did the same work as the women, and teenaged boys learned skills by working with the men.

There was a great deal of equality between men and women. The first explorers were astonished at the high status of plateau women compared with the status of women in other parts of North America. This equality could be seen in marriage proposals where the woman was always free to reject a suitor. Among the Spokanes, in fact, the woman could propose marriage.

Within the family, women had greater authority than men. For example, once food entered the house, it became the wife's exclusive property. Even if he had first provided it, the husband needed permission to take even a small piece of dried meat.

## Material Culture and Art

Because the Plateau Indians' time was spent mainly in obtaining food, there was little time for artistic pursuits. Most of the things they made were for practical purposes. Mats for lodge construction were woven from tule (rushes), or cattail. The skill that went into mat construction was even more evident in the elaborately woven and decorated baskets. Cradle boards were often decorated with beadwork.

A shy smile shows a mother's pride. This Spokane mother with her baby in a cradle board was taken in 1899. *Photo by Larry Allen*

By 1900, salmon runs were weakened. White commercial fishermen had taken too many salmon at a time. Indians continued to fish at Kettle Falls until the site was flooded by the reservoir created by Grand Coulee Dam in 1941.

Kalispel men fish in their unique bark-covered sturgeon nose canoe in 1908.

Ordinary clothing could become an object of art. Beautifully decorated deerskin shirts and dresses were sometimes decorated with elaborate porcupine quills and beadwork and worn only on ceremonial occasions.

Most Plateau Indians made very simple dugout canoes for river travel. But the Kalispels, who lived along the Pend Oreille River in northeast Washington, made a most unusual bark canoe. Constructed of white pine bark stretched over cedar ribs and sewn with black pine roots, these canoes were remarkably light and swift.

## Religion

Like the Coastal Indians, the Plateau Indians believed in a creator who was known as the "Old Chief," the "Ancient One," or "Father Mystery."

Young people were expected to go on a "vision quest" to find their guardian spirits. In keeping with gender equality, girls as well as boys were allowed to go on a vision quest.

The preparation for the vision quest began at an early age—between the ages of five and ten for boys, and seven and ten for girls. Elders supervised the quest, telling the children what to do and what they might expect. Children sought their guardian spirit by going off alone and fasting. They sang and prayed for a visitation. Their guardian spirit might appear as an animal such as Bear or Beaver. Sun, Moon, or Mountains could also appear as a spirit. A guardian spirit would help a person throughout his or her life.

Spirit power was the central religious belief. All significant or unusual events were explained in terms of this power. Indians with the greatest spirit power became shamans. Shamans had numerous powers, but their most important power was their ability to cure the sick. When their spirit powers failed to help them

cope with the dramatic changes in their lives—especially the measles and smallpox epidemics—some leaders turned to the white people for help. Indians thought that because the white men had a very rich material culture, perhaps they had the greater spirit power.

## Trade Connections

Trade took place at the intertribal fishing sites at Kettle Falls and The Dalles, as well as at major camas gathering fields. Goods were exchanged as ritual gifts, bartered for other goods, and won or lost through gambling. Gambling was so widespread that some scholars believe it was the primary method of trade.

Coastal tribes carried on extensive trading activities, none more so than the Chinook. The potlatch system became something like a series of elaborate and rotating yard sales. Up the Columbia River at The Dalles there was a thriving exchange between the Chinook and the various Plateau tribes. The Dalles became one of the most important inter-cultural trading sites in all of North America.

The Indians got horses from the Spanish in the 1700s. Horses allowed Indians to expand their trading opportunities. Plateau tribes traded as far south as California. Some tribes even attended the largest of native trade fairs—the Shoshoni rendezvous in Wyoming—where they could barter for goods from the Spanish settlements in New Mexico.

The lives of both the Coastal and Plateau Indians were enriched by this expansion of trade. But the result was more like the brighter flame of the candle just before it is blown out. As Indian trading networks expanded, they became routes for deadly germs. You will read more about disease at the end of the chapter.

The Dalles was an important fishing and trading center.

# The Horse

Horses were brought to Mexico by Spanish explorers. By 1700, horses had been traded to the Shoshoni in Idaho. The Cayuse people brought the horse to the Columbia Plateau about 1710. By 1750, most Plateau tribes had at least a few horses.

The Nez Perce and Cayuse, whose territory contained extensive grazing lands, had large herds. "Cayuse" became a term generally used for the tough wiry ponies of the region. Coastal Indians had little use for the horse, however, though there were some horses in the Puget Sound area.

David Thompson, a British explorer and trapper, wrote in his diary in 1810 this account of an Indian man's reaction to seeing horses for the first time:

*We were anxious to see a horse of which we had heard so much. At last we heard that one was killed by an arrow. . . . Numbers of us went to see him, and we all admired him. He put us in the mind of a Stag that had lost his horns and we did not know what name to give him. But as he was a slave to Man, like the dog which carried our things, he was named the Big Dog.*

Horses changed Indian life in many ways. Food gathering became more efficient. On horseback, it was possible to travel greater distances to get food and easier to bring food back to winter camps. Many tribes traveled to the Great Plains to hunt buffalo. An 1824 hunt consisted of more than 800 Indians with 1,800 horses. Dried buffalo meat and buffalo robes became important trade items.

Unfortunately, the greed for horses greatly increased the scale of violence. Horses became new **spoils** of war, and stealing horses became an important test of bravery. The Shoshoni began regular raids for horses and slaves. The Oregon Klamath people became fierce slave and horse raiders. "We found that we could make money by war," as one warrior put it, noting that "we rather got to like it anyhow."

Looking Glass, a Nez Perce chief, posed for photographs in 1887.

Lucy Nomee posed for this picture in 1941.

# GRANDFATHER CUTS LOOSE THE PONIES

Southern Columbia Basin tribes tell a colorful legend that explains how they got horses. Like all oral Indian history, this legend was passed down from generation to generation by what the native people called "Grandfather Tales."

*Speelyi, the Coyote Spirit who created the Indian world, decided one day that his people in this part of the country had walked long enough. Summoning one of his favorite shamans to a cave, he gave the medicine man a basketful of ponies and told him to turn them loose as a gift to his people. The shaman tipped the basket on a high bluff, where they spread to all the inland tribes as Speelyi's special gift.*

In modern times, artist David Govedare created fourteen life-sized ponies of steel. The ponies are placed in dramatic silhouette against a wide expanse of sky on a high ridge. You can see the ponies running across the ridge by taking the footpath off the eastbound lane of I-90, a few miles east of the town of Vantage.

*Grandfather Cuts Loose the Ponies,* a sculpture by David Govedare, is a stirring illustration of an old Indian legend. *Photo by Larry Conboy*

## WHAT DO YOU THINK?

**What were the positive and negative aspects of the Indian people's acquisition of horses? Think of a modern item that affects people's lives today in both positive and negative ways. Would you give up using the item because of the negative impact?**

Vantage

# Disease Frontiers

After devastating Indian populations in New England and the Great Lakes region, infectious diseases came to the Pacific Northwest. Native peoples had no immunity to such illnesses as smallpox, measles, malaria, typhoid, and diphtheria. Smallpox was the first to strike. Coming in waves, smallpox hit the eastern edge of the plateau in the 1760s and the entire northwest again ten years later. It reappeared in 1800. Malaria and measles followed smallpox.

The results were catastrophic for some tribes. By the 1830s, the Chinook had lost ninety percent of their population to smallpox and malaria. Overall, the smallpox epidemics reduced Indian populations by about one-third.

David Thompson recorded the life story of Saukamappee, who had raided deep into Shoshoni country when he and his group found a village *decimated* by smallpox:

*We entered for the fight; but our war whoop instantly stopped, our eyes were appalled with terror; there was no one to fight with but the dead and the dying. . . . This dreadful disease broke out in our camp and spread from one tent to another as if the Bad Spirit carried it. We had no belief that one Man could give it to another, any more than a wounded Man could give his wound to another. About one-third of us died. We believed the Good Spirit had forsaken us and allowed the Bad Spirit to become our Master.*

# Protohistoric Change

At least one hundred years before the actual arrival of the whites, Indians in the Pacific Northwest experienced wrenching changes in their lives as a result of indirect contact with the European explorers.

Scholars now recognize the importance of this period and they have given it a name: *protohistoric*. In the Pacific Northwest, this period runs from about 1700 to 1810.

Change came in the form of the horse, new trade goods, epidemic disease, and a steady flow of information. When Lewis and Clark met Indian peoples, for instance, the Indians had never met a white person, but they owned horses and guns. Some had smallpox scars.

The Lewis and Clark journals contain numerous examples. The Shoshoni described to Lewis and Clark the route to the Spanish settlements in New Mexico. The Chinooks astounded the captains with their detailed knowledge of the route over the Columbia Plateau and across the Great Divide. It was obvious that Indian traders traveled widely.

The explorer's trade goods such as cloth, blue and white glass beads, copper pots, and metal guns provoked questions among Indian peoples. Who made these goods? What are the people like? What is the source of their spirit power? Stories of the white man and his world were traded along with his trade goods.

In the summer of 1800, the sky went dark as a huge eruption from Mt. St. Helens blanketed the region with several inches of ash. This, together with a third smallpox epidemic, seems to have triggered a religious response.

The Prophet Dance, an unusual round of summer dances, swept across the Columbia Plateau. Accompanying the dances were prophecies describing the coming of the white men. The purpose of the Prophet Dance seems to have been a means of bringing together tradition and change and to prepare for what was expected to be a major disruption in Indian life.

So the protohistoric period ended. Northwest Indians awaited the coming of the white men. They did so more with curiosity and hope than with fear and misgiving.

## CHAPTER 3 REVIEW

1. What new information did archaeologists learn after the discovery of Kennewick Man?

2. Why did Native Americans object to the scientific study of Kennewick Man?

3. What evidence has been found that Paleo-Indians once lived in present-day Washington?

4. What were the two main groups of American Indians in Washington? What natural landform divided them?

5. How did living near the Pacific Ocean influence the lifestyle of the Coastal Indians?

6. Which group was famous for hunting whales?

7. What wood was important to the Coastal Indians?

8. What determined the social status of the Coastal people?

9. What was a potlatch? What was its purpose?

10. Who had special abilities to heal the sick and give spiritual guidance?

11. What part of the salmon life cycle made the Indians believe salmon were immortal?

12. What kinds of art did the people produce?

13. What river system was the most important to the lifestyle of the Plateau Indians?

14. What did the Plateau Indians do every season to provide food?

15. What were some of the jobs of the women? Of the men?

16. What was unique about the treatment of women in Plateau tribes?

17. What were some of the items Indians traded?

18. List three ways horses changed the lifestyle of the Indian people.

19. What does the term "protohistoric change" mean?

20. What were three ways the lifestyle of the Indian people changed even before they met the white people?

## GEOGRAPHY TIE-IN

1. Which dams on the Columbia River were responsible for the destruction of traditional Indian fishing sites?

2. Compare the ways the Native American people lived off the land with our use of natural resources today. How are they alike? How are they different? Which lifestyle appeals most to you?

## THE TIME
# 1492–1820s

### PEOPLE TO KNOW
John Jacob Astor
Frances Barkley
Captain Cook
William Clark
Marie Dorion
Pierre Dorion
Juan de Fuca
Robert Gray
Bruno de Heceta
Thomas Jefferson
John Ledyard
Meriwether Lewis
Ranald MacDonald
Alexander Mackenzie
Esteban Martinez
John McLoughlin
Juan Perez
Sacajawea
David Thompson
Jonathan Thorn
George Vancouver

### PLACES TO LOCATE
Asia
North America
South America
Europe
China
Spain
England
Canada
Hawaiian Islands
   (Sandwich Islands)
Vancouver Island
   (Nootka)
Pacific Coast
East Coast
Strait of Juan de Fuca
Puget Sound
Columbia River
Snake River
Missouri River
Boston, Massachusetts
St. Louis, Missouri
Montreal, Canada

### WORDS TO UNDERSTAND
aghast
barter
elusive
infirmary
lucrative
porcelain
voyageur

**1607** Colonists arrive at Jamestown on the East Coast.

**TIMELINE**   1492       1592       1607

**1492** Christopher Columbus discovers the New World.

**1592** Juan de Fuca claims to have sailed the coast of the Pacific Northwest.

# The Great Encounter

**4**

A replica of one of Captain Cook's ships was brought to Washington State to celebrate Cook's voyages up the Pacific Coast.

*Photo by Robert Esposito, Panorama Designs*

**1789** Esteban Martinez builds Fort San Miguel.

**1775** Bruno de Hezeta explores the Northwest.

Revolutionary War breaks out in the English colonies.

**1792** Robert Gray explores the Columbia River.

**1812** The War of 1812 is fought between Great Britain and the United States.

| 1770 | 1780 | 1790 | 1800 | 1810 | 1820 |

**1774** Juan Perez explores and claims the Pacific Northwest for Spain.

**1776** Declaration of Independence is signed in the English colonies.

Captain Cook sails to the Pacific Northwest.

**1787** U.S. Constitution is signed in Philadelphia.

**1803** U.S. buys the Louisiana Purchase from France.

**1804** Lewis and Clark travel to the Pacific Ocean.

**1806** Lewis and Clark return to St. Louis.

**1811** The Pacific Fur Company builds Fort Astoria.

**1824** Hudson's Bay Company builds Fort Vancouver.

**1780s–1840s The fur trade**

## The First Visitors

Different groups of Native Americans have lived in the region we now call Washington for thousands and thousands of years. Other groups of people also came from time to time. The first non-Indians probably came from China or Japan by accident when their small boats were blown off course and drifted ashore. The wind currents move in an easterly direction across the Pacific Ocean, explaining the ruins of many Asian boats that have been found on the coast. Chinese documents tell of Hui San, a Buddhist priest, who probably sailed to the Pacific Coast in the year 499.

To support this idea, archaeologists have found bits of Asian **porcelain,** or ceramic ware, along the Washington coast. Coastal Indians also told of early visitors from across the ocean. Whoever the visitors were, and why they came, we still do not know. We do know that they did not come in large numbers and that they did not establish settlements here.

## The Search for a Northwest Passage

There is a lot of written history about European explorers who tried to find a shortcut to China and the Indies. Instead of traveling over land across Europe and Asia to the markets of China, the merchants and government leaders spent money trying to find a water route that was shorter than

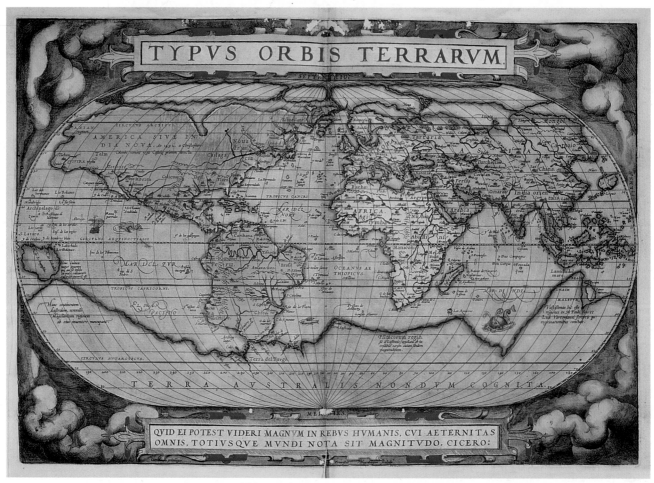

You can see on this early map from the 1600s why European explorers wanted a faster route across North America. They did not want to go all the way around South America to get to the West. Compare this map to our maps today. Which names and land shapes are similar and which are different?

Spanish explorers sailed in small wooden vessels called "galleons" that were powered by the wind and ocean currents. The hulls of some ships were filled with rocks to keep the ships from tipping over in violent storms. Water leaked into the ships and had to be carried up to the deck and dumped overboard.

going around Africa. In fact, that is how Christopher Columbus came upon North America. He found it accidentally when he and his crew tried sailing west to Asia.

Once the route to North America was used by the Europeans, ships from several countries kept searching for a way through North America so they wouldn't have to sail around South America to reach Asia. This *elusive* shortcut was called the Northwest Passage, and many explorers spent years trying to discover it.

## WHAT DO YOU THINK?

**If it had existed, how would a Northwest Passage across North America have affected the development and commerce of our country and our state?**

## Spanish Explorers

The Spanish may have been the first to sail ships along the Pacific Coast. In 1596, Juan de Fuca claimed that Spain had hired him to be the captain of an exploration ship to the Pacific Coast. He described a wide strait at the correct longitude, and he told of a pillar of rocks that stood at the entrance.

Whether or not Juan de Fuca had actually found the strait, mapmakers in Europe added his name to their maps, creating the Strait of Juan de Fuca—at least on paper.

Strait of Juan de Fuca

*"Your worship knows how I became poor, because Captain Candis took away from me more than sixty thousand ducats."*

— Juan de Fuca, sixty years old, 1597

It is now known that an English pirate named Cavendish had been robbing Spanish ships around that time.

### Juan Perez

Over 180 years after Juan de Fuca claimed to have explored the coast, Juan Perez, another Spanish sailor, sailed north from New Spain (now Mexico) to Alaska. He tried to claim the land for Spain. To do this, an explorer had to go on land, erect a cross representing the Catholic religion, and bury a bottle containing a written claim.

Perez and his crew traded with native people on what was later called Vancouver Island, but they were never able to go ashore on the mainland and properly claim the land. The weather was stormy, and the crew was sick with scurvy. Perez finally gave up and returned home.

### The Spanish Go Ashore

In 1775, another Spanish expedition arrived on the Washington coast. This time twenty armed sailors under Bruno de Hezeta went ashore, erected a cross, and claimed the Northwest for Spain.

Six men were ordered ashore to fill water barrels with fresh water and gather firewood. Before they could complete the work, 300 Indians attacked and killed them. Watching from the main ship, the captain was **aghast** when canoes of Indians then moved towards the ship. The Spanish fired their muskets, killed several Indians, and left.

The rest of the sailors found what they described as a "great river" (the Columbia) but did not explore it because so many of the men were sick and dying from scurvy.

### Why Didn't Spain Settle the Northwest?

Spain claimed the northern Pacific Coast but was not interested in exploring the interior of the region or settling it. Some possible reasons might have been:

- Spanish crews were very busy harvesting pearls off the western coast of Mexico and California.
- There was no mineral wealth, such as gold or silver, along the Pacific Coast.
- The native peoples lived in very small villages. There were no large populations to capture for slaves.
- The coastline was steep and rugged, with tall trees right to the shoreline, making development difficult.

Eventually, Spain lost out to the British in the Pacific Northwest.

## Scurvy and Vitamin C

Scurvy was a terrible curse to the Spanish sailors. Scurvy is a disease caused by a diet lacking in ascorbic acid, or vitamin C. It causes bleeding gums, swollen and weak arms and legs, and sores on the body. When a ship's crew got scurvy, they could be wiped out as quickly and completely as if they had been at war.

Scurvy developed aboard ships because crews were out at sea for such long periods and didn't have fresh fruits and vegetables. They didn't get enough vitamins from the dried meat, fish, and biscuits they ate. Their treatments for the disease, such as gargling with oil, were worthless.

It is ironic that Spanish sailors suffered so badly while Spain had many orange and lemon groves. No one realized the fruit would prevent scurvy.

# British Search for the Northwest Passage

In 1776, a year after the Spanish explorers quickly left the Pacific Coast, the American colonists were fighting the Revolutionary War along the East Coast. A British sea captain arrived in the colonial port of Plymouth, Massachusetts. His name was James Cook. He was already a famous explorer who had been around the world twice, in both directions. Cook had even discovered a group of islands in the Pacific that he named the Sandwich Islands. (They were later renamed the Hawaiian Islands.)

The American colonists supplied Cook with a crew and supplies, even though the colonists were at war with the English. Captain Cook again sailed around the tip of South America with two ships, the *Resolution* and the *Discovery*. He tried to establish a hold on the Pacific Coast for Britain.

*The weather was cold, the gales of wind were successive and strong, and sometimes very violent. Our ships complained. We were short of water, and had an unknown coast to explore.*

—John Ledyard, on the *Resolution*, 1778

Cook kept his ships far offshore, then stopped at Nootka Sound on what is now called Vancouver Island. He discovered that the Spanish were already trading with the Indians.

Feeling the trip had been a failure, the crew traded trinkets for some furs. The sea otter furs were warm and made good bedding and clothing for sailing in such a cold climate. The ships returned to the Sandwich Islands, where Cook was killed in a fight with natives.

## "Soft Gold" Changes History

After Cook's death, his crews left the islands and headed to China, where they were delighted to learn that the Chinese paid very high prices for the sea otter pelts they had brought from the Pacific Northwest.

While Cook's voyage did not result in a new trade route across North America, the word about the **lucrative** fur trade was out, and the world hurried in. It was the fur trade that resulted in the first European settlements on the Washington coast.

Captain Cook's expedition traveled far off shore, but they did stop at Vancouver Island and traded with the native people for furs. After sailing on to Alaska, the group returned to the Sandwich Islands (Hawaii), where Cook was killed.

*Captain Cook was looking for the elusive Northwest Passage. Whoever discovered it for Britain was to receive a cash prize equal to nearly a million dollars today.*

## Soda Pop at Sea?

Captain Cook's crews had a device that put carbonated air into water, creating fizzy "soda water." People thought the soda water might prevent scurvy. The men also ate a variety of foods that would not spoil at sea, such as portable soup (dried soup broth), malt, mustard, and carrot marmalade. At first, the crew refused the soured cabbage Cook insisted on, but once the captain ate it, his crew followed. The sauerkraut contained vitamin C and prevented the dreaded scurvy.

## Sea Otters

Between 1750 and 1790 thousands of sea otters were killed for their furs. Almost all of the otters were taken by explorers and trappers at sea before beaver trapping really got underway.

Why was there such a demand for the fur? Much of the fur was taken by ship to China, where it was traded for important things such as silk, spices, and tea. The Chinese used the soft warm furs as coats and blankets during the bitter cold winters.

The sea otter fur trade stopped when there were no longer enough otters alive to make the sea voyage worthwhile.

In 1977 the U.S. Fish and Wildlife Service placed the sea otter on the Endangered Species list. Sea otters have returned to Alaskan waters and the coasts of California and Washington, but their numbers are declining again. People think it is because of toxins in the paint on ships.

### The First English Woman in Washington

Frances Barkley, the seventeen-year-old bride of Captain Charles Barkley, sailed with her young husband to the Northwest Coast in 1787 to begin fur trading. She was the first English woman to come to the area.

Frances wrote in her diary:

*To our great astonishment, we arrived at a large opening [of land] the entrance of which appeared to be about four leagues wide [about twelve miles] and remained about that width as far as the eye could see. . . . My husband immediately recognized it as the long lost strait of Juan de Fuca.*

The Barkleys gave the strait that name, used on old maps, even though they were probably the first Europeans to actually discover it.

# Spain Builds a Fort

With the arrival of explorers from other countries, Spain worried that Americans might cross the continent to look for seaport locations on the Pacific Coast. They also realized that more and more people would come to take advantage of the riches to be made in the fur trade.

Esteban Jose Martinez and a crew of men arrived by ship at Nootka Sound. They built a Spanish settlement they called Fort San Miguel. A bake oven, blacksmith shop, and *infirmary* (a place where the sick were cared for) were built. Gardens were planted.

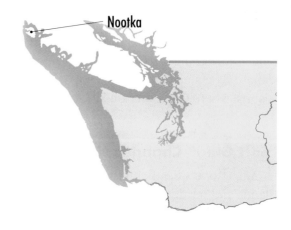
Nootka

Not just Spaniards did the work. Martinez had captured an English ship at sea and taken twenty-nine Chinese immigrants aboard, bringing them to Fort San Miguel to do the hard work.

*I have already [said] that we beat the Russians in taking possession of . . . Nootka, pretending, if . . . other foreigners arrive, that we already formally occupy it, and in order to assure our permanence, a . . . respectable body of troops go about on shore, with missionaries, settlers, cattle, and others.*

—Viceroy of New Spain

## The Nootka Sound Controversy

Russians, Spanish, British, and American traders all wanted to profit from the Pacific fur trade. Britain and Spain both claimed Nootka Sound on Vancouver Island. It seemed they might go to war over the issue. President George Washington worried that the new United States would be dragged into a war. Eventually Spain yielded Nootka to the British. Today the region is part of Canada.

# American Explorers

John Ledyard, an American, had dropped out of college to sail the Pacific with Captain Cook. When young Ledyard returned from the voyage, he went to Paris. In Paris, he met Thomas Jefferson, who was there as a United States ambassador.

As a young man, John Ledyard had a wild plan to go west to North America from Russia.

Ledyard and Jefferson planned a different route to the Pacific Coast—from western Asia.

John Ledyard walked part of the way across Russia, planning to cross the Asian continent, get a ride across the Pacific on a ship, then make his way overland across North America to the states in the East.

Ledyard started east across Russia with two dogs for company, but he was stopped by Russian troops in Siberia. When the Russian empress, Catherine the Great, heard about the upstart American, she ordered him deported back to Poland. That put an end to his plan to survey North America from the West.

## Pirates!

Pirates sailed the Pacific Northwest Coast, too. Between 1575 and 1742, there were at least twenty-five different pirate ships preying upon ships along the West Coast of North America. Pirates came from England, Holland, and France, looking for Spanish ships to plunder. Spanish ships on their way back to New Spain were filled with expensive goods from China and the West Indies.

## Americans Travel by Sea

The next exploration by an American was made by Robert Gray, who had heard about the huge profits to be made by trading furs in China. In 1792, Gray and his crew sailed out of Boston with a load of trade goods bound for the Pacific Coast. It was his second voyage to the Pacific Northwest.

After a long trip around the tip of South America and up the coast, Gray and his men discovered what seemed to be a river, but the water was so rough the ships could not sail into it. They sailed on to a wide inlet "which had the very good appearance of a harbor."

A few days later, the crew again tried to sail into the Columbia River. Sandbars filled the passageway between the sea and the river. Gray waited until the ocean tides were high, then carefully guided a small boat, and then his ship, over the foamy white waves. This time he made it, named the river, and claimed all of the land on both sides of the river for the United States.

The crew spent nine days on the river, trading with the Chinook Indians for furs. Realizing that the Indians captured the valuable sea otters in the ocean and not on the river, the group did no further exploring of the great Columbia.

Vancouver Island

Columbia River

*When Robert Gray's ship arrived at Nootka, the Spaniards at the small fort gave the American sailors gifts of fresh vegetables. "Considering the part of the world we were in, I thought it a very handsome present."*

— Joseph Ingraham, second mate

This art, titled *Entrance of the Columbia River*, shows the rough water dumping out the passengers of a small boat while the larger sailing ship is more stable. Gray's crew reported seeing entire trees being swept downstream in the huge river.

# Naming the Islands

In that same year a British sailor, George Vancouver, also sailed up the coast, passing the mouth of the Columbia River. Later, hearing of Gray's entrance into the Columbia, Vancouver returned and sent a small ship to cross the dangerous sandbar and explore farther up the river. "I never felt more alarmed and frightened in my life," wrote one of the sailors in his journal.

Vancouver spent the summer of 1792 exploring and mapping the Puget Sound region. He claimed all the land on both sides of the river for Great Britain and named Vancouver Island for himself. Among Vancouver's friends were men with last names of Baker, Rainier, Whidbey, and Puget. Can you find the locations named for them?

## Columbia

Do you know what the word "Columbia" means? Columbia was a female symbol that represented the United States. Columbia was a popular illustration in newspapers and magazines of the time.

Who created Columbia? Phyllis Wheatley, a brilliant young African slave in Boston, wrote poetry. She came up with the word and the idea of Columbia the goddess. She included Columbia in a poem she wrote to encourage General George Washington during the Revolutionary War.

The District of Columbia (Washington, D.C.), as well as many other places, were named after the goddess. When statehood was being planned for Washington, the people asked for the name Columbia, but were turned down and given the name Washington instead. Congress thought there would be confusion between a Columbia state and the District of Columbia.

### LINKING THE PAST TO THE PRESENT

**Do you ever hear confusion between our state's name— Washington—and the nation's capital? Naming our state Washington didn't solve the problem, did it?**

Columbia looked like a Roman goddess. She was a symbol of our young country. She may have been named for Columbus.

# LEWIS AND CLARK

In 1803, France had sold the Louisiana Purchase to the United States. It was an immense piece of new territory that needed to be explored and mapped. President Thomas Jefferson sent explorers to see if river travel all the way to the Pacific Ocean was possible, and to learn about the land, plants, animals, and native Indian people.

Jefferson chose his secretary, Captain Meriwether Lewis, to lead the expedition. Lewis, age twenty-nine, was a quiet man, a lover of solitude and nature. He chose an old friend from his army days, Lieutenant William Clark, as a partner. Clark, an outgoing redhead, was eager to take part in the adventure.

The rest of the party consisted of twenty-eight "good hunters, stout, healthy, unmarried men . . . capable of bearing bodily fatigue." York, Clark's black slave, was part of the group.

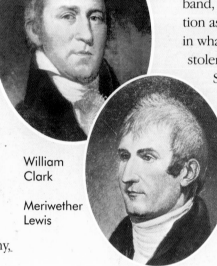

William Clark

Meriwether Lewis

The men traveled north from St. Louis and spent their first winter in the Dakotas—land of the Mandan Indians. There they met a sixteen-year-old Indian woman named Sacajawea and her French Canadian husband, Charbonneau, who joined the expedition as guides and interpreters. (Years before in what is now Idaho, Sacajawea had been stolen from her people by another tribe.) Sacajawea carried her baby son Pomp on her back the entire trip.

The group traveled by boat on the Missouri River and then trekked across the Rockies of northern Idaho. There Sacajawea met her long-lost brother, who had become a chief. His horses helped the group across the mountains.

Worn out but still hopeful, the group came to the winter camp of the Nez Perce Indians along the Clearwater River. The Nez Perce gave Lewis advice about the best route to the Pacific and provided vital

This is the Sacajawea one-dollar coin, first minted in 2000. Sacajawea's likeness was modeled from a living member of the Shoshoni tribe. No pictures or sketches were made of Sacajawea, so we don't know what she looked like, but there are more statues of her now than of any woman in American history.

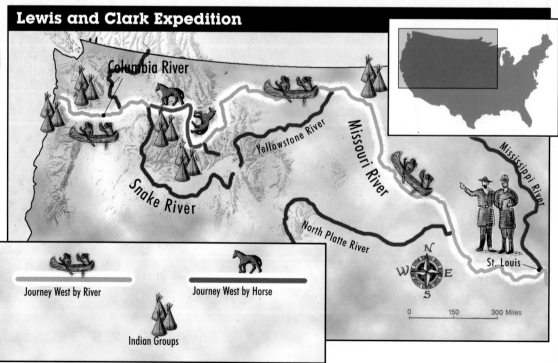

## Lewis and Clark Expedition

Columbia River

Snake River

Yellowstone River

Missouri River

North Platte River

Mississippi River

St. Louis

Journey West by River

Journey West by Horse

Indian Groups

0    150    300 Miles

## Clark's Diary
### November 6, 1805

*A . . . rainy morning. The Indians of the two lodges we passed today came in their canoes. . . . I purchased two beaver skins for which I gave five small fish hooks. . . . Dried out our bedding and killed the fleas which collected in our blankets. . . .*

### November 7, 1805

*A cloudy, foggy morning. Great joy in camp. We are in view of the ocean, this great Pacific Ocean which we have been so anxious to see.*

Sacajawea, voted to build a small shelter, called it Fort Clatsop, and waited for spring.

## The Journey Home

The next spring the group began the long trip home. Along the way, they drew maps, collected plants, and made notes about the native people. They even sent a live prairie dog and bones from a forty-five-foot dinosaur back to President Jefferson.

When the explorers finally arrived in St. Louis over two years after they started, local people were astonished. Many thought the explorers had died. However, it was not until their extensive journals were published—many years after their deaths—that Lewis, Clark, and Sacajawea became heroes.

*Lewis and Clark on the Lower Columbia was painted in 1905 by Charles M. Russell.*
*Amon Carter Museum*

*Lewis and Clark first saw the ocean from Washington, then the group voted to cross the Columbia River into Oregon to wait for spring where the weather was milder.*

food and assistance with building boats. The explorers then moved downriver to the rough Columbia River and continued to the ocean.

Finally, in November of 1805, Clark spied the blue waters of the Pacific. They had reached their goal after nineteen months. The group hoped to meet a ship to take them back to the East, but none appeared, so the entire party, including York and

# American Fur Traders Build Fort Astoria

The Pacific Fur Company, an American company started by John Jacob Astor, was already well-established east of the Rockies, but Astor wanted to expand to the Pacific Northwest. Captain Jonathan Thorn, a strict military man who often angered his crew, sailed from New York to open a trading post on the Pacific Coast.

After the long trip around South America, the *Tonquin,* Thorn's ship, sailed through a storm to the mouth of the wild Columbia River. Instead of waiting for better weather, Thorn ordered five men to get into a small boat and find a safe passage into the river; the boat flipped over in the white foam, and the men drowned. Three other men and a second boat were also lost in the raging waters.

The main group finally made it through and landed the ship. Thorn left some men to build Fort Astoria, named for John Jacob Astor. They built the fort on a hill with a magnificent view of the river below.

Thorn, impatient to begin trading with the Indians for furs, took the rest of the crew and sailed on to Nootka to trade. Later in the summer, word came back that Thorn had made some local Indians so angry that they killed him and all of his men. With many of their original crew and most of their supplies lost, the group at Fort Astoria barely survived the winter.

## Traders Come by Land

Meanwhile, another group of the company was coming by land. They got lost, ran out of food, and were attacked by Indians. More than half of the group died. Marie (a Native American), her husband Pierre Dorion (the expedition's translator), and their two children were among the few who made it to Fort Astoria. Marie had given birth to a third child in Oregon, but he did not live.

A supply ship arrived in the spring, and the Pacific Fur Company survived. They built trading posts where they could trade with native people and even Russian traders who had posts along the coast. They took the furs to China, bought Chinese silk, spices, and rugs, and sailed to New York to sell them.

## The Oregon Country

Unfortunately, the United States and the British became involved in the War of 1812. The Astorians were forced to sell their fort to the British, who renamed it Fort George after the King of England. At the end of the war, Great Britain and the United States signed a treaty that gave both countries ownership of the Oregon Country. The land stretched from the Rocky Mountains to the Pacific Ocean.

**OREGON COUNTRY**

Russian Territory

British Territory

OREGON COUNTRY

United States Territory

Spanish Territory

In the treaty that ended the War of 1812, Britain and the United States agreed to peacefully settle the location of the border. In 1818, they agreed on the 49th parallel as the border from the Great Lakes to the Continental Divide in the Rocky Mountains, but neither country was willing to give up the Oregon Country. They agreed to postpone that decision.

# British Fur Traders

Two years before Lewis and Clark, the Canadians explored British Columbia. Alexander Mackenzie made it all the way to the Pacific. His trading company, the Northwest Company, did a lot of business with Indian traders.

While the Americans were building Fort Astoria, David and Charlotte Thompson, British traders, brought their children into the Oregon Country. They founded Spokane House, the first trading post in what is now Washington State, months before Fort Astoria was built.

Thompson recorded in his journal about the land and the native peoples. He also made excellent maps, using stars as reference points for surveying land. The Indians called him "Kookoo-sint," meaning "the man who watches stars."

Thompson is credited for locating the source of the Columbia River.

## The Hudson's Bay Company

In 1821, the Northwest Company merged into the Hudson's Bay Company. The HBC controlled the fur trade in Canada and the Oregon Country. It was directed from England and Montreal, Canada.

The HBC needed a director of operations in the Oregon Country, and chose an excellent trapper, medical doctor, and ambitious leader to run the affairs of the region. Dr. John McLoughlin soon gained a reputation as a good and fair businessman.

Dr. McLoughlin traveled by canoe and horseback across Canada for four months and reached Fort George in the fall. He wrote in a letter:

*Since my arrival on the 8th of November, we have not seen one clear sun shining day and not ten days without rain. . . .*

McLoughlin built a new fort near the mouth of the Willamette River and called it Fort Vancouver. He wanted a fort nearer to other forts on the north side of the Columbia. He thought it was important to keep a British hold on the land there. The company moved all the trading goods, animals, and people to the new location. Fort Vancouver grew to contain a hospital, small houses for employees and their Indian wives, storehouses for furs, trade goods, and workshops for blacksmiths, carpenters, and other craftsmen. There was a sawmill to provide lumber and a gristmill to grind grain.

Outside the fort there were extensive orchards, farmlands, a dairy, and herds of cattle. Ships brought the latest news and supplies.

The people at Fort Vancouver came from many places. There were local Chinook Indians, Delaware and Iroquois Indian fur trappers from the East, French Canadians, Hawaiian laborers (called *Kanakas*), Indian women who had married employees of the HBC, and Scottish traders.

McLoughlin was called the "White-Headed Eagle" by the Indian people. He treated them with respect and gained their trust. Indians supplied most of the furs the HBC needed for trade to distant cities.

There were very few women at Fort Vancouver, so Eloisa McLoughlin was treated as the "princess" of the fort. Her father was in charge of all operations. Her mother was a Native American. Like many other children of the day who had white fathers and Indian mothers, Eloisa grew up as a child of two cultures.

Fort Vancouver was a trading post, not a military fort. It was the main source of supplies and information for early trappers, missionaries, and settlers.

Today you can visit Fort Vancouver in the city of Vancouver and see things almost as they were 200 years ago.

*M*any of the Hudson's Bay Company fur traders were from Scotland. A tall, red-haired Scottish Highlander in plaid kilts played bagpipes for the local Indians. It awed the Indians, who had never heard anything like it.

## Voyageurs

Traders used canoes to move piles of furs on the rivers. French-speaking Canadians called **voyageurs** paddled the canoes. When crossing land, they carried both the furs and the canoes on their backs. The voyageurs became famous for their strength, their colorful dress, and the songs they sang while paddling canoes down the rivers.

## Furs, Forts, and Farms

The main business of the forts was trading for furs. Company trappers traveled out along the many streams to kill animals and take their fur. Indians also brought furs to the fort and traded them for glass beads,

muskets, and metal objects such as knives and cooking pots.

From Fort Vancouver, British traders **bartered** for furs from French and Indian trappers up and down the Columbia River. The fur in demand was the beaver pelt, called a plew. Plews were stretched, dried, and shipped to London, where the long soft fur was made into felt. The felt was then made into hats. Beaver top hats were a very popular style for men in Europe and the United States until fashion replaced them with silk hats. By the time silk hats replaced beaver hats, the beavers in the Pacific Northwest had been nearly trapped to extinction.

The HBC set up farming companies at Fort Nisqually and at Cowlitz Farm, south of Tacoma. Crops were grown for trade. Fort Colville, up the Columbia River, was both a trading and a grain-growing center. Fort Vancouver remained an important settlement in the Oregon Country.

A few American fur trade companies tried to set up fur trading posts in the Pacific Northwest, but they were not successful. Fort Astoria faded when the War of 1812 broke out between the United States and Britain in the East. Other attempts were failures because traders had little chance of making a profit as long as the powerful Hudson's Bay Company controlled the region's trade.

**FUR TRADING LOCATIONS**

## The Fur Trade Ends

By the late 1840s the fur era was over. The fur-bearing animals were nearly gone. Styles had changed. Pioneers were beginning to move into the area. They used the trading posts, trails, and information they got from traders. The fur traders had come from all over the world and reported knowledge about the area, its natural resources, and its native people to others. The Pacific Northwest would not be forgotten. Unfortunately, the everyday life of the American Indian had changed forever. You will read more about this in later chapters.

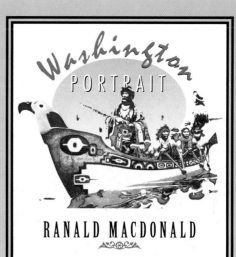

## RANALD MACDONALD

Ranald MacDonald's father was a Scottish trader with the Hudson's Bay Company and his mother was a daughter of a powerful Chinook chief. He grew up at Fort Vancouver, where he met three Japanese fishermen. He heard about the exotic land of Japan and decided to go there someday, but at that time, Japan would not allow foreigners to enter the country.

Eventually, Ranald got a job on an American whaling ship. On the coast of Japan, he went ashore in a small boat. He had an English dictionary, a history book, and a world map that he thought would reassure the Japanese that he meant no harm.

Local villagers quickly discovered him and put him in jail. He was treated well, however, and spent his time teaching Japanese youths to speak English.

A year later Ranald was sent back to the United States, where he discovered his Chinook relatives had died from diseases. When Commodore Perry of the U.S. Navy later negotiated a trade treaty with Japan, he used MacDonald's former Japanese students as interpreters.

## WHAT DO YOU THINK?

From what you have read about the fur trade, what do you think were some positive and negative effects on the development of our state? On the native people? On the animals? In the lives of the explorers and trappers?

## Washington Place Names

One advantage to being an explorer is getting to name places for yourself and your friends. Many of the early Spanish names have survived. Are you familiar with these Spanish names?

**San Juan Islands** — named for Saint John the Baptist
**Guemes Island** — named for the viceroy of Mexico
**Rosario Strait** — named for Our Lady of the Rosary
**Port Angeles** — named for Our Lady of the Angels
**Cape Alava** — named after the governor of Acapulco

Fort Walla Walla was another trading post of the Hudson's Bay Company. This sketch by Joseph Drayton is called *Fur Traders and Indians.*

## Chinook Jargon

How did sailors and coastal Indians talk when neither knew the other's language? The problem was complicated by the many different languages the Indian tribes spoke and the variety of countries the traders came from. American Indians who spoke different languages were already speaking a trade language when white trappers and settlers came. Called Chinook Jargon, the language had about 300 words.

Here are a few words from Chinook Jargon:

| Chinook Jargon | English |
| --- | --- |
| Boston | American |
| cultus | worthless |
| muckamuck | food; eating |
| skookum | strong |
| tillicum | man |
| tyee | chief |
| gleece | grease |
| pire | fire |
| gleece-pire | candle |
| mahkook | trade |
| chuck | water |
| tenus | small |
| hyas | big |

## CHAPTER 4 REVIEW

1. What were the early explorers looking for? Why?

2. What country sent the first explorers?

3. What disease killed sailors during long sea voyages? What was the cure?

4. What was accomplished by the voyage of Captain Cook's crew to Asia?

5. What American walked across Russia to find a new passage to the Northwest?

6. Name the American who sailed to the Northwest. What places are named after him?

7. What African slave girl created the concept of Columbia as a symbol of America?

8. Who sent Lewis and Clark to the Pacific Ocean? What were three things the men were supposed to do?

9. Who was the young Indian woman who helped Lewis and Clark get to the Pacific Ocean?

10. What was the name of the largest fur trading company in the region? Which country started the company?

11. Why did trappers want beaver pelts?

12. What three factors ended the fur trade?

13. How did the fur trade affect settlement of the Pacific Northwest?

## GEOGRAPHY TIE-IN

1. Discuss with your class how Washington's location on the Pacific Coast contributed to early exploration by the Spanish and British. How would our history have been different if Washington were not on the Pacific Coast?

2. On the map of the Lewis and Clark expedition on page 66, look at where they started and where their journey ended. What were the main rivers they followed? Why was early travel easier on water than on land?

3. Can you locate a place by its latitude and longitude? Use a globe to find the point that is 46 degrees N and 127 degrees W. What river enters the Pacific Ocean there?

4. What natural features caused early sea explorers to miss both the mouth of the Columbia River and the Strait of Juan de Fuca for 150 years?

## PEOPLE TO KNOW

Father Blanchet
George Washington Bush
Isabelle Bush
Mother Joseph
Daniel Lee
Jason Lee
John McLoughlin
John Mullan
President James Polk
Sager Children
Father de Smet
Eliza Spalding
Henry Spalding
Isaac Stevens
Elijah White
Marcus Whitman
Narcissa Whitman

## PLACES TO LOCATE

Vancouver
Walla Walla
Willamette Valley
Bush Prairie
East Coast
Pacific Ocean
Pacific Coast
Vancouver Island
Puget Sound
San Juan Islands

## WORDS TO UNDERSTAND

abolitionist
bounty
compromise
entrepreneur
grade (roads)
immunity
negotiate
ransom
vengeance
veteran

*Caught by Snow*, a painting by Glen Hopkinsen, shows the trials of families who left too late in the year and got caught by an early snowstorm.

**1834** Jason and Daniel Lee start the first mission in the Oregon Country.

**TIMELINE**   1780   1830

**1780s–1840s** The fur trade era begins and lasts sixty years.

**1831** Four Indian men travel to St. Louis and ask Clark to send Christian missionaries to Oregon.

**1836** Marcus and Narcissa Whitman leave New York State to start a mission in the Oregon Country.

# Looking West

**Chapter 5**

**1843** First Wolf Meeting is held.

**1844** The George Washington Bush family goes to the Oregon Country.

**1848** Oregon Territory is created.

Gold is found in California.

**1856** Mother Joseph comes to Vancouver.

**1840**

**1850**

**1860**

**1838** Father Blanchet builds the first Catholic mission in the Oregon Country.

**1842** Elijah White and 100 people travel the Oregon Trail.

**1847** The Whitmans are murdered by Cayuse Indians.

**1846** The U.S. gains full control of the Oregon Country.

**1853** Washington Territory is created. Isaac Stevens is the first governor.

The Mullan Road is completed.

# Christian Missionaries

In the early 1800s, people in New England were excited about religion. The church was the center of village life, and crowds of enthusiastic worshippers attended prayer meetings and revivals. Preachers shouted out sermons of heaven and hell, and congregations enthusiastically sang religious songs. Many people, especially women, supported a worldwide missionary effort. Protestant missionaries and teachers were sent to Africa, China, and the American West. Missionaries tried to teach the people how to read the Bible and dress, speak, and live like Christian Americans.

## A Request for Christianity

In 1831, three Nez Perce and a Flathead Indian went to St. Louis to visit William Clark, who, along with Lewis, had visited them during the famous exploration trip. The Indian men asked Clark to send someone to teach the Christian religion to their people. They thought Christianity would help them understand the white people's ways and their powerful God. A religious newspaper printed the story.

## Methodist Missionaries

Jason Lee and his nephew Daniel Lee, both Methodist ministers from the East, were the first to answer the request of the Nez Perce. Instead of staying with the Nez Perce, however, they stopped at Fort Vancouver, where John McLoughlin advised them to settle in the Willamette Valley. The Lees converted few Indians. The Indian people there did not take to the white people's religion or lifestyle, and their children did not like the strict rules of the mission school.

Jason Lee returned to the states and brought fifty more settlers to Oregon. They opened new missions and started settlements. Lee was active in setting a new government for the settlements, and he educated the children in his mission schools. Accused of neglecting his commitment to the Indians, Lee was later recalled by the mission board and his mission was closed.

## Catholic Missionaries

Some members of the Hudson's Bay Company were Catholic and wanted priests. Father Francis Blanchet answered the call. He spent most of his time with the French Canadian Catholics and not with Indians. Later, a Jesuit priest, Peter John de Smet, and other priests came and worked with the Coeur d'Alenes and Flatheads. Many of the Coeur d'Alenes were baptized Christians, mixing in their own religious customs with that of their new religion.

## Presbyterian Missionaries

Narcissa Prentiss was a kindergarten teacher in rural New York State who dreamed of being a Presbyterian missionary. A minister put her in touch with Marcus Whitman, a young doctor who was planning a mission in the West. Only married people were sent to missions, so the two agreed to marry. They set out to build a mission in the Rocky Mountains. They were joined by Reverend Henry Spalding and his wife Eliza, who were also on their way to an Indian mission.

The Whitmans and Spaldings traveled to the Oregon Country with a party of fur traders. Eliza and Narcissa rode horseback on sidesaddles most of the way because the small wagon Eliza's parents had given her could not make it up the rugged trails. Eliza and Narcissa were the first white women to travel across the entire continent.

The Whitmans and Spaldings finally arrived at Fort Vancouver, where Dr. McLoughlin sold them supplies and advised them about locating a mission. During the long trip, which had taken 207 days, the Whitmans and Spaldings had a hard time getting along with each other. As a result, they decided to build two missions. The Spaldings went to live with the Nez Perce Indians along the Clearwater River. The Whitmans built a mission among the Cayuse Indians on the Walla Walla River.

*"We have plenty of dry buffalo meat which we purchased from the Indians and dry it for meat. I can scarcely eat it, it appears so filthy, but it will keep us alive and we ought to be thankful for it. . . ."*

— Narcissa Whitman

## More Missionaries

Two years later, Congregationalist missionary couples joined the Whitmans and Spaldings. Mary and Elkanah Walker, along with Myra and Cushing Eells, built a mission among the Spokane Indians near present-day Spokane.

Missionaries built log houses and schoolrooms and taught the American Indian men and women how to raise animals, grow and harvest crops, grind wheat to make flour, and weave wool into cloth. Missionaries translated the Bible into the Indian languages so they could teach the Indians to read.

The missionaries wrote many letters to their friends and families in far-off New England. It took two years for a letter to receive a reply because everything had to be sent by ship around the tip of South America. The letters were published in newspapers back east and read aloud in church meetings.

## Missionary Children

Several children were born at the missions—the first white Americans to be born in the region. The children learned how to read and write from their parents. There were few supplies. Mary Walker once drew on a bird's egg to show the children where the earth's continents and oceans were.

The Whitman Mission along the Walla Walla River was built to bring Christianity to the native Indian people. Called the Waiilatpu Mission, it also served as a rest stop for pioneers. This drawing was made in 1847.

Sometimes tragedy struck the children. The Whitman's only child, two-year-old Alice, drowned in the river near their home. The Whitmans eventually adopted sixteen more children.

## WHAT DO YOU THINK?

**Do you think people should share their religious beliefs with others? Do you think people should try to change the lifestyle of other people? Why or why not?**

Narcissa Prentiss Whitman

Marcus Whitman

**EARLY MISSIONS**

Fort Nisqually (Demers)
Lapwai Mission (Spaldings)
•ASTORIA
Waiilatpu Mission (Whitmans)
Mission Bottom (Lee)
The Dalles Mision (Lee)
St. Pauls (Blanchet)
*Columbia R.*
*Willamette R.*

Both Catholics and Protestants opened missions in the Oregon Country.

# Disease and Death

Something terrible and unexpected happened to the Indian men, women, and especially children when explorers, missionaries, and pioneer settlers arrived. Indians had no ***immunity*** to European diseases. Ship's crews brought smallpox, measles, cholera, influenza (flu), and malaria. Entire villages along the coast were wiped away by sickness.

In 1847 nearly 5,000 American pioneers passed

*Whitman College and Whitman County are named after the Whitmans.*

through the Whitman's mission. The last wagon train of the season brought many sick travelers infected with measles. The Walker children got sick, and at the Whitman mission there were both children and adults in sickbeds. Several people died from the infection.

At the same time, there was a measles epidemic among Coastal Indians. The Cayuse Indians near the Whitman mission had no immunity to the disease. When they came down with measles, over half the tribe died. It was horrible and frightening for everyone. Dr. Whitman with his simple medicines could do nothing to save the people he had tried so hard to help. Some Cayuse, in fact, accused Dr. Whitman of starting the disease and trying to kill the Indians. They thought that since he was a

doctor, or a shaman, he had special powers over disease.

The angry Cayuse attacked the Americans, killing Marcus and Narcissa Whitman and eleven others. They took forty-seven women and children hostage. After bargaining with the Hudson's Bay Company officials, the angry Indian men **ransomed** the prisoners for blankets, shirts, tobacco, and muskets.

The Whitman Massacre caused American settlers in Oregon to clamor for **vengeance** and protection. Five hundred volunteers assembled a militia. The first war between Indians and whites erupted across the region. The Cayuse War lasted for two years, until the Cayuse people turned over five men involved in the killings. The men were tried and hanged.

## Seven Alone

Eight Sager children were orphaned when their parents died while traveling west on the Oregon Trail. One was only an infant. Another child was on crutches, having broken her leg when she was run over by a wagon.

Members of the wagon train cared for the children for the rest of the journey. Like most other pioneers, the group stayed for a while at the Whitman mission. The Whitmans, whose own daughter had drowned, adopted all of the children.

The Sagers later experienced the tragic murder of the Whitmans. Two of the Sager boys were killed during the assault. Years later, the Sager girls wrote about their experiences in their new land. A movie called *Seven Alone* was made about them.

This homemade doll once belonged to one of the Sager girls while they lived with the Whitmans. It is on display in the museum at the Whitman Mission National Historic Site at Walla Walla.

## Mother Joseph

Esther Pariseau, a young Catholic girl, joined a convent and was sent to Vancouver. During her forty-six-years in the Northwest, she was known as Mother Joseph. She built hospitals, Indian schools, academies, and orphanages. She did men's work—unusual in those days—drawing plans, checking construction, laying bricks, and carving beautiful woodwork.

Mother Joseph raised money for her projects by traveling around the country on horseback with other nuns. In towns and mining camps, the woman in the black robe asked for donations to her causes.

There is a statue of Mother Joseph in the Capitol Building in Washington, D.C.

# GO WEST!

After the explorers, traders, trappers, and missionaries came to the Pacific Northwest, pioneer families in wagon trains rode or walked to the rich new land. The first pioneers settled near Fort Vancouver or Oregon City, but later groups spread out over the fertile land.

Traveling across the flat plains was relatively easy. The main problems were crossing the wide rivers and dealing with the weather on the six-month journey. It was often hot and dusty or wet and muddy.

Crossing the high Rocky Mountains was difficult, however. Weary families who did not make it through before the snows fell had to wait until spring. Finding passage through steep mountain ranges was not easy. A government explorer found South Pass in Wyoming in 1832, and two men made it through the Blue Mountains of Oregon in 1840. This opened up the way for more pioneers to follow.

Elijah White, a former missionary to Oregon, brought a group of 100 settlers from Independence, Missouri, to Oregon's Willamette Valley in 1842. Their route became known as the Oregon Trail. For the next thirty-five years, the trail was used by over 300,000 men, women, and children.

## Reasons for Going West

Why did people go west?
- There was a chance to see new country and to be part of an adventure.
- Good farmland was available for a low cost. In the eastern states, land was crowded, and the overworked soil had lost its fertility.
- Merchants, doctors, and lawyers came to start businesses.
- Many people wanted to escape the problems of slavery, including disagreements between slaveholders and *abolitionists*.
- People wanted to live in a mild, healthful climate.

Most of the earliest pioneers settled near Fort Vancouver or in Oregon City. This is Oregon City in 1846.

## THE OREGON TRAIL

Follow the trail from Independence, Missouri, to Oregon. What rivers did the trail follow? What kinds of land did people travel over? What landmarks did they see along the way? At what forts did they stop to rest and get supplies?

Lucia Loraine Williams wrote in her 1851 diary:

*Some . . . were going for wealth and honors. Others, who had suffered from ill health for years, and to whom life had become a burden, expected to regain health . . . For some, life was too prosy and tame in their old environments. They wanted more action, more diversity, more thrilling experiences with man and beast.*

Many young people went west because their families did. Sixteen-year-old Eugenia Zieber learned that she would be going on the Oregon Trail when she was a student at a seminary for young ladies in Pennsylvania. A letter came from her father just two days before Christmas, telling her about the plan. He wanted to move the family to a healthier climate.

LINKING THE PAST TO THE PRESENT

How would a trip to a new place change a person's life? What changes would a person have to make to move to a place that was wild and unsettled?

### Getting Ready

Despite rumors of Indian attacks and other hardships on such a long trip, hundreds of settlers took the gamble. A family needed a strong wagon and a team of either four oxen or six mules. People had to prepare enough food for the trip and some to live on once they reached the new land. Families who planned to farm (and most planned to do that) also had to take tools and seed.

During the winter before the trip, families spent the evenings drying apples and grapes, making jerky, baking crackers, and sewing cloth sacks and quilts. Even the wagon cover, made of canvas, had to be stitched by hand. Flour, sugar, tea, salt, and other items were packed in cloth sacks or barrels.

People purchased almanacs or guidebooks and took them along on the trail for guidance. Some books were reliable, while others were written by authors who had never left New York City. After making the trip westward, travelers joked that they had tossed their guidebooks away when the going got rough and the book proved to be useless.

## Overland Travel

Traveling by wagon was both difficult and exciting. Many people took diaries with them and wrote about what they saw and experienced. Later, diaries were copied and sent back to relatives, encouraging others to make the trip.

Most people came as family units. Some traveled with neighbors with whom they would settle when they reached the Oregon Country. Other wagon groups were made up of people who belonged to the same church.

People traveled west in groups for several reasons. One was the safety of traveling with others. Bandits, who were sometimes dressed as Indians, robbed wagon trains. Another reason was for help with emergencies. When animals sickened and died, when wagon axles or wheels broke, or when someone got sick, there were other people to rely on.

Pioneers had to wait for spring and the grass to grow up before making the journey. With oxen and horses to pull their wagons, they needed to be sure there would be grass along the way. The first weeks of travel were usually pleasant. The spring weather was mild and there were grassy plains and wild flowers along the way. Rain and mud were sometimes a problem, however.

As the trip went on, the trail dried to dust. The thousands of oxen and mules kicked up so much dust that it was nearly impossible to breathe if your wagon was in the rear of the train. Other times, the rain made the road so muddy the animals couldn't pull the wagons through it. The people got wet and cold. It was hard to prepare and cook food.

Children were expected to gather buffalo chips, care for younger children, and not get lost. *Painting by Glen Hopkinson*

## Roles of Men and Women

Men did the heaviest work and probably had the most fun. They hunted, bartered with Indians, drove wagons, and herded cattle. They also raced around on horseback, fired guns, and went swimming.

Women also worked hard driving wagons, setting up camp, cooking over a fire, tending the sick, and caring for bored, tired, and hungry children.

### Animals of Choice

Oxen were the best choice for pulling wagons. They ate prairie grass, could pull heavy loads, and were not as likely to be stolen by Indians as horses were. Those who could afford it took an extra team in case anything happened to the animals on the trip.

Cows were taken along to provide milk. One traveler wrote: "The milk can stood nearby and always yielded up its lump of butter at night, churned by the movement of the wagon from the surplus morning's milk."

Families took horses for riding and exploring and to have in the new home. Chickens, goats, and dogs also walked the thousands of miles to Oregon.

"*Sometimes the dust is so great that the drivers cannot see their teams at all though the sun is shining brightly.*"

— Elizabeth Wood, 1851

*The trip went quickly from awe to boredom. "If we were only in Willamette Valley, for I am so tired of this."*

— Elizabeth Wood

*The wagon roads were so heavily traveled that they looked like highways. Father de Smet, a Catholic missionary, wrote that the trail was "as smooth as a barn floor swept by the winds, and not a blade of grass can shoot up on it on account of the continual passing."*

### Effect on the Land and Native People

Thousands of oxen, mules, and horses grazed their way west. They often spread out for a mile or more beside the wagons. So many animals passed through each summer that watering holes were drained by heavy use. Natural grasslands were depleted, so wild animals had trouble finding food.

Always looking for fresh meat, the travelers hunted along the way. This meant that the supply of deer, elk, and buffalo that Indians relied on for food dwindled.

Pioneers observed Indians and wrote about them in diaries. One woman observed:

*Indians ketch crickets and dry them, pound to powder, mix with berries, and bake it for bread.*
— Catherine Washburn, 1853

At first the Indians had been friendly and helpful to the travelers, but after a while they grew angry. Sometimes Indians tried to get the pioneers to leave the area by burning the prairie grass. When this happened, the pioneers' animals had nothing to eat.

*The Indians had set all on fire except here and there a spot. The blackness of praire under our circumstances presented a dismal sight. We found the grass mostly burned ahead. . . . we had to stop because of the fire and smoke.*
— Levi Jackman

## LINKING THE PAST TO THE PRESENT

- **Why were the American Indians angry at the pioneers for killing buffalo?**
- **How are wild animals protected today? Why?**

### Bartering

In the Oregon Country, trading between Indians and pioneers was common. Indian men offered large pieces of dried salmon in exchange for needles, thread, tools, shirts, and socks. Blankets were also in high demand. Indians also made moccasins for trade. "Swap, swap" was a common term.

### End of the Trail

As settlers arrived in the Oregon Country, Hudson's Bay Company officials directed them to settle south of the Columbia River. The British company wanted to keep Americans out of the area north of the river, hoping that the region would one day be under British rule.

Americans thought differently. They wanted the excellent harbors of Puget Sound for American ships. Some people settled around Puget Sound and in the Cowlitz River Valley. Places such as Tumwater, Tacoma, Olympia, Centralia, Alki Point (Seattle), and Port Townsend were founded. At first, however, most people settled south of the Columbia River in Oregon.

GEORGE WASHINGTON BUSH was a war *veteran* and successful cattleman in Missouri. Then Missouri passed a law making it illegal for free Negroes to live there. Afraid his property would be taken because he was black, Bush sold his home and business and outfitted six large wagons full of supplies.

George, his wife Isabelle (a white woman who had been a nurse), and their sons left for the Oregon Country. One of the Bush children later remembered his father hiding $2,000 in silver underneath the floorboards of a wagon. The money made the trip safely.

A few other families joined the Bush family, and the group joined a wagon train. When the Bushes arrived in the Willamette Valley, they discovered they could not stay. A law had been passed that said no Negroes could live in Oregon.

So the Bush party headed north of the Columbia River. They figured there would be few Americans there to challenge them. They were right. Bush and about thirty others spent another month walking beside their wagons to their new home.

The little group built log homes, plowed the ground, and farmed. Nisqually Indians taught the new settlers to gather oysters, dig clams, and fish for trout and salmon. The farms prospered, but within a few years the Bush family once again faced the loss of their land.

A law said that only white Americans and mixed-blood Indians could own land. New settlers wanted the Bush farm because it was so valuable. Fifty-three neighbors signed a petition asking that Bush be allowed to keep his 640 acres of

Bush Prairie

The town of Bush Prairie is named after George Washington Bush.

# GEORGE WASHINGTON BUSH

George Washington Bush brought his family and neighbors to settle in the West. *Painting by Leandro Della Piana.*

land. Congress responded, giving Bush legal right to his original homestead.

A few years later, the Bush farm was

one of the most productive in the area. George Washington Bush was always interested in improving his farm and spent his last years studying new techniques. Bush's son was elected to the legislature in 1889.

*He provided the settlers with food for their first winter and with seed for the first sowing. If they had no money, he still supplied them with what they needed.*

— Bush's neighbor

## Slavery, or Not?

The people who moved to the Pacific Northwest brought one big problem with them—what to do about slavery. To keep the question of slavery from creating problems, Oregon residents passed laws to keep all blacks—free or slave—out of the territory.

# The First Local Government

The first rules were made by the British Hudson's Bay Company. As the number of people grew, and the people spread out away from Fort Vancouver, the settlers wanted an American government, with a sheriff and courts.

> *As [there] is no laws in this country we do the best we can.*
>
> — Early trapper

## Wolf Meetings

"Wolf Meetings" were the earliest forms of local government in the region. Settlers held meetings to decide how to handle the many wolves that were killing cattle and sheep. Panthers, bears, and bobcats were also a problem. Settlers agreed to pay a tax that would be used to pay hunters **bounties** for dead wolves. The meetings led to the first real government in the Oregon Country.

## BOUNTIES

A bounty was a fee paid for killing an animal:

$5.00 panther
$3.00 large wolf
$2.00 bear

After the Wolf Meetings, about a hundred Americans and French Canadians gathered in the Willamette Valley store to start a local government. There was much discussion about whether or not the group should make laws at all. A popular story says that Joe Meek, a fur trapper, finally suggested that the noisy group go outside. He directed the men in favor of government to stand in one place and those against to stand in another place. The vote was close, but several officials were elected and laws were written. The first laws banned alcoholic drinks.

# The Oregon Territory

Thousands of American settlers had located in the Willamette Valley. They organized a temporary government in 1843 and asked the U.S. Congress for the creation of the Oregon Territory. But the area was still claimed by both Britain and the United States. Both countries wanted the rich farmland in a mild climate and the natural harbors of Puget Sound.

In the East, James Polk used as his presidential campaign slogan the phrase "Fifty-four Forty or Fight." This meant that the U.S. wanted land north of today's present boundary, all the way to the 54th latitude line, the southern border of Alaska. Polk won the election and became president.

Britain and the United States **negotiated** a **compromise** in 1846. They agreed that Britain would give up its claims to the land below the 49th parallel—the area that forms the border between the United States and Canada today. The United States gave up the land above the 49th parallel.

In Washington, D.C., there was a lot of discussion about the Oregon Territory. Senator Stephen Douglas of Illinois had already proposed that Oregon be admitted as a free territory—free of slavery. Southern senators opposed this because it would upset the even balance of free and slave states and territories. The arguments went on and on.

Finally, on the last day that Congress was in session, President Polk created the Oregon Territory. It was August 1848. Salem, Oregon, became the capital. A young man from Illinois, Abraham Lincoln, was offered the job as governor of the territory, but he turned down the job.

## What Is a Territory?

Territories were different than states. The people in a territory could vote for leaders to send to Washington, D.C., but the representatives could not vote there. They could only try to persuade Congress to make laws that were favorable to the people in their territory. Back home, most officials and judges were appointed by Congress instead of being voted in by the local people.

## THE OREGON TERRITORY

Oregon Territory 1848–1853

Unorganized

Continental Divide

The new territory included both present-day Washington, Oregon, Idaho, and parts of Montana and Wyoming. Two of its borders were the Pacific Ocean and the Continental Divide. Slavery was not allowed in the territory.

## Dividing up the Land

Because so many Americans wanted to come to Oregon, Congress passed the Donation Land Claim Act of 1850. It was a homestead law that allowed each white male over eighteen years of age to claim 320 acres of land for free. If he had a wife, they could claim another 320 acres. All they had to do was live on the land and grow crops for four years. Because the law gave land only to white people, few minorities came to the region.

# Washington Becomes a Territory

Soon, settlers living north of the Columbia River wanted to separate from the Oregon Territory and form their own government. They thought the government leaders in Oregon were too far away and that the territory was too big. After several requests, Washington Territory was created in 1853.

The people wanted the territory to be named Columbia, but Congress changed the name so there would be no confusion with the District of Columbia. It was a huge piece of country but had only 4,000 American residents and 17,000 American Indians.

## Pig War

The agreement between Britain and the United States left one thing unclear: who owned the San Juan Islands? Citizens from both countries had settled there and each thought the other was trespassing.

Tempers were short when a British neighbor's pig got into an American farmer's garden and ruined the potato patch. The farmer shot the pig. This set off a fight between the Americans and British on the island. Sixty-six American soldiers took a position near the wharf.

The British were furious and sent three British warships to remove the men without firing on them. They refused to budge. Eventually five British warships and over 2,000 soldiers came. Americans, with 155 men stationed behind earthen walls, waited it out.

When news reached Washington, D.C., President James Buchanan sent a commander of the army to solve the situation. The British retreated to one end of the island and the Americans to the other. It stayed that way for twelve years, until a German leader was asked to study the situation. He declared that the islands belonged to the United States.

The "Pig War" was settled. The only casualty? One pig.

## Who Owns Oregon?

• **Convention of 1818**—Great Britain and the United States agree to joint occupation of the Oregon Country.

• **Adams-Onis Treaty, 1819**—Spain gives its claims to the Oregon Country to the United States.

• **Oregon Treaty, 1846**—Great Britain retreats northward. International boundary is drawn at the 49th parallel. The Oregon Country is finally owned by the United States.

The new territory, created in 1853, included parts of present-day Idaho and Montana. Six years later, Oregon became a state.

### The First Governor

The first governor of Washington Territory was Isaac Stevens. He was also appointed as Secretary of Indian Affairs. Stevens had been born and raised in Massachusetts. He was smart, with lots of energy and ambition. He dreamed that a railroad would cross the continent, bringing people to Washington Territory.

Stevens traveled west with a group of men who helped survey the route. In Olympia, the territorial capital, he worked to organize the first legislature and create laws and schools.

*"Below us, in a deep mud, were a few low wooden houses at the head of Puget Sound. My heart sank. . . ."*

— Mrs. Stevens, after arriving by ship

Isaac Stevens was appointed the first governor of Washington Territory.

## The Mullan Road

Lt. John Mullan was given the job of building a road between Fort Walla Walla and Fort Benton, Montana. The road was needed to move supplies and men between the two distant forts.

Mullan hired ninety men to do the work. They took fifty pack mules, a herd of cattle for fresh meat, and teamsters to drive forty-five freight wagons. A hundred soldiers went along to protect workers from Indian attacks.

The work was hard. The men had to chop down huge trees. Then they cleared the brush and **graded** the roads, using mules to drag logs over the ground.

Workers had accidents with axes and falling trees. One hunter was lost for days. His legs had to be amputated because of frostbite. Finally the workers made it to Fort Benton.

Settlers, traders, and gold seekers used the road more than the soldiers did. One **entrepreneur** used a pack train of seven camels loaded with merchandise. The odd-looking camels frightened horses and caused them to run off.

## Indians and Settlers

When sea traders and fur trappers first came to the Pacific Northwest, Indians were willing to trade with them and most got along well. Indians worked for the fur companies and helped missionaries build homes and churches.

As thousands of settlers came west on the Oregon Trail, relations between Indians and whites changed. After 1848, so many gold seekers used the trail that wild game could hardly be found. Disease wiped out whole Indian villages. An era of warfare lasted thirty years.

You will read more about the conflict between settlers and Native Americans in the next chapter.

## CHAPTER 5 REVIEW

1. Why did Christian missionaries come to the Oregon Country?

2. Who were some of the early missionaries to Oregon Country?

3. How did disease affect Native Americans? Why did the Cayuse murder the Whitmans?

4. Why did the Hudson's Bay Company want Americans to settle south of the Columbia River?

5. What were the main reasons people wanted to move to the West?

6. What preparations did people make before heading west on the Oregon Trail?

7. What laws did the early Oregon settlers make to handle the problem of slavery?

8. Why did George Washington Bush settle north of the Columbia River?

9. What were some of George Washington Bush's admirable personality traits?

10. Why did Britain and the United States both want the Pacific Northwest?

11. How was the question of ownership of the Oregon Country and its boundary an example of negotiation and compromise?

12. After the Pig War, which country finally got ownership of the San Juan Islands?

13. What year was the Washington Territory separated from the Oregon Territory? What was the capital city of Washington Territory?

14. Who was the first governor of the Washington Territory? What was his other title?

15. What road was built to connect army forts in Washington and Montana? Who used the road?

### GEOGRAPHY TIE-IN

1. What landforms along the coast were important to both the British and the Americans? Why is shipping important to the economy of a place?

2. People choose natural landforms such as rivers, oceans, and mountain ranges as boundaries. What natural features formed boundaries of the Oregon Country? Of Washington Territory?

3. Today, the largest population of Washington lives near water. Why is living near water important to people? How do people who don't live near water get the water they need?

## THE TIME
# 1850–1883

### ▶▶ PEOPLE TO KNOW

Patrick Clark
David Douglas
Ulysses Grant
Chin Gee Hee
Robert Hume
John James
Chief Joseph
Kamiakin
David Maynard
James Monaghan
Chief Moses
George Pickett
Chief Sealth
Isaac Stevens
Sarah Winnemucca
Erskine Wood
Henry Yesler

### ▶▶ PLACES TO LOCATE

China
Japan
Ireland
Canada
Alaska
California
Idaho
Montana
Nevada
Issaquah
Olympia
Pasco
Seattle
Tacoma
Walla Walla
Washington, D.C.
Colville Reservation
Yakama Reservation

### ▶▶ WORDS TO UNDERSTAND

decade
Kanaka
menial
retaliate
witness tree

# Washington

The Nez Perce were a plateau tribe who lived in Washington, Oregon, and Idaho. Their leaders were friendly to white settlers and some joined the Christian faith. Like other Indian peoples, the Nez Perce were forced from their lands onto reservations.

**1862** Homestead Act gives settlers 160 acres of land for $200.

**1854** Governor Stevens' first Indian treaties are signed in western Washington.

**1859** Oregon becomes a state.

**TIMELINE** 1850      1860

**1850** Donation Land Act gives white men 320 acres of free land and their wives another 320 acres.

**1855** Governor Stevens holds a meeting with plateau tribes near Walla Walla. Treaties are signed and reservations are determined.

**1855–1858** Yakama war

**1853** Washington Territory is separated from the Oregon Territory. It contains parts of Idaho and Montana.

**1861 1865** Civil War

# Life in Territory

**1869** First transcontinental railroad is joined in the Utah desert; it did not go through Washington.

**1878** Timber and Stone Act is used to provide forest land to timber companies.

**1882** U.S. Congress passes the Chinese Exclusion Act.

▼

## 1870

## 1880

▲

**1867** Robert Hume builds the first salmon cannery in Washington.

**1877** Chief Joseph surrenders to the U.S. Army and gives his famous speech.

**1883** The Northern Pacific Railroad joins Seattle to the cities of the Midwest. Tracks meet in Montana.

# Property Lines and Boundaries

The early years of territorial settlement were years of establishing boundaries. American and British boundaries had to be established. The Washington Territory had to be separated from the Oregon Territory. Cities had to be laid out, homesteads marked, and maps drawn. How was this done?

In order to plot and map the land holdings for legal title, the land was surveyed, then marked on a grid pattern. That pattern was based on latitude and longitude, and was divided into townships and sections.

- A township was a square six miles in each direction.
- A township was divided into thirty-six sections.
- Each section was one mile each direction, or 640 acres.
- Each section was numbered.
- Sections were divided into quarter sections of 160 acres each.

A homesteader checked with the land office in the nearest town and located on a

*The Donation Land Claim Act of 1850 stated that each white male over eighteen years of age could claim 320 acres of free land. If he had a wife, they could claim twice as much land.*

Government survey parties mapped the West. Trains of pack mules took surveyors into remote areas where wagons couldn't go.

map a quarter section he wanted to claim. After going out to see the land, he marked the corners. Corners could be marked by driving posts in the ground, or by marking a ***witness tree***. A witness tree was the nearest tree to a corner. A homesteader sliced away a piece of bark and carved the township and section number with a knife.

After marking the land, the homesteader went back to register the claim at the land office. In order to make his claim valid, he also had to advertise it in a newspaper so anyone else claiming that land could challenge him. During the homestead era, newspapers were published throughout the West because land claim advertisements were a source of profit for the newspapers.

## WHAT DO YOU THINK?

**What problems might have occurred when people tried to choose pieces of land in the vast wilderness? What made some land more valuable or desirable than other land?**

## ACTIVITY

**Using this map, find 160 acres in the SW Quarter of Section 16.**

6 mile square township

| 6 | 5 | 4 | 3 | 2 | 1 |
|---|---|---|---|---|---|
| 7 | 8 | 9 | 10 | 11 | 12 |
| 18 | 17 | 16 | 15 | 14 | 13 |
| 19 | 20 | 21 | 22 | 23 | 24 |
| 30 | 29 | 28 | 27 | 26 | 25 |
| 31 | 32 | 33 | 34 | 35 | 36 |

1 square mile section

N

| 320 | |
|---|---|
| 80 | 160 |
| 40 | |

# Everyday Pioneer Life

Surviving on a pioneer homestead was difficult. Chas Ross, a young man in Pierce County, said:

*Pioneering here meant clearing land, hunting, fishing, and driving and feeding cattle. In this little home our family spent the most strenuous winter of our existence. That was the terrible winter of 1861-62. That winter opened with the freezing over of the Columbia River, which cut us off from the outside world. Then on top of this the snow began to fall and fell to the depth of four feet, then it would settle and freeze. For fear we would run out of matches, we kept the fire burning all night.*

## Disease

Many people came west for the clean air, clean water, and mild climate they thought would give them good health. In the mid-1800s doctors did not know that germs caused disease. Most people thought sickness was caused by bad odors such as the smell from sewage or rotting garbage.

Eva Brown, a girl in Waterville, said, "To be sick was unfortunate for the patient. There was no doctor. The neighbors did what they could and the patient either got well or died."

## Food

One boy on Whidbey Island remembered:

*As late as 1866 pork—fresh, salted, or smoked—was about the only meat other than venison that was obtainable, except that occasionally a farmer would kill a beef and share the meat with his neighbors, who later would return an equal quantity of beef after butchering their cattle. Flour, for years, was almost unobtainable.*

Pioneers spun wool fibers into yarn. Then they wove the yarn into cloth. They made candles from melted animal fat.

Kelsey Congor, in Cowlitz County, said:

*We seldom had coffee—we used brown peas instead. The first settlers suffered from lack of food. I've heard William Whittle say that when he went to work, many times all he had in his lunch were some cold boiled potatoes and sometimes not even salt.*

## Fun and Games

Clara Gray was a teenager in Spokane in 1879. She told about getting ready for a neighborhood dance:

*When I started to dress for the dance I found that the dress I wanted to wear was frozen fast to the side of the house, and it took me quite a while to thaw it loose with a hot iron. I had hung my spare clothing on nails against the rough boards. Two fiddlers played at the dance, and a collection was taken up to get money to build a schoolhouse.*

"Horseback riding in the summer and skiing in the winter were the stand-by sports. I made my skis from barrel staves. I got about all over the country on them," one pioneer remembered.

Erskine Wood wrote about a game he played with the Indian youths. They used little whips to spin three or four egg-shaped stones. "They would start the rocks spinning on the ice with their hands and then whip them like everything and they would spin as good as a top."

**LINKING THE PAST TO THE PRESENT**

Compare the games you play today with those of pioneer times. How have activities changed?

## Newspapers

The first newspaper in Washington was the *Columbian*, first published in 1852 in Olympia. Because the territory was so spread out, many people did not get a chance to read it regularly. "President Lincoln was assassinated a year before I heard of it," said Barney Owsley, a freight packer.

## Mail Service

There was no mail delivery in rural areas until the twentieth century. Mail might come and might not," one pioneer remembered.

Getting mail to the East meant sending it on the Columbia River by steamboat to Wallula, where a pony express rider picked it up and raced overland on the Mullan Road to Montana. In Montana, the letter was put on a steamboat headed down the Missouri River to St. Louis. From there it was sent eastward by boat, stage, or railroad. Sometimes letters were sent aboard ships that had to round the tip of South America before reaching the East Coast. Letters could take a year to reach their destination.

The lifestyle of the Nez Perce people, including children, changed forever when the white settlers came.

*As part of the treaties, Indians had to agree to stop stealing, buying, and selling Indian slaves.*

Building a home meant chopping down trees—lots of trees. The side branches were cut off and the logs were cut into even lengths. Cabin roofs were logs, boards, mud, and sometimes grass.

# Pioneer–Indian Conflict
## Governor Stevens' Plan

Following the murders of the Whitmans in 1847, there were three **decades** of conflict between settlers and the native peoples called the Cayuse War. The U.S. Army finally prevailed, and Indians were confined to smaller and less desirable lands.

By the 1880s, most Indians had been forced against their will to move to reservations. Some Indians were paid a little for the land. Some were promised they could retain hunting and fishing rights. Most Indians, however, lost their land and their traditional way of living.

What events led up to this drastic change for the Native American? As Secretary of Indian Affairs, Governor Stevens planned to make treaties with Indian tribes, pay them for their lands, and teach them to farm.

Stevens held treaty meetings, or councils, throughout Washington Territory to negotiate terms with the Indians. The treaties were legal agreements between the tribe and the United States government that demanded that the tribe sell most of its land. Then the U.S. government would reserve, or set aside, part of that land for the Indians to live on.

Indian people in the territory did not all have the same ways of living. Those who lived along the coast remained where they had always lived and continued fishing as they always had. They were not as upset with the land treaties as those Indians who lived inland on the plateau. Plateau Indians needed more space to hunt and travel to gather seasonal plants. They were not willing to give up their land because it would change their lives too much.

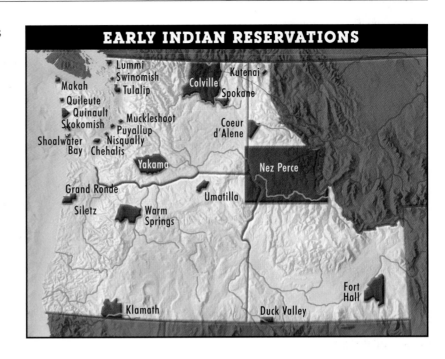

**EARLY INDIAN RESERVATIONS**

Peu-Peu-Mox-Mox, head of the Walla Walla Indians, resisted the idea of a reservation. He was later killed by a volunteer army.

## The Yakama and Kamiakin

Governor Stevens met with 5,000 Indians at Walla Walla to discuss the division of land on the Columbia Plateau. Nez Perce, Cayuse, Walla Walla, Umatilla, and Yakama people gathered for the meeting.

Until the meeting, the Yakama people were not considered a tribe. Fourteen related bands who spoke the same language, shared hunting grounds, and intermarried were grouped into the new tribe by Governor Stevens.

At the recommendation of a Catholic priest who had worked among the scattered bands and had come as an interpreter, Stevens appointed Kamiakin, a respected Indian man, to be the leader of the group. He was to sign the treaty for all of them. Kamiakin was named "head chief" of what became known as the Yakama Nation. Men from other bands were named as "subchiefs."

Kamiakin was a proud man who did not talk much. He had not wanted to come to the council at all. When the subject of a reservation for the newly formed Yakama Nation was brought up, he responded:

*The forest knows me; he knows my heart. He knows I do not desire a great many goods. All that I wish for is a [government] agent, a good agent, who will pity the good and bad of us and take care of us. I have nothing to talk long about. I am tired. I am anxious to get back to my garden. That is all I have to say.*

At the large meeting, where English, Chinook Jargon, and various Indian languages were all spoken, interpreters tried to negotiate between Governor Stevens and Indian leaders. Stevens agreed to give the larger tribes—the Nez Perce and Yakama— large reservations in their homelands. Smaller groups, who did not have much bargaining power, were forced to agree to this arrangement.

## The Yakama War

Only a few years after the treaty agreements, something happened that changed everything—gold was discovered along the upper Columbia River. Gold seekers rushed into the area, trespassing on lands given to the Yakamas in the treaty. The Indians were angry. Stevens prohibited whites from entering Yakama lands, but they came anyway.

Angry bands of Yakamas sought revenge and started killing white intruders. Chief Kamiakin and his followers were captured by the U.S. Army. This ended the fighting for a while.

At almost the same time, Seattle, still a village, was attacked by neighboring Indians. It seemed as if the entire region was at war. An army was sent from Fort Walla Walla to look over the situation, but as they reached the open grasslands near Rosalia, they were surrounded by Indian warriors from several tribes. During the night, soldiers escaped and retreated to their fort, abandoning weapons, horses, and several soldiers who had been killed.

The army sent a group of 600 soldiers to punish the tribes. They captured and slaughtered 700 Indian horses and hanged 24 of the Indian leaders. They also forced the Indians to sign peace treaties, ending the Yakama War.

Kamiakin was given a chance to return to the reservation, but he would not. He spent the rest of his life alone in remote parts of Washington and Canada.

# Indian-White Conflict

Why were there so many problems? Why couldn't both groups live side-by-side in the vast territory?

• **Getting Food** was done differently by Indians and settlers. In some parts of North America, Indians had farmed before Columbus arrived, but not in the Pacific Northwest. Native people here lived by hunting, fishing, and gathering plant foods. Farmers and ranchers expected native people to settle down on one spot of land, grow crops, and raise livestock.

• **Land ownership** meant different things to each group. American Indians had hunting and fishing grounds within tribal boundaries but did not own land individually. They used the natural resources on the land to provide food and shelter. They were satisfied with ways they used the land.

The settlers, however, each wanted to own a piece of land. They wanted to grow crops on the land. They also wanted to make money by mining, cutting down trees to sell, and raising food and cattle to sell to others. They needed buildings, roads, railroads, and shipping harbors. They didn't mind changing the land so they could make a living.

• **Language** was another problem. When people spoke different languages, treaties were easily misunderstood. Governor Stevens had treaties translated in to Chinook Jargon, but terms were not exact.

• **Leadership** ideas were different. Settlers chose leaders to speak for them and make rules and laws. Native Americans had tribal councils that made decisions. After signing a treaty, the Indian chief still had to get the support of the council.

• **Concept of superiority** by the white settlers gave them the belief that "good" meant "civilized our way." They did not respect the cultures of the native people. The settlers thought the Indians needed to eat, dress, talk, and worship like the white people.

## Chief Moses

Chief Moses, of the Columbia-Sinkiuse tribe, was forced to take his people to the Yakama Reservation. He told how the settlers created problems for Indian survival:

Chief Moses

*There are white men living in my country. Some can stay forever and some must go. . . . People who raise hogs in my country must go with their hogs, because they kill out the young camas, and to kill that is to starve us. It is our bread and we cannot eat earth. . . . We must fish and hunt and our squaws must dig camas and other roots, and when you touch us on any of these points, then we carry our rifles on the right and left of us.*

—From a letter from Chief Moses, 1879

## Chief Sealth

Chief Sealth was leader of the Duwamish. He welcomed the protection of the federal government against local Indian enemies.

Wanting peace for his people, Chief Sealth tried to help the white settlers. When it was time to move to a reservation, he encouraged his people to go peacefully. Here is part of a famous speech he gave to Governor Stevens:

*The White Chief says that Big Chief in Washington sends us greetings. . . . His people are many. They are like the grass that covers vast prairies. My people are few. . . . They are ebbing away like a rapidly receding tide that will never return. . . . Let us hope that hostilities between us never return. We would have everything to lose and nothing to gain. My people will retire to the reservation you offer them. Then we will dwell apart in peace.*

### Sarah Winnemucca

**S**arah was the daughter of a Northern Paiute chief in western Nevada. She spoke English, Spanish, and two Indian languages. She worked as an army scout and an interpreter. When members of the Bannock tribe were held by the army at Fort Vancouver, Sarah opened a school for the Bannock children.

Sarah sought to gain proper treatment for her people by making a trip to Washington, D.C. to plead for understanding of the Native American situation. When the wife of President Hayes visited Vancouver in 1880, she broke into tears as she heard Sarah's plea for help for her people.

Sarah had a difficult life trying to walk between two cultures and was not always appreciated by white people or Indians.

## WHAT DO YOU THINK?

• **Do you think it was morally right for the settlers to assume that they could take, or buy, land already occupied by Native Americans?**
• **Was it fair or good to force the Native Americans to move to the reservations? What problems did this cause for the Indian people?**

When settlers came to the Elliott Bay area in the 1850s, Chief Sealth stayed friendly to the newcomers and urged his people to do the same. The city of Seattle was named after him. This portrait was taken in 1864 and is the only known photograph of him.

# CHIEF JOSEPH AND THE LAST INDIAN WAR

One band of Nez Perce Indians was led by Hin-maton-Yal-a-kit, which meant Thunder Traveling to Loftier Mountain Heights. The white settlers called him Chief Joseph. Like his father, whose tribe had assisted Lewis and Clark, Joseph had worked peacefully with fur traders and missionaries. Many of the tribe had been baptized as Christians. They had made an art of breeding horses and grazed them on rich grass-lands. They signed the treaty at Walla Walla and lived peacefully on a reservation until gold was discovered there.

The government responded by opening some reservation land for mining and white settlement, and forced the native people to move yet again. In 1877, a few young men whose fathers had been killed by white set-tlers killed four white men in revenge. When Chief Joseph found out, he knew the U.S. Army would **retaliate**. He prepared a band of 200 young men, some older men, and nearly 600 women and children for flight. Chief Joseph was thirty-six years old.

The U.S. Army caught up to the Nez Perce, who sent out a small party under a truce flag. Someone fired a shot, however, and the fight-ing began. Two Nez Perce were wounded, but they killed a fourth of the U.S. soldiers.

Chief Joseph was photographed by Edward Curtis about a year before Joseph's death in 1904. It is said that he died of a broken heart.

This began a series of battles that were recorded by journalists. Readers in the East followed the stories in the papers, and the Indian war and Chief Joseph became famous.

One reason for the success of the Nez Perce was that they did not fight in traditional Indian ways. They took the high ground, dug rifle pits, and surrounded a force six times their size. They used bows and arrows, shotguns, and rifles. They outshot and out-rode the army.

The Nez Perce fled to the east and crossed into Montana, but were caught by a surprise attack in Big Hole Valley. Again they fought back. Warriors pinned the soldiers down with rifle fire while the rest of the Nez Perce gathered their wounded and dead and escaped into the hills.

Finally, the army sent about six hundred men to overtake the Nez Perce, who were resting at Snake Creek thirty miles from the Canadian border. The combat was fierce, with hand-to-hand fight-ing between the soldiers and the Indians in the canyons and gullies. The battle went on until nightfall. Many Indians were dead. Joseph knew that his people were finished.

The next day a snowstorm blew in, adding to the misery. October 5, 1877, heartsick, freezing, and hungry, Chief

*Chief Joseph's Surrender*

*Chief Joseph kept track of the time with his own calendar, made by notching a small white stick each day. On the seventh day, Sunday, he made a dot. He tied a bundle of the sticks together with rawhide to keep track of the months and years.*

Joseph and his people had little choice but to surrender. Chief Joseph's surrender speech shows the strong feelings of a leader for his people.

> *Our chiefs are killed. . . . It is cold and we have no blankets. The little children are freezing to death. My people, some of them, have run away to the hills and have no blankets, no food. . . . Hear me, my chiefs, I am tired. My heart is sick and sad. From where the sun now stands, I will fight no more forever.*

The army moved the band to a reservation in Oklahoma. Later, they were returned to the Colville Reservation in northern Washington.

> *We could have escaped from Bear Paw Mountain if we had left our wounded, old women, and children behind. . . . We were unwilling to do this. We had never heard of a wounded Indian recovering in the hands of white men.*

— Chief Joseph

## Erskine Wood and Chief Joseph

A teenaged white boy spent summers living with Chief Joseph on the Colville Reservation. His name was Erskine Wood. His father had met Chief Joseph when they were negotiating treaties. In his diary, Erskine described the way the Indian families combined ten tepees into one long lodge during the winter, with four cooking fires down the center. Fresh venison strips were hung on racks over the fires and smoked to make jerky.

Erskine wrote that Chief Joseph refused to accept the overalls distributed by the Indian Agency, wanting to wear the traditional style of leather leggings.

Erskine had a camera and tried to develop his photography skills on the reservation. He described the camera he used:

*This was a clumsy affair, about a foot square. I used to [make] a darkroom under my blankets, using a small patch of red blanket, with sun coming through it, for a lantern. Some of the Indians objected very strongly to having their picture taken—especially older women. The younger ones, if dressed up in their finery, did not mind at all.*

When Erskine was preparing to go home to Portland, he asked Joseph if there was any gift that his father could give to repay the kindness of keeping the boy through the summers. Joseph thought about it, and then asked for a horse. To young Erskine, that did not seem like much of a gift—Joseph already had many horses. He never told his father about Joseph's request.

Years later, in 1997, relatives of the Erskine Wood family purchased a fine Appaloosa and gave it to Joseph's 250 descendants on the Colville Reservation.

# White Support of Indians

John James was a boy when his three older brothers were asked to join volunteers to fight Indians. The James family was against fighting the Indians. This aggravated their neighbors. The neighbors thought everyone should join together to get rid of Indian problems.

An Indian was lured to the James' property and then murdered by neighbors. The neighbors thought that if Indians retaliated against the James family for the murder, the Jameses would join the volunteer forces in fighting the Indian wars. There was no retaliation against the James family, though, and they still refused to fight the Indians. Their farm was frequently looted by white neighbors, and their sheep and butter were stolen.

*My father thought we should not have to fight the Indians . . . as there were no settlements over there . . . with the exception of one or two army posts. This created considerable feeling among the families that wanted to [fight the Indians]. . . I am satisfied it takes just as much nerve and courage to oppose a war as actual participation in the fighting.*

—John James

> *" At the time I arrived in Whitman County, the people lived in or near government forts, as the Indians were hostile in these times. The forts were built of logs which stood close together on end twelve feet above the ground."*
>
> —Robert Farr

**WHAT DO YOU THINK?**

**Why do you think it would be difficult to take an anti-war stance if everyone around you supported the fight?**

# New Towns

After the first burst of settlement on farmland, people began to locate in towns where they could sell goods or profit from offering services. They settled where shipping and transportation were available. In the mid-1800s, that meant along waterways. There were few roads—no good ones—and shipping by water was the easiest way to transport wheat, vegetables, animal hides, and even timber. Merchants also settled in towns that they thought would grow. More people meant more customers.

Cities competed with each other to be the largest. They wanted to be the seat of government and the place where successful businesses would open. Larger cities meant modern conveniences and a better supply of store-bought goods.

---

Several things contributed to the growth of cities around Puget Sound and in eastern Washington:

| Natural Resources | Human Elements |
|---|---|
| • natural harbors | • hard working people |
| • rivers | • buildings |
| • trees | • roads |
| • fish | • railroads |
| • farmland | • ships |
| • gold and coal in nearby territories | • advertisements |
| • mild climate | |

---

**Walla Walla**, a wheat farming community, became a supply point for mining camps when gold was discovered in Idaho. It became the largest settlement in Washington Territory.

**Olympia** started out being called Smithfield. Mike Simmons, a friend of George Washington Bush, owned one of the two stores in town. Views of the stunning Olympia Mountains, however, soon led to the name of Olympia. Two years later, settlers on the other side of the mountains named their settlement Tacoma. The word sounded like the Indian name for Mount Rainier.

**Seattle** grew as a shipping port for lumber. Dr. David Maynard was one of the first residents. He had visited Mike Simmons in Olympia and learned of the need for logs in San Francisco, California. After a trip there to investigate shipping logs to California, he returned with a ship full of goods and opened a store next to Simmons. He cut prices, too. Simmons' friends told Dr. Maynard that he should open a store somewhere else, and suggested a place at the mouth of a river several miles north.

Seattle started as a shipping port for lumber.

Dr. Maynard did move, and started the city of Seattle.

Maynard met a few other entrepreneurs who had come to the area, including Henry Yesler from Maryland. Yesler was a lumberman who sought timber for the California market. The Puget Sound, with its tremendous forests nearby and easy shipping access, was perfect. Yesler immediately set out to build a steam sawmill.

*Where did Seattle get its name? Dr. Maynard met the leader of the Duwamish tribe. The leader's name was Sealth, pronounced like Seattle.*

## Civil War in the West

During the 1860s, the United States was bitterly divided by the Civil War. That conflict reached the Pacific Northwest, too. There were rumors that a Confederate ship, the *Shenandoah,* was attacking Union ships off the Pacific Coast. The Union Army had troops at Fort Vancouver, where a military fort was built near the old HBC fort. Troops were also stationed at several smaller posts. When the Union soldiers were called east to fight, local volunteers took their places.

General Ulysses S. Grant was at Fort Vancouver when he was called to lead the Union Army in the East.

After serving as governor, Isaac Stevens went to fight for the Union and was killed in Virginia. General Ulysses Grant and General Philip Sheridan had both served at Fort Vancouver and were called to lead troops for the Union Army. General George Pickett, who had been stationed on San Juan Island during the Pig War, also went east to fight. He fought in the Confederate Army and is famous for "Pickett's Charge" at the Battle of Gettysburg.

Dr. Maynard

# TIMBER!

This clever house built from a stump gives an idea of how large the trees were. The house was located between Marysville and Arlington.

David Douglas was a Scottish botanist who toured the Pacific Northwest in the early 1800s. He sent hundreds of plants back to Scotland to study, and also identified the huge tree named for him—the Douglas fir. Douglas died by falling into a pit meant for wild bulls in Hawaii.

Many people worked along the waterways. They earned money by supplying timber to other places. Down south, in San Francisco, the gold rush of 1848 brought thousands of people who needed logs to build docks, buildings, and sidewalks. The huge forests of the Pacific Northwest were cut down near waterways, the logs floated downstream, then bundled together and towed by ship to San Francisco.

San Francisco had the misfortune of burning down in six major fires between 1849 and 1851. Each rebuilding effort meant greater demand for northern lumber. This meant more mill workers were needed in the Puget Sound. More people moving to the area meant increased sales of local farmers' milk, vegetables, and hay. Coal and oysters both found ready markets in San Francisco.

Loggers needed to cut the huge logs into smaller pieces. They built sawmills near streams so waterpower could run the gigantic saws. A new steam sawmill, which was much faster, was built at Port Gamble. Men boiled water in huge boilers. The boilers gave off steam that pressed against moving parts of engines that moved saws.

Once the tree was down it had to be cut into smaller sections by buckers. Logging was dangerous work, buckers could be crushed when a log rolled over them on a steep slope. This photo was taken near Brennan.

*L*ouisa Sinclair was the only girl who lived at the logging camp. Her mother was a Skagit Indian and her father a white storekeeper. "My mother taught me the use of the needle and I obtained patterns for shirts for men. I was well paid for them."

Horses pulled heavy logs out of the forest. This horse had been working in the logging industry for seventeen years when the photograph was taken.

When the first settlers came, most of western Washington was covered with evergreen forests. They were different from most of the forests we see today. Many of the trees were hundreds of years old. Today we call forests with these old trees "old growth forests." This photo was taken after 1900.

Oxen hauled heavy logs to the sawmills or to the freight wagons. To make pulling the load easier, a log road was greased with oil. This made the logs easier to slide across. The oxen, of course, had to step over the slippery logs. The roads were called "skid roads."

## Trees, Trees, Trees

There were so many trees in Washington when the early settlers came that they thought they would never run out. They were not concerned about replanting trees. They were not concerned about how much wood they wasted.

One man wrote:

*We cut down good, solid Douglas Fir, White Fir, Hemlock, and even Tamarack, lopped the limbs and burned it, leaving barren areas that today have grown up to brush. I'm ashamed of the wasted wood fiber. . . the loss of soil through erosion, the loss of trees that results in higher temperatures that melt snow swiftly and produce greater floods.*

# Fishing

The great Pacific Ocean was the natural home to fish that could be harvested by American Indians and settlers. Fish were sold to local people and dried and shipped to other cities.

The fishing industry changed quickly when Robert Hume developed and built a plant that used cans and high heat to preserve fish. Salmon was canned in over thirty canneries that sold salmon to far-away places in South America, Great Britain, Australia, and China.

C. O. Rhodes was a young teen when he went salmon fishing with his uncle on the North Palix River in the 1880s.

*In those days there would be tens of thousands of these fish in shallow streams. . . . Not being content to stand on the bank, I crawled out on an old slippery log that projected out into the creek some ten feet, right among the fish. I picked out a good big one and did I hook him! He landed me right off that log among all those fish. The water was only about two feet deep, and there were fish over me, under me, and on all sides of me, and as fast as I'd gain a footing, down I'd go again with fish splashing salmon eggs in my ears, eyes, and mouth.*

These men are unloading one of the huge salmon catches on Puget Sound in the 1880s. Fish were canned or salted and then exported.

## Whaling

Indians who lived on the northern coast of Washington had a long tradition based on whaling. An early settler, Jim Hunter, wrote about the Makah people at Neah Bay who were whaling when whites arrived.

*The killing of a whale meant a great celebration in the village at Neah Bay. The capture of these immense animals was attended with great danger, and only the Indians skilled in casting the harpoon or in rowing the large canoes were permitted to engage in the hunt. One of the most successful hunters was "Lighthouse Jim" who at the end of his life had established the reputation of having killed 59 whales.*

## LINKING THE PAST TO THE PRESENT

**Today, Washington residents are working hard to bring back wild fish runs that diminished from over-fishing and destruction of natural habitats. Salmon are also being grown commercially in the waters of the Puget Sound area, but they are susceptible to disease, while wild fish are not.**

A Makah canoe party returns from the whale hunt.

Whale products included lubricating oil, fertilizer, meat, animal food, glue, and bone meal. Whale oils and fats were also used in cosmetics, soap, and crayons. In this photo, several men sit on the baleen in the mouth of a whale.

### The Whaling Industry

During the early 1800s, American whaling ships set sail from New England ports. During peak years, 700 whale ships embarked on a voyage that averaged four years. Ships sailed from New England around the tip of South America and up the Pacific to hunt whales off the coast of Washington State and Alaska.

Whale oil was the most valuable product. It was used for home lighting and was very expensive. A ship full of barrels of whale oil brought $100,000.

Baleen was another valuable whale product. Baleen whales didn't have teeth. They had baleen instead, which strained a whale's food. Baleen was used for carriage springs, corset stays, fishing rods, hoops for skirts, ribs for umbrellas, and horsewhips.

So many whales were killed that it became hard to find enough to hunt. Then, in 1859, petroleum was discovered in Pennsylvania. It could be made into kerosene for home lighting. Whaling was no longer a large industry.

### LINKING THE PAST TO THE PRESENT

**Today, the Makah people are reviving their tradition of whaling, which has caused controversy because many people do not want to support the killing of whales. The Makah claim it is their heritage and a right guaranteed them by treaties written in the mid-1800s. They see the whale hunts as opportunities for families to bond with one another during the hunt.**

# New People in a New Land

The story of Washington's growth is a story of immigrants. They came from many parts of the world, bringing their culture with them. Their many voices and ideas created a dynamic society. Sometimes different groups got along. Other times, discrimination made life miserable.

## Hawaiians in Washington

Hawaiian men, called **Kanakas**, had agreed to work for the Hudson's Bay Company for a period of years. They worked as fur trappers, boatmen, cooks, and laborers. After the HBC moved their fur trade into Canada, many of the Kanakas returned to Hawaii, while some remained in the Washington Territory. Some Kanakas married Indian women and blended into the local Indian communities.

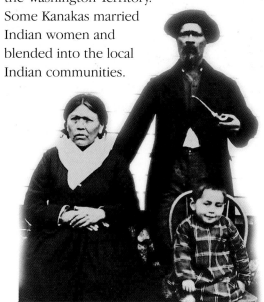

John Kahana, his wife Mary (a Lummi Indian), and son Robert lived on San Juan Island.

Some Kanakas moved to San Juan Island, where they worked for the HBC and were involved in the Pig War. After it was determined that San Juan Island belonged to the United States, most of the Hawaiians left and moved to British-held islands nearby. The British allowed the Hawaiians to own land and vote—things they could not do in the United States.

Patrick Clark's home in Spokane was lavish. He made a fortune in the mining industry. Most Irish, however, lived in humble homes.

## Irish Immigrants

In the 1840s a terrible disaster hit Ireland, where most people existed on a diet of potatoes. A fungus infected the potato crop, causing them to turn black and shrivel up. Men and women took their starving children and moved away to the "Promised Land" of America. Most Irish immigrants settled in the cities along American's Eastern Coast, where they usually lived in poverty.

Irish men had come from California in the wake of that state's gold rush. They settled first in Walla Walla. Many ran for government offices. Some of the Walla Walla Irish moved north, where they started the first agricultural communities in the Columbia Basin. Other Irish came as laborers on the transcontinental railroads.

James Monaghan and Patrick Clark were Irishmen who made fortunes in mining, business, and real estate. The Irish also worked as housemaids, mill hands, miners, or enlisted in the army.

*The army adopted many of the Irish tunes. The rhythm kept the group in unison when marching or riding. A favorite tune was "Garryowen."*

Chin Gee Hee, a Chinese labor contractor, brought men from China to work in fish canneries, logging camps, coal mines, and to help build the railroads. Chin Gee Hee later returned to China to build that country's first railway.

*"There is a wash house occupying a prominent position among business houses and hotels. This is not a credit to our town. If Chinese must come, let no man encourage them to locate where their presence will make white residents uncomfortable."*

*— Spokane Falls Review*

## Chinese Laborers

In the middle 1800s, China's government seemed ready to collapse. There was war, flooding, and famine. People were desperate to find jobs to provide for their families.

Chinese men came to work in the mining camps of the Pacific Northwest. By 1870 there were twice as many Chinese miners in eastern Washington as white miners. Chinese men were also brought to build the transcontinental railroad.

Chinese laborers were not given full rights. They could not vote or testify in court cases involving whites. They were paid much less than white men for the same work. They did **menial** labor such as washing clothes and cooking. They also did the most dangerous and difficult jobs on the railroads and in the mines. For the Chinese, life was generally miserable.

In China, cutting off the queue (pony tail) was a crime punishable by death. If a Chinese man in America ever wanted to return home, he needed to maintain his long hair.

## Anti-Chinese Laws

Americans were worried that too many Chinese laborers were coming into the country and taking jobs. Congress passed the Chinese Exclusion Act, which stopped Chinese laborers from entering the country.

A few years later, when many white workers were jobless, they turned their anger against Chinese residents. Violent riots erupted in Issaquah, Tacoma, and Seattle. Over a thousand Chinese people were expelled from Washington Territory. Their homes and businesses were burned. Chinese men in Walla Walla and Pasco were attacked by white residents.

Like many other times in history, racial prejudice made life miserable for immigrants. It was many years before laws were passed that made it illegal to hire or pay a person differently because of race. It was even longer before people's attitudes changed.

## Japanese Workers

Japanese men and boys also came to find jobs. Here is one story from a boy who came to work on the railroad:

*My work was to cut down trees or to dig and fill in land in the mountains. I was only a boy of 15, having just graduated from grade school. When I worked ten or twelve hours a day, the next morning I couldn't open my hands. I dipped them in hot water in order to stretch the fingers back to normal and sometimes I secretly cried.*

*My pay was $1.75 for ten hours. I had good reason to work my hardest, gritting my teeth, for when I left Japan, I had promised my mother, whose health was not good, "I'll surely come back to Japan in a year."*

## CHAPTER 6 REVIEW

1. What did a person have to do in order to take legal ownership of land in early Washington? Include at least three steps.

2. Describe three ways pioneer life was different from your life.

3. Getting and sending mail was difficult. What route might a letter travel to get from Seattle to the East Coast?

4. What were three reasons there was often trouble between native people and the white settlers?

5. How did Sarah Winnemucca help Bannock Indian children at Fort Vancouver?

6. Who was the town of Seattle named for?

7. List four things you read about Chief Joseph and his people.

8. Who was Erskine Wood?

9. Why was John James' family unpopular with their neighbors?

10. Were there any real Civil War battles in Washington?

11. What famous Union general left Fort Vancouver to fight in the Civil War in the East?

12. Name at least five things that contributed to the growth of early towns in Washington.

13. A fire in what California city created a market for Washington lumber?

14. What man had a tree named for him and died while exploring the Washington wilderness?

15. How did Robert Hume change the salmon fishing industry?

16. The Makah people at Neah Bay had been hunting what animal long before the white settlers came?

17. Name at least three immigrant groups who came to Washington to work.

18. What did Chin Gee Hee do for Washington industries? For workers? For his native country?

## GEOGRAPHY TIE-IN

1. How did landforms contribute to the growth of Seattle and other port cities? (Remember, landforms include land and water.)

2. Choose one of the immigrant groups that came to Washington to work. Research the group's native land, climate, and food. What things in Washington's climate, food, and land were very different? How might this have caused problems for the immigrants?

# Leaving the

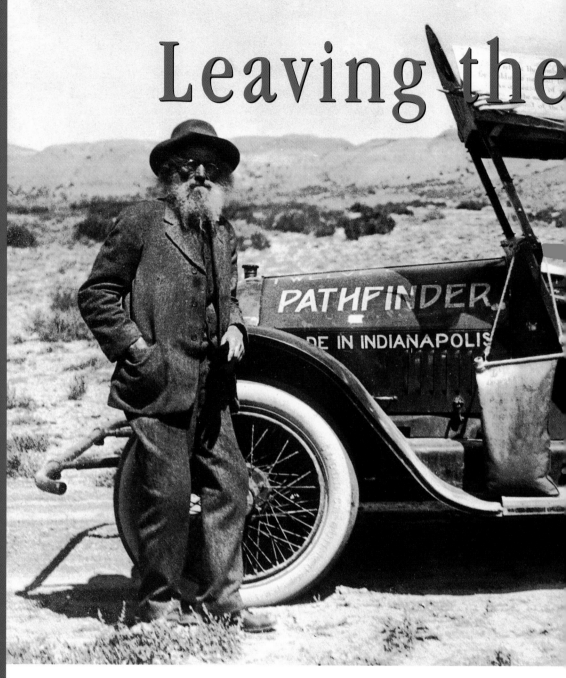

Ezra Meeker came to Washington by covered wagon in 1852. He lived long enough to retrace the Oregon Trail—first by wagon and then by car—to promote marking the trail with monuments. Then, in the 1920s, he retraced the route in an airplane.

**TIMELINE** ▼ **1875** ▼ **1885**

**1875**
Congress passes the Indian Homestead Act.

**1883**
Northern Pacific Transcontinental Railroad is completed.

**1885/86**
Tacoma and Seattle expel all Chinese.

# Frontier Behind

## Chapter 7

**1889**
November 11, Washington and Montana gain statehood.

Fires burn down much of Ellensburg, Spokane, and Seattle.

**1900**
Weyerhauser buys 900,000 acres of timber from Northern Pacific R.R.

**1895**

**1905**

**1887**
The Dawes Act deeds reservation land to individual Indian people.

**1890**
Idaho gains statehood.

**1893**
Great Northern Transcontinental Railroad is completed in Seattle.

**1897**
News of gold discovery in Klondike reaches Seattle.

**1899**
Mount Rainier National Park is created.

**1905**
Washington takes the lead in U.S. lumber production.

## PUBLIC ATTENTION

Is now largely directed to the

### VAST NEW REGIONS

Opened for Settlement by the completion of the

## NORTHERN PACIFIC RAILROAD

Through MINNESOTA, NORTH DAKOTA, MONTANA, NORTHERN IDAHO, WASHINGTON and OREGON,

The widely known and prosperous

# Northern Pacific Country

☞ The important Geographical Divisions traversed by this New **TRANS-CONTINENTAL LINE,** possess unusually large and varied Natural Resources.

**THERE ARE** New Towns growing into important trade centers, and there is a steady advance in the values of all property.

**THERE ARE** Large unoccupied areas of FERTILE LANDS especially adapted to Wheat Growing and General Farming.

**THERE ARE** EXTENSIVE GRAZING RANGES, the best in the United States for Stock Raising.

**THERE ARE** RICH MINERAL DISTRICTS to be developed and HEAVY BODIES OF TIMBER for lumbering purposes.

**THERE ARE** Navigable Rivers, Lakes and larger waters and innumerable water powers ready to be utilized.

**THERE ARE** Profitable Fisheries on the Rivers, Lakes and Puget Sound. The fish are of great commercial value.

**THERE ARE** Exceptionally good opportunities for Merchants, Manufacturers, Professional Men, Mechanics and Traders to engage in business.

## The Diversified Resources of this Grand Region

ready to be developed into innumerable paying industries, will put in use much capital AND REQUIRE A LARGE NUMBER OF OPERATORS AND WORKING MEN.

# THERE IS AMPLE ROOM

*In this Great Belt of Productive and Prosperous Country*

# For Millions of Settlers

To secure COMFORTABLE HOMES and become INDEPENDENT.
☞ Each State and Territory traversed by the NORTHERN PACIFIC possesses abundant resources to support a compact population. The countries are well watered, the soil is rich and productive, while the climate is superior in the qualities which assure healthful and pleasant living, is favorable for the production of crops, and usually more propitious than elsewhere found for the growth of wheat, oats, rye, barley, fruits and the vegetables.

**FREE!** For Maps and Publications, SENT FREE OF CHARGE, and for all information relating to Lands and the Northern Pacific Country, apply to or address,

PAUL SCHULZE, Gen'l Land Ag't, PORTLAND, OREGON.

R. J. WEMYSS, Gen'l Land Ag't, ST. PAUL, MINN.

P. B. GROAT, Gen'l Emigration Ag't, or, ST. PAUL, MINN.

CHAS. B. LAMBORN, Land Commissioner, ST. PAUL, MINN.

Railroad posters promoted the West. How did this poster entice settlers?

## The Railroad Age

The frontier period in the Pacific Northwest ended on September 8, 1883. On that date, the tracks of the Northern Pacific's rail line from the Great Lakes to Puget Sound were joined. Now a journey that once took three to five months could be made in only five days—or even less.

Other transcontinental railroads finally reached Washington, too. The companies extended lines into the mining, timber, and farming regions.

### Federal Land Grants

It would have been almost impossible for private companies to build a transcontinental railroad. The vast unsettled nature of the land was a harsh fact. There were deep gullies, raging rivers, thick forests, and steep mountains to cross. There would be trouble with Indians who would resent railroad tracks crossing their hunting grounds. Land had to be cleared, bridges built, and tunnels blasted. Heavy steel rails, lumber, and supplies had to be delivered to the sites by teams of wagons. Thousands of workers had to be hired, trained, and paid. The trains themselves had to be purchased. It was clear that help from a very large company or the national government was needed.

At one time, the federal government owned all of the land in the West. As settlement progressed westward, the government gave land grants to farmers, ranchers, timber companies, and railroads. Huge amounts of land were given to the railroad companies to improve transportation for everyone. Then the railroad could sell some of the land to settlers. This would raise money for construction of the rail lines.

The Northern Pacific Railroad received a land grant *subsidy* of 40 million acres (an area about the size of the state of Washington) to build a rail line from Lake Superior to Puget Sound.

The government deeded every other section (one square mile) on both sides of the tracks to the railroad upon completion of every twenty-five miles of track. The government kept the alternating sections for other uses. This resulted in a vast "checkerboard" across the region.

The Northern Pacific Railroad was the most important corporation in the state's history. No other business had a greater influence on Washington's settlement and economic development.

An article in the *Spokane Falls Chronicle* described the excitement surrounding the arrival of the first passenger train of the Northern Pacific:

*About half past 6 o'clock in the evening, Graham's band struck up a lively tune, and then almost the entire population of the town left homes, stores, shops, and offices, and hastened to the depot. At 7:14 the train came into view . . . the crown cheered, the band played, and greetings were extended to those who came to Spokane by rail.*

## Railroads and Immigration

In order to earn **revenue** from their land grants, railroads hired land agents to sell pieces of the land to businessmen and settlers. Northern Pacific land agents spread out across the United States, the British Isles, and northern Europe. There were 831 agents in Great Britain in 1883. They distributed advertisements at weekly farmers markets, while another 124 agents carried the same message across northern Europe. Brochures were published in English, French, Swedish, Norwegian, and other languages.

The Northern Pacific, and later the Great Northern Railroad, published detailed instructions on how to travel to the Northwest. Both railroads ran special trains at reduced rates to carry immigrant families and their belongings. Settlers could buy railroad land as low as $1.25 an acre, though

*Washington* PORTRAIT

# HENRY VILLARD

The individual most responsible for the completion of the Northern Pacific was a man of remarkable talent and energy. Villard had emigrated from Germany to the United States when he was eighteen years old. He worked as a journalist, reporting the Lincoln-Douglas debates, the election that Lincoln won, and the Civil War.

During a visit to Europe to recover from overwork, Villard met a group of German men who were interested in investing money in American railroads. They persuaded him to handle their financial affairs in the states. In a daring move, Villard raised $16 million for the venture.

Villard used the money to form the Oregon Railway and Navigation Company. The company built the ORN tracks along the Columbia River to where they met the tracks of the Northern Pacific Railroad. Then Villard bought the Northern Pacific and directed the completion of the tracks through Idaho and Montana.

Horse teams pulled the heavy iron rails and wooden cross beams to the track site.

some land cost more. If immigrants didn't have the money to buy the land, the railroad sold it to them on credit.

The result was a tidal wave of immigration into Washington. Railroad-sponsored migration was the principal cause of the state's growth after 1880.

# Who Were the Immigrants?

By providing a faster way for immigrants to travel to the Northwest, the railroads were actually responsible for the ethnic mix of the state. In the late 1800s and early 1900s, mostly Canadian, English, German, and Scandinavian

immigrants came. People also came from many other countries.

By 1910, forty-six percent of the state's people were either born in another country or their parents were. These new immigrants joined the Chinese and Irish already here.

## Scandinavian Immigrants

Puget Sound attracted Scandinavians because its wet climate, high mountains, and many ocean inlets reminded them of home. Norwegians started a colony at Poulsbo on the Olympic peninsula because it looked like their native **fjord** in Norway. Swedes worked for logging companies, doing work that was familiar to them. For the same reasons, Norwegians and Finns were attracted to fishing and Danes to dairying.

Scandinavian families worked together on a dairy farm in the 1860s.

## German Immigrants

German farmers established small settlements across the Palouse and Big Bend regions. Mathias Reinbold was so impressed by the railroad's message in Germany that he persuaded nine of his fourteen children to emigrate. Today their descendants are found in Lincoln County.

## Italian Immigrants

Washington's Italians arrived with railroad construction crews. Others came as skilled stone masons to help rebuild Spokane, Ellensburg, and Seattle after the terrible fires of 1889. Italian farmers located in the Walla Walla Valley, where they became famous in later years for their sweet onions.

German families built round barns. Mr. Steinko's barn actually has twelve sides.
*Photo by Barbara Murray*

### Fire!

In 1889, the same year Washington became a state, people living in Seattle, Ellensburg, and Spokane had to deal with the devastation of huge fires.

In Seattle, a craftsman was heating glue in his shop when the pan boiled over. When the glue hit the hot stove it caught fire. Soon entire blocks of wooden buildings were burning. Flames were jumping from roof to roof and even across dirt streets. By evening the entire business district was in ruins. Soon people were doing business from tents.

Italian, Chinese and other workers cooperated in rebuilding the cities—this time with fireproof brick and cement.

*Swedish, Norwegian, Italian, Japanese, and German newspapers were published in Seattle at the turn of the century.*

This pile of basalt rocks is actually an oven. Italian railroad construction crews in eastern Washington made the ovens to bake their bread.

### LINKING THE PAST TO THE PRESENT

**Today, Seattle's International District remains a thriving reminder of the origins of diversity. It is also a stronghold of Asian and Pacific Island cultures.**

After tracks were laid to the forests, logs were carried by rail.

# A Natural Resource Economy

Washington's explosive growth depended on the productive use of its natural resources. The manufacturing of wood products was important. Exports also included metals, canned fish, livestock, grain, and fruit.

## Lumbering

Lumber was our most important industry for many years. Washington became the nation's leading lumber state in 1905.

Seattle had grown up as a sawmill town around Henry Yesler's steam-powered sawmill. Soon larger mills were built throughout the Puget Sound region. Tall timber next to deep water meant that trees could be cut, milled (sawed into boards), and easily exported by ship.

In California, the demand for lumber seemed *insatiable*. Huge log rafts were towed to San Diego to be processed in a mill built specifically for Northwest timber.

Timber companies were helped by the Northern Pacific Railroad. Huge tracts of timberland, first given to the railroads by the federal government, were sold at bargain prices to timber companies.

Timber companies also benefited from the passage of the federal Timber and Stone Act, which they abused. Timber companies found out-of-work sailors and hoboes and paid them to file homestead claims on forest lands. Then the sailors and hoboes deeded the land to the timber companies for $50. In some cases, the price was as low as a large glass of beer. One timber company acquired more than 100,000 acres with this scheme.

**The largest timber companies in the Pacific Northwest today—Boise Cascade, Potlatch, Plum Creek, and Weyerhauser—bought much of their first timberland from the Northern Pacific Railroad.**

Amazed by the majesty and abundance of the Northwest's old-growth timber, Asahel Curtis, a noted photographer, made this self-portrait in 1910.

## Fishing

As the fishing industry grew, salmon became a popular symbol of the Pacific Northwest region. The fish had been the basic food source for most of the region's Indian tribes; then fish became not only a food source, but a way to make money. Fresh, canned, and dried fish were sold to other states and countries. Most of the fishermen were Scandinavians and Finns.

The dirty, smelly work in canneries was done by Chinese. All day long they stood on the wet floors in front of piles of fish, using sharp knives to gut and sort the fish. After the turn of the century, a new machine called the "Iron Chink" was used. ("Chink" was a **derogatory** term for Chinese.) The machine cleaned salmon at the rate of one per second. Each machine could do the work of dozens of workers.

Like the lumber industry, fishing was a victim of careless disregard for a natural resource. The huge salmon runs on the Columbia River were already in decline by 1900, long before the dams were built. Over-fishing was the major reason. Water pollution and destruction of spawning habitats by mining and logging companies had already begun, too.

**Today, many salmon runs are on the verge of extinction. Salmon are an indicator used to measure the *degradation* of our environment. The Columbia River salmon harvest peaked in 1895, when an incredible 40 million pounds of fish were canned! The commercial catch today is less than one percent of that.**

## Mining

Washington and Oregon never developed significant gold or silver mining districts, but three Washington cities—Walla Walla, Spokane, and Seattle—were greatly affected by mining rushes in other places. Merchants grew rich by supplying food, tents, tools, and clothing to miners on their way to the gold fields of Canada, Alaska, and Idaho. You will read more about them later in this chapter.

Some ordinary people struck it rich in the mines and returned to Washington to spend their money. May Arkwright Hutton, a boardinghouse cook and advocate of miners and unions, and her railroad engineer husband, Al, put their savings of a few hundred dollars into a seemingly unproductive mine in Idaho. However, their Hercules Mine became one of the richest strikes in Silver Valley, and the Huttons became overnight millionaires. In the next chapter we'll look at how this wealth changed their lives and influenced the Spokane community.

Coal was discovered in the Puget Sound Lowlands and the Cascade Mountains. Coal was burned to heat homes and to provide the power that ran machines in factories. Some of the early miners were Chinese. Others came from England and Wales. The first large group of African Americans in Washington came to dig coal. Even children were hired to sort the pieces of coal.

Discovery of high-quality coal in 1886 in Kittatas County led to the rapid development of the Roslyn coal field. Two towns, Roslyn and Cle Elum, sprang up overnight. Coal mining was important well into the 1900s.

*Coal production declined rapidly after World War II as hydropower replaced coal. The last mines closed in 1963.*

Roslyn and Cle Elum in Kittatas County

Many Europeans came to work in the coal mines. Mining was very dangerous work. Hundreds of miners died on the job each year. Notice the lamps on the hats, a bag for water, and the lunch pails.

# Agriculture

From its earliest beginnings in the Walla Walla Valley, wheat farming spread rapidly across the Palouse region of eastern Washington in the late 1800s. Soon wheat made up forty-five percent of the value of all Washington crops. Whitman County, in the heart of the Palouse, was the wealthiest county **per capita** in the United States. Later, a series of wet years encouraged farmers to raise wheat in the drier Big Bend region.

Farmers put wheat in sacks and hauled it in wagons to landings on the Snake and Columbia Rivers. Then steamboats took the wheat to Portland. Later, wheat was shipped by rail to the ports of Tacoma and Seattle.

Most wheat farms were small by today's standards, averaging 160-320 acres. There were dozens of small farm towns, most of which have disappeared.

## Apples

Washington apples had become an important crop by 1900. Irrigation projects made it possible to run successful orchards in the Yakima, Wenatchee, and Okanogan Valleys. Washington fruit growers planted over one million trees in one year. The transcontinental railroad and the development of refrigerated cars in 1902 made it possible to ship fruit to eastern markets before it spoiled. By 1917, Washington led the nation in apple production.

## Ranching and Dairying

After farmers started growing wheat on the Palouse Hills, cattlemen could no longer graze their cows on the grass there. In other places, new settlers filed land claims along the rivers and streams and then fenced their land so cattle could not get to the water. Cattlemen retreated to the drier uplands and the foothills of the Cascades.

Harsh winters thinned the herds in the 1880s. The winter of 1889–90 killed half the cattle in the Yakima Valley and nine out of ten animals in the Big Bend.

Machines that both reaped (cut) and threshed (separated the wheat from the shaft) were called combines. They were widely used by the 1890s. Some required as many as forty-four horses. Later, self-propelled steam combines were used in the Palouse region.

Wheat came down the chute into sacks. A fast worker could sew up to 1,000 sacks per day. Sack sewers in 1911 made $3 per day.

Wheat sacks weighed as much as 140 lbs. and were moved by hand many times. Wheat was shipped down the Columbia to Portland, then by ship to overseas markets.

*Large families of eight to twelve, and sometimes even fifteen, children made up the rural population. Farming was a way of life for these families.*

Cowgirls try "spinning the wedding ring" in 1912.

The mild moist climate of the Puget Sound Lowland and the Oregon Coast was good for raising dairy cows. There was a growing market for fresh milk, cream, and butter in the rapidly growing cities. Establishment of **condensed milk** plants and cheese factories provided additional export markets. Carnation Company built a large canned milk plant in Kent in 1899.

# Urbanization

The years from 1880 to 1910 were a time of spectacular population growth in the Pacific Northwest. Some places that were inhabited by Indians and an occasional trapper were transformed within a generation into bustling communities with brick buildings, paved streets, trolley cars, and electric lights! In all of American history, there had been nothing quite like this. Nowhere was the transition to the urban age as rapid as it was in the state of Washington.

Most of the urban population was found in the region's four largest communities—Portland, Seattle, Tacoma, and Spokane. By 1910 these four cities contained almost one-third of the entire population of Washington, Oregon, and Idaho.

## Population Growth

### Washington's Cities 1880-1890

| City | 1880 | 1890 |
| --- | --- | --- |
| Tacoma | 1,098 | 36,006 |
| Seattle | 3,553 | 42,837 |
| Spokane | 350 | 20,000 |

### Washington State 1880-1910

| | |
| --- | --- |
| 1,200,000 | 1,142,000 |
| 600,000 | |
| 300,000 | 357,232 |
| 150,000 | |
| 75,000 | 75,116 |

1880  1890  1900  1910

## LINKING THE PAST TO THE PRESENT

**A time of rapid population growth causes problems with transportation, education, housing, law enforcement, and the environment. What problems has a growing population caused in your city?**

## Tacoma and the Northern Pacific

Leaders of the Northern Pacific Railroad planned to run tracks from St. Paul, Minnesota, all the way to the harbors of Puget Sound. Company officers planned the route, knowing that wherever the tracks ended there would be tremendous growth and new business for cities along the route.

Cities were often built up around train stations, especially cities that also had a seaport. Goods and raw materials such as coal,

Tacoma in 1911 boasted a large business district. Business signs on the buildings give clues to the type of work the people did in the city.

*The famous English writer Rudyard Kipling visited Tacoma in 1889 and noted that on the city's muddy streets "men were babbling about money, town lots, and again money."*

ore, lumber, and grain could be shipped from mines, mills, and factories across the country by rail, then shipped to other countries and cities on the East Coast by sea. People who rode the trains started businesses near train terminals.

When Tacoma was chosen for the railroad terminal, the railroad company bought land cheaply, had it surveyed, and drew land plots. Tacoma's growth rate in the 1880s boomed.

The world's largest sawmill was built there in 1886. Then growth slowed down. An economic depression in the 1890s was especially hard on Tacoma, and opened the way for its rival, Seattle, to forge ahead.

## Spokane

Spokane, first called Spokane Falls, was built next to the waterfalls of the Spokane River, so the city's first advantage was water power. The water power was first used to run a saw mill and to grind grain into flour.

Then the water power produced Spokane's first electricity.

After both the Northern Pacific and Great Northern railroad lines came through, the city's growth seemed assured. Its location made it a transportation hub. Soon branch rail lines linked Spokane to mining, timber, and agriculture areas.

Spokane reaped the benefit when silver was discovered in Idaho's Coeur d'Alene region in the 1880s. People brought their new wealth from the mines and settled in Spokane. Silver from mines in Idaho and British Columbia provided the money to build many of the mansions in Spokane.

*I am today selling four times the quantity of merchandise [to miners] of which I disposed one year ago. I can scarcely order goods rapidly enough to meet the daily requirements.*

—Spokane Review, 1890

*If the rate of growth had continued, the state's population in the year 2000 would have been 37 million—more than six times the actual figure. If the growth had continued, think of the trouble you would have getting to the mall or a Mariners' game!*

The competitive exuberance of the times took different forms. Towns took pride in baseball teams and the height of their grain elevators. Building a courthouse more extravagant than anyone else was important. Town leaders chose the plan of 29-year-old Willis Ritchie for the Spokane County Courthouse, completed in 1895.

*"Spokane Falls is simply the most marvelous city the American continent has ever witnessed."*

— A traveling newspaper reporter

Reporters wrote the following newspaper articles about the city:

*My next stop was Spokane Falls, where I was greatly surprised to find the improvements that have been made there within two years. Electric lights, telephones, and other metropolitan conveniences are available. Every face expresses vitality, every voice is cheerful, and everyone has a little money.*

—*The Morning Review,* 1886

*Spokane Falls is well supplied with churches. It is a sure sign of peace and prosperity. . . . People in the East always locate in a place where there are good influences, whether they follow them or not.*

—R.P. Elliot, *Spokane Falls Review,* 1890

## Seattle

Seattle was only one of a number of possible port cities on Puget Sound. However, the Cascades cut it off from the interior of the region. The city, according to historians, grew by sheer will power and a "booster spirit" that produced some spectacular results.

Seattle took on several ambitious engineering programs between 1890 and 1910. It created its own electric power system,

Steamships carried goods on the Columbia River to Portland, 1888.

Powerful hydraulic water cannons shot out streams of water to slice away the steep hills of Seattle. Leveling out many hills was a huge engineering project. *Photo by Curtis.*

built a sewer system, and built a water system adequate for a much larger city. The city leaders spent millions of dollars lowering its steep hills and leveling out land in the downtown area to facilitate growth and better transportation. Today you can take an "underground tour" in the Pioneer Square area to see a bit of the old Seattle at the end of the 1800s.

Seattle boosters persuaded James J. Hill to bring his Great Northern Railroad to town and the Northern Pacific Railroad to move its headquarters from Tacoma to Seattle. The crowning achievement of the Seattle spirit, however, was its successful promotion of the city as the only gateway to the gold of the Klondike.

## Portland

Urban rivalries pitted city against city, for the stakes were high. Growth meant more railroad and steamship connections, higher land values, and more business. All of these meant more money.

Portland, Oregon, achieved its importance because of its location. Portland's position at the confluence of the Willamette and Columbia Rivers meant that all the trade of the inland regions flowed down to it. Its deepwater harbor opened it to ocean-going commerce.

*Every city on the Pacific Coast aspired to become the metropolis of the West. More business meant more money. More money meant better transportation, stores, schools, and homes.*

Expecting large crowds, outfitters stacked prospector's supplies on the sidewalks in front of stores. Summer, 1897. *Photo by Curtis*

# THE KLONDIKE GOLD RUSH

The discovery of gold in the Klondike region of Canada's Yukon Territory in 1897 was an important event in Seattle's history. The city **exploited** the Klondike rush to gain the advantage over all of its rival cities.

No American port was closer to Alaska and the main trails that led from there to the Klondike. 1500 people fled north on the first ship to Alaska, with nine other ships crowded in the harbor waiting to follow them. Even the mayor of Seattle quit his job and went to the gold fields.

Stores ordered in so many provisions that the merchandise was stacked ten feet high in downtown Seattle. Each miner had to take about a ton of supplies with him, including tents, cooking pots, tools, winter clothes, and over 1000 pounds of food. All the provisions were called an "outfit." Outfits were sold in Seattle. So were hotel rooms, restaurant meals, and many forms of entertainment. Shipyards bustled with construction. All this meant a booming business for Seattle.

Erastus Brainerd of the city's Chamber of Commerce was directed to promote Seattle as *the* gateway to the Klondike. And he did! Brainerd let loose on the United States and foreign countries a flood of advertisements and articles in magazines and newspapers.

The Klondike region was part of Canada's Yukon Territory and part of Alaska. The "rich man's route" was an all-water route that included more than 2,000 miles on the Yukon River to the gold fields.

The "poor mans route" was shorter but much harder. It included taking a boat to southern Alaska, climbing over steep mountains on foot, then building a boat to go 500 miles down the Yukon.

He wrote letters to government leaders, all touting Seattle as a place for miners to buy their provisions and as the nearest seaport where miners could board a ship for Alaska and Canada.

The frenzied result was a stampede. In fact, the crazed gold seekers were actually called stampeders. Some **deluded** souls took gunnysacks to carry back the gold nuggets they assumed were just laying all around. The truth was that less than half of the 100,000 people who left for the Klondike actually got there. The extreme cold and isolation of the Klondike was daunting. Waterways froze solid. Miners faced blizzards, hikes across glaciers, and falls into crevasses or off icy cliffs.

In the warmer months, deep mud holes, floods, and mosquitoes made life miserable for men and beast. When men reached the tops of icy peaks with part of their provisions, they had to go down again to bring up another load. They repeated this process as much as thirty times.

Finally, the town of Dawson City welcomed them at the edge of the gold fields. Anxious to begin finding gold, miners would often find that the best claims were already staked. They sold their provisions to other miners for a fraction of what they had paid and made the long journey home.

A newspaper correspondent

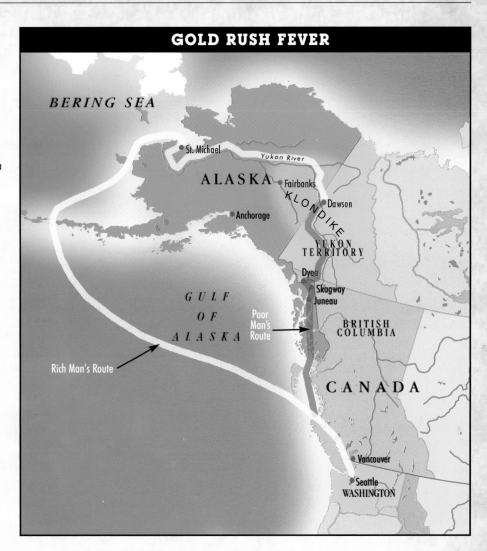

**GOLD RUSH FEVER**

described the arrival of the stampeders in Dawson:

*It is a* motley throng—*every degree of person gathered from every corner of the earth and from every state of the Union—weather-beaten, sunburned, . . . Australians with upturned sleeves and a swagger, young Englishmen in golf stockings and tweeds; would-be miners in macki-naws [raincoats] and rubber boots or heavy highlaced shoes; Japanese, Negroes—and women, too, everywhere.*

Some successful stampeders who returned to Seattle invested in local businesses. John Nordstrom invested $13,000 of his gold into a shoe store. The store was owned by a man he had met in the Klondike. That modest start was the beginning of the Nordstrom department store chain. Edward Nordoff, a Seattle merchant who capitalized on his success during the Klondike rush, turned his small store into the Bon Marché stores.

The gold rush was not good for many miners, but it was very good for Seattle businessmen. New businesses meant more growth. By 1910, Seattle was the largest city of the Pacific Northwest.

A woman stands by a canoe at the Seattle waterfront in 1898. Native people from many parts of the Northwest Coast came to Seattle to trade and buy supplies. *Photo by O.P. Anderson*

# The Vanishing Indian

The flood of new settlers overwhelmed the Indian people. Indian tribes were crowded out of their original territory, and most were assigned to reservations. There were, however, many Indians who had not moved to a reservation. They tried to hold on to their small farms and ranches, believing that the federal government would protect their land titles.

Congress passed the Indian Homestead Act in 1875. It gave individual Indians the right to own a piece of property. But Indians rarely had complete papers for their claims or took the necessary steps to protect their land titles if they did get them. When whites wanted the land, they often **coerced** the Indian owner to sell it to them, or managed to get it through **fraud**. There were many loopholes in land laws and the Indian people usually did not know how to fight the legal system.

## Dividing up Reservation Lands

Trying to be **humane** to Indians, Congress passed the General Allotment Act. Often called the Dawes Act, the law divided reservation land into individual allotments (usually 160 acres) and encouraged Indians to become farmers.

Under the new act, Indians could not sell their land for a period of time. When they finally got title to their land, they would become American citizens. It was a great **irony** that the first Americans had to wait to become citizens.

The Dawes Act was a catastrophe. Most reservations were on land that was dry and unsuited for agriculture so Indians often sold their land as soon as they got title to it. Whites bought reservation land that was never deeded to Indian people. When the law was **repealed** in 1934, more than 30 percent of the Colville and Spokane reservation land was owned by non-Indians.

## Boarding Schools

Unfortunately, American Indian policy was based upon the idea that there was nothing of value in Indian culture. The majority of whites thought that it was in the best interest of Indians to abandon their old ways and adopt the ways of the white culture.

To accomplish this goal, the federal government took Indian children from their families on the reservations and sent them far away to boarding schools. Children from Northwest reservations were often sent to Oklahoma. Most did not see their parents again for many years.

The boarding school experience was a culture shock. Indian students had their long hair cut short, they were dressed in uniforms, and given new names. They were punished if they spoke their native language. The students washed their own clothes in tubs of water and kept their dormitory rooms clean. They helped prepare and clean up after meals.

Boys and girls were taught English, reading, spelling, geography, and arithmetic. The course of study for older children emphasized **industrial** and **domestic** arts. Boys learned carpentry and to run machines. Girls learned how to make clothes on sewing machines.

Sid Bird was sent to the Genoa School in Nebraska when he was six years old. Returning years later, he found that he could not talk to his grandmother:

> *My own language had been beaten out of me. I was no longer an Indian. I guess I was an imitation white man.*

## LINKING THE PAST TO THE PRESENT

**In 2000, Kevin Grover, a Pawnee Indian and head of the Federal Bureau of Indian Affairs, offered the first official apology for this national "legacy of racism and inhumanity." With tears streaming down his face, Grover said:**

> *Never again will we seize your children or teach them to be ashamed of who they are. Never again!*

## WHAT DO YOU THINK?

**"White makes right" was a typical idea of the time. It affected the treatment of many races of people. How did treatment of the American Indians compare with ways African Americans and Asian Americans have been treated in American history?**

Carrie Anderson, Annie Dawson, and Sarah Walker were the new names given to these girls on their arrival at the Indian Agricultural Institute.

Carrie, Annie, and Sarah are playing checkers in this posed photograph fourteen months later. The picture was taken in 1880.

## Statehood

Washington's long 36-year wait for statehood ended on November 11, 1889, when it was admitted to the Union along with Montana, North Dakota, and South Dakota. Why did it take so long to gain statehood? There were certain rules about how many people had to live in a territory before it could become a state. The major cause of the delay, however, was the concern of Democratic congressmen in the nation's capital about admitting states that were apt to vote Republican. This obstacle was removed when Republicans captured the White House and both houses of Congress.

In a special election, Washington's male voters overwhelmingly approved their new constitution. They also overwhelmingly rejected the right of women to vote. Olympia was chosen for the state capital.

*Women were allowed to vote only for school board members. They were not allowed to vote in any state or national elections.*

The Fourth of July was the most important holiday of the year. Young girls raced in Davenport, 1900.

## ACTIVITY

### VISIT A CEMETERY

Cemeteries contain a wealth of information. Visit a cemetery with graves from the late 1880s and write a summary of what you find. What can you learn?

The dates on tombstones give clues to the life expectancy of people a hundred years ago. Places of birth indicate patterns of migration. Names show ethnic origins. Gravestone art reveals the religion of the people.

In German communities, graves are found in precise rows. Many older graveyards separated people according to race and religion. Mining and logging towns, where people moved in and out often, often have a haphazard layout with no regard to ethnic backgrounds.

### Earliest Photograph

Your county, city, or local universities may have a historic preservation office that could give you a copy or photocopy of the earliest photograph of your community. Or, they may be able to help you find a record or photograph of the oldest building in your area, or the first school or church building, or of early commerce, or people celebrating a special event or holiday. In a few paragraphs, describe what you find. Use descriptive words to give an "I was there" feel to the writing.

### Examine an Old Catalog

Go to a library and ask a reference librarian if the library has a reprint of a turn-of-the-century *Montgomery Wards* or *Sears* mail order catalog. They are filled with information on what people used in their everyday life—clothing, medical equipment, recreation items, and tools.

Choose a category and compare the items with those you use today, or with items found in catalogs today.

## CHAPTER 7 REVIEW

1. What event ended the frontier era and was responsible for Washington's huge population growth?

2. Describe the federal government's assistance to the railroad companies.

3. List some achievements of Henry Villard.

4. What methods did the railroad companies use to get revenue from federal land grants?

5. List the three largest groups of immigrants brought by the railroads.

6. Which three cities were burned in 1889? What other important event occurred that year?

7. Which natural resources contributed to the state's explosive growth?

8. How did the timber industry benefit from the land given to the railroads? List some modern timber companies that bought much of their timberland from the railroads.

9. Which ethnic groups were fisherman? Which ethnic group did a lot of the canning of fish? What invention helped the men can the fish?

10. What contributed the most to the decline of the salmon fishing industry?

11. What mineral was mined in the Lowlands and the Cascades? What was it used for?

12. What part did the discovery of gold and silver in surrounding states and in Canada have on the prosperity and growth of Washington cities?

13. What important agricultural products (crops and livestock) were grown or produced in Washington?

14. Which three large Washington cities had the highest population growth between 1880 and 1890?

15. How did Tacoma get its start?

16. What event in Alaska and Canada did Seattle exploit to increase business? Who benefited the most—the miners or the merchants?

17. What did the Indian Homestead Act attempt to do? Was it successful? Why or why not?

18. Describe the purpose of Indian boarding schools. What methods were used to try to change the culture of the children?

19. What did the Dawes Act attempt to do? Was it successful? Why or why not?

20. What year was Washington made a state? What city was chosen as the new capital city?

The students on this page went to the Baldridge School in 1898. Like so many other buildings in the wheat country, it was abandoned in the 1920s but still stands today.
Photo by Mike Green

# Reform, War

➡ **PEOPLE TO KNOW**

William Boeing
Major John Butler
Horace Cayton
Wesley Everest
Elizabeth Gurley Flynn
May Arkwright Hutton
Rev. Mark Matthews
James O'Sullivan
Anna Louise Strong
William U'Ren

➡ **PLACES TO LOCATE**

Germany
Russia
British Columbia
Puget Sound
Columbia Basin
Grand Coulee
Columbia River
Seattle
Spokane
Everett
Centralia

➡ **WORDS TO UNDERSTAND**

1 ardent
2 capitalist
3 capitalism
4 communism
8 conspiracy
6 deficient
7 exploit
8 incense
9 initiative
10 libel
11 radical
12 recall
13 reclamation project
14 referendum
15 repeal
16 sabotage
17 suffrage
18 suppress
19 suspend
20 vigilante

Men made makeshift "trucks" with automobile engines. The trucks replaced horse-drawn wagons for hauling logs. Since lumber was plentiful, it was used to make a "road" for the trucks in the early 1920s.

**1911**
Washington adopts the initiative, referendum, and recall.

Washington enacts workmen's compensation and an eight-hour workday for women.

| TIMELINE | 1900 | | 1905 | | 1910 |
|---|---|---|---|---|---|

**1902**
Oregon adopts the initiative and referendum.

**1905**
Birth of the Industrial Workers of the World (IWW)

**1909**
IWW Free Speech Campaign in Spokane

**1910**
Washington approves women's suffrage.

and Inventions

Sandison

**1914**
Prohibition is adopted in Washington.

**1916**
Everett Massacre

**1919**
Seattle General Strike

Centralia Massacre

The Eighteenth Amendment prohibits making or selling alcohol in the United States.

**1929**
Stock Market collapses.

**1933**
Prohibition is repealed.

**1915**

**1920**

**1925**

**1930**

**1914**
World War I
**1918**

**1920**
The Nineteenth Amendment gives women the right to vote.

**1917**
United States enters the war.

**1931**
Butler report favoring construction of Grand Coulee Dam is released.

# Progressive Reform

The rapid growth of industries at the beginning of the twentieth century caused many problems. Cities were crowded and were without proper **sanitation.** No one collected the garbage, and water was not always clean. The cities needed sewer systems. There were few paved roads or public transportation. Factories, mines, and lumber camps were unsafe places to work. There was widespread political corruption.

People wanted to reform government and clean up the cities. The Progressive Movement was a collection of many different reforms. Local laws were passed to protect consumers and workers.

The United States Constitution was amended to give women the right to vote, to establish a federal income tax, and to provide for the direct election of U.S. senators by voters.

## Prohibition

Prohibition was part of the Progressive Movement. People, especially women, tried to make the production, selling, and buying of all alcoholic drinks illegal. They said alcohol was responsible for much of the abuse of women and children, most of the crime, and that buying alcohol wasted money a family needed for food.

The Eighteenth Amendment to the United States Constitution made alcohol illegal all over America. However, Washington was still very "wet" because liquor from British Columbia was smuggled into the state by "rumrunners" who could legally buy it north of the border. Rumrunners brought the illegal alcohol to private clubs or roadhouses called "blind pigs."

Millions of Americans seemed willing to break the law if it interfered with having a good time. Violations became so widespread that local police stopped enforcing Prohibition in many cities. Bribery of the police to ignore the selling of alcoholic drinks was so common that one Spokane man said years later that it was a shock to find an honest law officer.

## LINKING THE PAST TO THE PRESENT

**How do the issues of Prohibition compare with today's illegal drug problems? How are the problems alike?**

*P*rohibition *was finally* **repealed** *in 1933. The fourteen-year effort to make alcohol illegal had been a failure.*

Remains of stills that had made alcohol pass by the Spokane County Courthouse.

## Legislative Reform

The Progressive Movement owed much to the leadership of William U'Ren in Oregon. He encouraged Oregon's voters to approve two new ways citizens could make or reject laws themselves. Washington State voters also adopted the initiative and referendum.

- The *initiative* let citizens pass laws themselves by gaining enough signatures on a petition. Then the public voted on the law at the next election.
- The *referendum* allowed citizens to vote for or against laws already passed by the legislature.

Voters also established the *recall*. If they did not approve of the way an elected official was doing his job, he could be removed from office.

## Regulating Business

As part of the Progressive Movement, the government started regulating the fees charged by railroads and utilities. Laws were passed to limit the number of hours people could work. Women could only work eight hours a day. Children could no longer work all day in mines and factories. They had to go to school.

## The Suffrage Movement

Washington's most significant victory was voting rights for women. The state constitution had denied women both the right to vote and to serve on a jury. Women were leaders in all areas of Progressive reform, and they understood how much more effective they would be with the right to vote and hold office. Across the state, women's groups campaigned for political rights.

Finally, a state constitutional amendment gave women the right to vote in state and local elections, hold public office, and serve on juries. Washington was the fifth state to do this, ten years before the national *suffrage* amendment gave all women in the United States the right to vote.

### Washington PORTRAIT

# MAY ARKWRIGHT HUTTON

A colorful and energetic campaigner for women's suffrage was May Arkwright Hutton. She was a former mining camp cook who had struck it rich in the silver mines in Idaho. May was always on the side of striking miners. She spoke bluntly. Her language often embarrassed both men and women, but her speeches were effective. "Criminals and idiots can't vote," she said, "and neither can women."

Hutton enjoyed being driven to her many social and political activities in Spokane by a chauffeur in a fire-engine-red car. She loved to wear scarlet dresses, a tiger-striped coat, and a hat with billowing ostrich plumes.

After her death, her husband opened an orphanage in her memory. Hundreds of the children raised there returned as adults for a celebration in 1994.

May Hutton fought male opposition to women's suffrage.

## MARK MATTHEWS

**M**uch of the Progressive Movement in Seattle revolved around the Reverend Mark Matthews. Matthews came to Seattle from the South in 1902. A tall slender man, he was a powerful speaker and a dynamic leader. Matthews turned Seattle's First Presbyterian Church into an instrument of social change. His congregation worked for public hospitals, parks, and playgrounds, as well as a juvenile court system.

Matthews said:

*It is cheaper to establish schools, parks, . . . and places of refinement, culture and morality, than it is to support hundreds of policemen, jails . . . and asylums for [alcoholics].*

Matthews fought against the "moral evils of liquor, gambling, and prostitution." He was particularly *incensed* with political corruption in city government. He directed a campaign that used the recall to remove the mayor from office because the mayor supported illegal activities.

Mark Matthews and his church members were champions of Progressive reform.

# Washington's Workers

**B**y 1900, most of the Northwest's workers were young single males. Workers went from job to job. They earned wages in mines, logging camps, lumber mills, and farm fields and orchards.

During the winter months, workers gathered in Spokane, Portland, and Seattle, where they were eager customers for Skid Road saloons, gambling halls, and places of prostitution. These workers created a less than respectable feature of Seattle's growth.

## The IWW

From its creation in 1905 into the 1920s, the Industrial Workers of the World championed the concept of "One Big Union" and the overthrow of *capitalism.* Capitalism is private ownership of land, property, and business. *Capitalists* were business owners who made money by hiring workers, usually at very low wages. It was workers against owners, poor against the rich.

Unlike other unions, the IWW welcomed women and African Americans. The union also gave dignity to unskilled workers who were barred from other unions.

Called "Wobblies," union members were not satisfied with just Progressive reforms. They wanted *radical* change. They agreed to strike if necessary. Workers fought for the right to speak freely to bosses and government leaders to get safer working conditions and higher wages. Wobblies spoke on street corners and in public parks. Their "free speech fights" created much sympathy for their cause.

### LINKING THE PAST TO THE PRESENT

**Has there been a union strike in your town? If so, what were the causes of the dispute? What was the outcome for workers and management?**

## The Everett Massacre

The IWW spent most of its time campaigning for basic rights, especially better conditions in the lumber camps and the eight-hour workday. IWW literature, however, openly discussed **sabotage**. Sabotage is the destruction of a company's tools or materials so it can't do business.

The record, though, is clear on this point—the IWW received far more violence than it ever started. A tragic example is the Everett Massacre. In Everett, a mill town north of Seattle, Wobblies were giving speeches criticizing World War I and capitalism. Many were arrested, then repeatedly beaten by police and **vigilantes**. Vigilantes are men who take it upon themselves to punish criminals.

To give support, a boatload of nearly 300 more Wobblies landed at Everett. As they sang union songs and tried to get off the ship, they were met with gunfire. Five workers and two vigilantes were killed.

Seventy-four Wobblies were charged with murder. After a trial, the defense showed that no one could tell who fired the first shot, and no guns were found on the ship. The Wobblies were freed.

### Workers Lingo

**Bindle** Blanket roll

**Bindle Stiff** Worker who carries his bedding

**California Blankets** Newspapers used for bedding

**Dingbat** A tramp considered "homeless, helpless, and harmless"

**Fink** An informer or strikebreaker

**Jungle** A place, usually near a railroad yard, where migrants cooked and slept

**Rattler** Fast freight train

**Scab** Person who takes the job of a striking union member

**Skid Road** An area of town where there were saloons, gambling, and prostitution

## ELIZABETH GURLEY FLYNN

One of the most popular IWW free speech fighters was Elizabeth Gurley Flynn. As an eighteen-year-old girl, she led a free speech fight in Spokane in 1909. Speaking on Wobbly philosophy on the city's street corners, she and several hundred IWW members were arrested for disturbing the peace.

Flynn was only in jail one night, but it was long enough to get material for a report of illegal prostitution going on in Spokane's county jail. The city's chief of police knew what was going on and did nothing to stop it. Flynn's account, printed in the next edition of *The Industrial Worker*, provoked outrage across the country.

Flynn was the inspiration for the popular IWW ballad "The Rebel Girl."

Flynn speaks in Patterson in 1913.

## ACTIVITY

### POSTERS PROMOTE THE CAUSE

These posters show some of the powerful messages that the IWW was trying to promote. Read the posters, and then discuss the questions.

1. What did the union mean by the phrase, "We have fed you all a thousand years"?

2. Look up the meaning of the word "proletariat." Discuss how it relates to poor workers who were fighting against the wealthy business owners.

3. The Rebel Girl was a popular union ballad. What do the terms "blue blooded" and "thoroughbred" refer to?

### The Rebel Girl

*There are blue-*
*blooded queens*
*and princesses,*
*Who have charms*
*made of diamonds*
*and pearls;*
*But the only and thor-*
*oughbred lady*
*Is the Rebel Girl.*

**Chorus:**

*That's the Rebel Girl!*
*That's the Rebel*
*Girl!*
*To the working class*
*she's a precious*
*pearl.*
*She brings courage, pride and joy*
*To the fighting Rebel Boy.*
*We've had girls before, but we need some more*
*In the Industrial Workers of the World.*
*For it's great to fight for freedom*
*With a Rebel Girl.*

---

# The First World War

The Great War, as it was called at the time, raged in Europe from 1914 to 1917 before the United States became involved. On one side were the Central Powers of Germany, Austria-Hungary, and Turkey. On the other side were the Allied Powers of England, France, Italy, and Russia. Many American businesses sold weapons, supplies, and food to England and France. The companies made enormous profits.

Most Americans ***ardently*** expressed their opposition to American participation in the war. Then Germany started fighting with a new weapon—submarines, or U-boats.

> "*The world must be safe for democracy.*"
>
> –Woodrow Wilson, 1917

They attacked without warning, sinking both military, commercial, and passenger ships.

When a ship carrying American tourists was sunk off the shore of England, Americans were outraged. Still U.S. President Woodrow Wilson fought to keep America neutral. Later, when other ships were also attacked, killing more Americans, the U.S. Congress declared war.

Men were asked to join the war effort. When not enough men signed up, Congress passed the Selective Service Act. It required all men between twenty-one and thirty to sign up for military service. They called it "being drafted." About 75,000 Washington men fought in the war.

## Political Hysteria

During the war, Germans were the enemy in Europe. Thinking German Americans were disloyal or even enemies of the United States, some Americans beat up Germans and vandalized their farms and businesses. German was banned as a language taught in many schools. Things with German names were given American names. Hamburger became "liberty sausage;" sauerkraut became "liberty cabbage."

## The IWW Fights Against the War

Members of the Industrial Workers of the World were against America's involvement in the war. They claimed the war was being fought to enrich big businesses who supplied war materials, not to make the world safe for democracy. The Wobblies engaged in strikes against companies that

Girl Scouts collected peach pits to help the United States win the war. The pits were turned into charcoal. Charcoal was used in gas masks to filter out poisonous gas.

supplied tanks, guns, uniforms, and other war materials. They gave fiery speeches against those who profited from war.

The IWW's greatest accomplishment was a 1917 strike for the eight-hour workday. The federal government forced the region's lumber companies to accept this demand so workers wouldn't strike again and would continue to provide lumber for planes and warships.

## The Sedition Act

Since so many Americans were against the war, Congress made laws to **suppress** criticism. The Sedition Act prohibited any speech that was "disloyal, profane, . . . or

## Russian Revolution and the Red Scare

Life in Russia was desperate. There had already been a huge loss of life and materials during the war. People wanted to end it. There was no food and no fuel to heat homes. Everyone blamed the government, and the czar was forced to step down from power.

Vladimir Lenin established a communistic government where all the people, not individuals, owned all property and all businesses. No longer, they said, would wealthy capitalists take all the profits and **exploit** workers who lived in poverty. No longer would there be a struggle between the "haves" and the "have nots." "All the people" quickly came to mean only the government, however.

The Russians called on the world's workers to revolt against capitalism. Some Americans regarded striking workers in America as part of a world-wide **conspiracy** against democracy. Some people in the United States did join a Communist Party, but no evidence was found of any communist plot to overthrow the American government.

Since Russian communists marched under a red flag, they were called Reds.

abusive" about the government, flag, Constitution, or armed forces.

The IWW continued to campaign against the war, however. Wobblies were arrested for breaking the Sedition Act.

# Economic Boom

The war created many new jobs. The country suddenly needed warships. At the end of the war, there were more than twenty-five shipbuilding companies where there had been only one before the war.

The war was also responsible for what eventually became Washington's largest industrial employer—the Boeing Company.

Lumber was used for building ships, airplanes, and new houses for workers. The federal government sent army men to help the lumber industry meet production demands.

Since there was a shortage of food in Europe, Washington's crops were shipped overseas. To increase production, farmers

**Capitalism:** *private (individual or company) ownership of land, property, and business*

**Communism:** *government ownership of all land, property, and business*

A jubilant soldier returns from the war.

Who was responsible for building the planes? When young Bill Boeing took his first plane ride just ten years after the Wright brothers made their first flight in South Carolina, he wanted to build a better plane. Boeing and two friends planned, built, and tested ideas. In 1916, the three men completed a seaplane on the shores of Lake Union.

The next year the Boeing Company built fifty airplanes for the government. At first, airplanes were used for observation in the war. Later they were equipped with machine guns.

Within fifty years, the Boeing Company was the largest company in Washington.

## WILLIAM BOEING

William Boeing (right) flew air-mail between Seattle and Vancouver in 1919.

found new ways of using machines to grow and harvest more food for everyone. Workers came from Mexico and the Southwest.

Men too old to be drafted, who had had a hard time finding good jobs before the war, found better jobs once the soldiers left for Europe. Many minorities came from other states to work in Washington's industries.

Washington women, like others in the United States, took the jobs of the men who were fighting in Europe. Women became factory workers, auto mechanics, printers, and farmers. Some even worked in lumber camps. Everyone hated the horrors of war, but business was booming.

### The War is Over

Finally peace came to America once more. For lucky families, Washington's soldiers and nurses came home. For those whose sons and husbands had been killed or injured, there was relief, at least, that the killing had stopped.

## From Boom to Bust

The economic boom of the war years was followed by a sharp collapse of farm and lumber prices. Europe no longer bought as much food from Washington. There was too much food to sell locally, and prices dropped. Shipyards suddenly had no orders and laid off their workers. Lumber mills no longer needed to supply wood for ships and planes so they closed, throwing thousands of people out of work. Weyerhauser lumber sales dropped fifty percent. Many smaller mills went bankrupt. Men talked in quiet voices of how they would feed their families.

Anger increased toward immigrants and ethnic workers. Women were once again told that they should stay home and give jobs to men.

## The Seattle General Strike

At the end of the war, Seattle shipyard workers struck for wage increases that had been **suspended** during the war. Other unions voted to go on strike to show their support. Since members of so many unions in many jobs were on strike, it was called a general strike. The city almost shut down. People could not get a ride on a streetcar or a meal in a restaurant.

The strikers wanted to prove to people that workers, not just business owners, could run things, so strikers made sure that food was brought into the city and that hospitals were kept running. The Seattle General Strike was headline news across the country.

People were afraid that the strike was the beginning of a communist revolution. Unions never made any clear demands, however, and the peaceful strike ended in less than a week.

*Washington* PORTRAIT

# ANNA LOUISE STRONG

At the center of the Seattle General Strike was a remarkable young woman, Anna Louise Strong, who had just come to Washington. She was a published writer and the youngest woman ever to receive a Ph.D. from the University of Chicago.

An accomplished mountain climber, Strong led the first winter climb of Mt. Hood. She quickly became a Seattle favorite and was elected the first female member of the school board.

When Wobblies were on trial for the Everett murders, Strong covered the story as a reporter for a New York newspaper. The testimony she heard in court changed her life. She came to sympathize with the Wobblies, who were "waging a stark fight for human rights."

Two days before the Seattle strike, Strong wrote a famous newspaper editorial, admitting that no one really knew what the outcome of the strike would be, but saying that it was important for workers to be heard. She wrote:

*We are undertaking the most tremendous move ever made by Labor in this country, a move which will lead NO ONE KNOWS WHERE. . . .*

Anna Louise Strong

After the strike, Anna Strong left Seattle and worked for reform in Russia and China.

## The Centralia Massacre

Centralia, a lumber mill town south of Olympia, was the center of a dispute between mill owners and the IWW. The mill owners had recruited World War I veterans called Legionnaires to harass local Wobblies.

The Legionnaires were tricked into thinking the Wobblies were a real threat to America. After marching in a parade celebrating the end of the war, the Legionnaires went on to attack the IWW meeting hall. The Wobblies, forewarned, had armed themselves and met the attack with gunfire. Three Legionnaires were killed.

Wesley Everest, a Wobblie, shot into the crowd, killed a man, and ran. He was caught and taken to jail. Other Wobblies were also arrested.

That night, an angry mob of over a thousand men kidnapped Everest from jail.

They hanged him on a bridge outside of town. Mobs persecuted Wobblies throughout the state for days.

No one was ever charged with the murder of Wesley Everest, but eight Wobblies were convicted of murdering Legionnaires. They were given long prison sentences, though no one could prove who shot first.

Centralia demonstrated the fear caused by the Red Scare.

# Washington in the Twenties

The twenties were years devoted to the pursuit of pleasure. It was the Age of Jazz—a truly American music form. Sports spectaculars, flappers (dancers), bathing-beauty contests, and soap operas on the radio and in newspapers entertained people.

For the first time, women cut their hair short and wore skirts above the ankle. They hung long bead necklaces around their necks, colored their cheeks with rouge, and wore nylon stockings with seams down the back. Men wore wide ties and black-and-white shoes. They slicked back their hair and tried to look as modern as the ladies.

## New Inventions

Inventions, many of them dating from the late 1800s, became more available to everyone in the 1920s. It was the first "modern decade." Americans used electric power, telephones, phonographs, radios, and washing machines. They went to motion pictures on the weekends.

## LINKING THE PAST TO THE PRESENT

**Interview someone who can remember the 1920s. This might be difficult, but not impossible. Ask questions that will help you compare life in that time period with your life today.**

With the widespread use of electricity, radios became popular. For the first time in the history of the world, airwaves brought music and stories into homes.

The price of Henry Ford's Model T dropped from $850 in 1908 to under $300 by the mid-twenties. Auto ownership was within the reach of many Americans.

The engine that powered automobiles was also used in farm machinery, logging trucks, freight trucks, and school buses. School districts replaced one-room schools with larger ones since children could now be bused many miles from their farm homes to schools in town.

Every family wanted a refrigerator instead of the old ice box.

No single invention has had a greater impact on American life than the automobile. It changed where and how people lived, worked, shopped, and played.

The automobile helped to end rural isolation. Farm families could drive to major cities to shop and see concerts and movies.

# Racial Intolerance

The World War and the Red Scare that followed aroused fear of foreigners. In fact, of all the labels that might be given to the twenties, the "Intolerant Decade" is one of the most accurate. Oregon and Washington passed laws barring the growing number of Japanese residents from owning and leasing land. Politicians urged Congress to restrict further Asian immigration.

An unfortunate event of the Automobile Age was a streetcar and an automobile collision on the crowded streets of Spokane in 1929.

## ACTIVITY

### The KKK—a Primary Source Document

During a huge Ku Klux Klan ceremony in a field south of Yakima, over 1,000 robed Klansmen escorted 700 new members before a crowd of 40,000 viewers. Wooden crosses burned, and fireworks exploded in the sky.

The Klan blamed all the problems of the United States on immigrants, Catholics, Jews, and African Americans. Hiding under white hoods, Klan members terrorized families by burning crosses on lawns, and whipping, shooting, or hanging people they were trying to get rid of.

An ugly event developed in Washington's Yakima Valley in the early 1920s. The Klan tried to evict Japanese American farmers who were leasing land. However, the Klan became weaker over the next two years and the Japanese farmers remained on the land.

### Some of the questions on the application below are:

8. Are you a Gentile or a Jew?
9. Of what race (color)?
15. What is your religious faith?

This document has strong language that is very much against the ideals of Americans who work for racial equality and freedom of religion. As a class, talk about the words in the document and how the Klan used the words for their purposes. Discuss how you feel about the document.

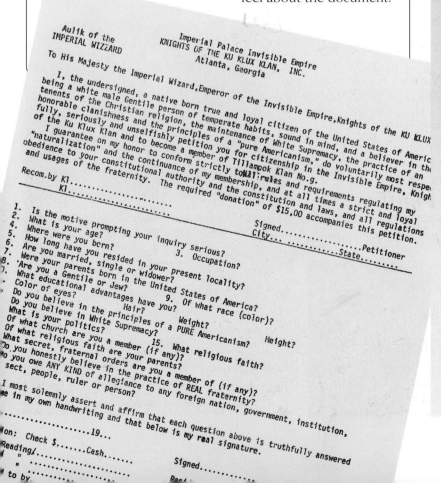

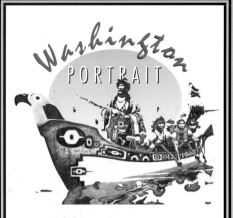

## HORACE R. CAYTON

Cayton was a prominent African American who worked for civic reform and racial equality in Seattle. He told a story of a woman who was told to move to the back of the bus and replied, "God's getting awfully tired of this."

Cayton published a weekly newspaper, *The Seattle Republican*. A scathing article on Seattle's police chief, W.L. Meridith, accused the chief of accepting bribes and allowing prostitution and other vices to go unpunished. The article led to Cayton's arrest for *libel*, but it also produced a huge outpouring of support. Charges were dropped.

# Help from Hydropower

Because electricity was essential to run the new inventions, producing hydropower became important. The Pacific Northwest had about forty percent of the nation's hydropower potential. Since the region was ***deficient*** in other energy sources (oil, natural gas, and large coal deposits), the use of hydropower was a necessity.

The depressed economy of the Puget Sound region, together with the drought on the east side of the state, also encouraged the state to use its rushing rivers to produce electricity. The Washington State Grange, the state's leading farm organization, proposed a county Public Utility District (PUD) bill. PUDs could condemn the property of private power companies and establish public power systems. This would give the public more control over prices.

Opposition to high rates and the unwillingness of private companies to serve rural areas strengthened the PUD bill. But, it was voted down by the 1929 legislature. It was narrowly approved the following year. PUDs were eventually established in twenty-nine of the state's thirty-nine counties.

## The Campaign for Grand Coulee Dam

Farm families of the Columbia Basin had a hard time making a living in the 1920s. Adding to the frustration of lower income from crops after the end of the war, a drought made it hard to grow crops. The major push for a dam came from farmers who saw it as the only way to bring irrigation

water to reclaim the Basin's parched lands.

Supporters of a dam at Grand Coulee were called "pumpers." A dam across the Columbia River would generate more than enough electricity to pump irrigation water uphill to a reservoir. It would be stored there and released as needed to the dry farmland below.

James O'Sullivan led the pumpers. They had a lot of support, but they faced powerful opposition from Spokane's privately owned Washington Water Power Company (WWP). The WWP was horrified at the prospect of a huge block of cheap public power becoming available.

The WWP came up with a different plan to irrigate the Columbia Basin. They used newspaper articles to promote a gravity canal. It would bring water from the Pend Orville River to farmland in the basin.

James O'Sullivan is one of the most honored figures in the struggle to build Grand Coulee Dam.

Throughout the twenties, both pumpers and gravity plan promoters tried to convince the federal government that their plan was the most efficient.

In 1928, the U.S. Army Corps of Engineers began a survey of the Columbia River system. Directed by Major John Butler, the engineers' report showed that the

Washington's wheat country today contains hundreds of farm homes abandoned in the 1920s.
*Photo by Mike Green*

pumping plan could be built for much less because it would bring income from the sale of electricity produced at the dam.

The dam was finally approved. Construction of the massive project, however, did not start until years later. The Columbia Basin was the largest *reclamation project* in U.S. history.

## LINKING THE PAST TO THE PRESENT

**Interview someone who can remember the Columbia Basin before irrigation. Does he or she remember the controversy around the project? Does the person think the project has been beneficial?**

## ACTIVITY

### Debate the Issues

Divide the class into two or four groups. Choose a topic, take a side, and research your topic. Present your ideas to the class in a persuasive manner. Let the class decide whose views are the most convincing.

### Choose from these topics:

- Prohibition—good or bad for citizens?
- Labor Unions—good or bad for America?
- The Columbia Basin Irrigation project—good or bad for the Columbia Basin?

## CHAPTER 8 REVIEW

1. What were some of the reforms Progressives worked for?
2. What was Prohibition?
3. How was Washington ahead of the rest of the nation in regards to women's suffrage?
4. What two new laws made it possible for ordinary citizens to make or repeal laws?
5. What was the nickname of the IWW union members? What were some of their objectives?
6. Who was a popular free speech fighter and the inspiration for "The Rebel Girl"?
7. Which groups participated in the Everett Massacre?
8. Name the two sides of the Great War (World War I) and which countries fought on each side.
9. What was outlawed in the Sedition Act?
10. Why did Americans think that strikers might be part of a communistic takeover?
11. Define capitalism and communism.
12. How did the war help Washington's economy?
13. What happened to Washington's economy after the war ended?
14. Who started the airplane company that became Washington's largest industry?
15. What famous strike was Anna Louise Strong involved in? How did the strike end?
16. Which groups shot at each other during the Centralia Massacre?
17. Describe life in the twenties, including some inventions that everyone wanted.
18. Who was Horace R. Cayton?
19. What groups did the Ku Klux Klan think were responsible for all the problems in America?
20. What was the solution to Washington's need for hydropower and irrigation water?

## GEOGRAPHY TIE-IN

1. On a map of the world, locate the countries involved in World War I. How could our lives be different today if the Central Powers had won the war?
2. Refer to pages 19, 150, and 151 and read more about the Grand Coulee Dam. How has the dam changed life for people in Washington?

## THE TIME
# 1929–1945

### ⟫ PEOPLE TO KNOW

John Collier
Albert Einstein
Jim Emmett
General Leslie Groves
Woody Guthrie
Gordon Hirabayashi
Henry J. Kaiser
Richard Neuberger
Franklin D. Roosevelt
James D. Ross
C. Ben Ross

### ⟫ PLACES TO LOCATE

Germany
Italy
England
Russia
Japan
New York
Yakima Valley
Spokane
Tacoma
Longview
Hanford
U.S. 30 (Highway)

### ⟫ WORDS TO UNDERSTAND

adamant
affluence
censorship
conservation
dilapidated
destitute
exodus
fastidious
inferior
longshoremen
migrant
reactor
subsistence
superior
transient
warehousemen

Hard Times and

Making new sidewalks in Seattle provided jobs under the New Deal's Works Progress Administration (WPA) program.

**1932** Franklin D. Roosevelt is elected president. The New Deal begins.

**TIMELINE  1929**

**1933**

**1929** New York stock market crashes. The Great Depression begins.

**1933** Construction of Bonneville and Grand Coulee Dams begins.

Civilian Conservation Corps (CCC) is created.

**1934** Indian Reorganization Act is passed.

**1939**
Roosevelt gets letter from Einstein warning of a potential German atomic bomb.

**1941**
Japan attacks Pearl Harbor, Hawaii, on December 7. The United States enters World War II.

**1945** Germany surrenders May 7.  Atomic bombs are dropped on Japan August 6 and 9.  Japan surrenders August 14.

**1937**

**1941**

**1945**

**1936**
Roosevelt is re-elected.

**1938**
Bonneville Dam starts producing electricity.

**1939** • • • • • • • • • • • • • • • • • • **1945**
World War II.

**1941**
Grand Coulee Dam is completed.

**1942** Japanese Americans on the West Coast are given relocation orders.

## The Great Depression

The Great Depression was a worldwide economic collapse. It began with the New York stock market crash in 1929, and it lasted through the 1930s.

The banks closed first. Many banks had invested recklessly in stocks. When the stocks became worthless, the banks lost their money. People who had saved their money in the banks were now broke. Soon many factories and businesses closed because no one had money to buy anything. Thousands of workers lost their jobs.

United States President Herbert Hoover did not have a workable plan to help end the depression. Blaming him for not doing enough, homeless people built housing developments out of scrap lumber, metal, and cardboard and called them "Hoovervilles."

*"With the help of 240 agencies and churches who helped with sewing, the Red Cross distributed 2800 shirts."*

*– Spokesman-Review,* January 11, 1932

Every major Northwest city had communities of homeless and unemployed people living in wretched makeshift shelters often made from discarded packing boxes. "Hoovervilles," like this one on Seattle's waterfront, were pathetic examples of hard times.

Since people with little or no income could not pay their taxes, there was not enough tax money in government funds to help people. Washington counties maintained twenty-four shelters, or "poor farms," for homeless people but turned away many of the homeless.

### How Hard Were the Hard Times?

Looking back from our time of relative **affluence** today, it is difficult to imagine how much suffering people endured. Hunger, misery, fear, and anger were found in every community.

Four-year-old Angeline D'Ambrose died after eating poisonous weeds in her backyard. Her father, a Seattle shoemaker, had been out of work for a year. "I guess my baby was hungry," he sobbed. "We haven't had anything in the house to eat for two days."

In later years, people wrote what they remembered about their family's struggle during the depression:

"We wore clothes made out of material from old clothes. We put cardboard in our shoes, and when they wore out we wore any shoes that we could get our feet into. They hardly ever fit."

"We shared an egg for breakfast, with bread."

"We ate potatoes three times a day—fried for breakfast, mashed at noon, and in potato salad for dinner. My mother even learned how to make potato fudge."

## Bargains Galore

One person's hardship could be another person's opportunity. There were bargains for those with ready cash. A long-time resident of Cheney remembers an entire block of twelve lots selling for $38. Farms, homes, and businesses sold for a fraction of their true value.

# Drought and the Dust Bowl

One of the most severe droughts in the nation's history came to the Great Plains states in 1928 and lasted in some areas for twelve years. Strong winds turned dry farming regions into a gigantic "dust bowl."

The drought also reached the Pacific Northwest. Billowing clouds of topsoil from the Columbia Basin were visible to ships hundreds of miles off the Washington coast. Dust storms plagued the basin for years. One lady with a reputation for **fastidious** housekeeping decided she could not keep

up with the dust. "She just opened her front door and opened her back door and let the dust blow right through," reported a neighbor.

The dry hot winds turned forests into a fire waiting to happen. In 1936, with drought conditions at their worst, the Forest Service reported that 450,000 acres of national forest in the Northwest had been destroyed by fire.

### Fires for Jobs

A tragic measure of those desperate years was the fact that some of the fires were deliberately set by the unemployed in an effort to get jobs as fire fighters. During the summer of 1931, Idaho's Governor Ben Ross ordered the National Guard to prevent people from entering the forests.

## Agriculture Disintegrates

Agricultural distress took many forms. Crops rotted in the fields because the cost of harvesting and shipping them to market would be greater than their sale price. In Oregon, thousands of sheep were slaughtered and fed to the buzzards and coyotes because the money farmers could get for the meat and wool was too low to make a profit. In Washington, some farmers burned fruit trees for fuel.

## Migrants by the Thousands

"We loaded up our jalopies [old run-down cars] and rattled down the highway never to come back again," said the words of a Woody Guthrie song.

With such grim conditions, it was a shock to people in the Northwest that their region was regarded as a land of opportunity by people from the Great Plains. Most **migrants** traveled Highway 66 that went all

*During the 1930s, companies that made home canning jars were one of the few businesses that made money. People wanted to make sure they had food on their shelves.*

*Within a 100 mile radius of Spokane, 18 million jars of fruit and vegetables were canned by women.*

*A young girl in Seattle with no money for Christmas shopping spent weeks making gift necklaces of paper clips. She wrapped each clip in colored tape.*

the way across the country to California, but many others "rattled down" Highway 30 to Oregon and Washington.

With crops ruined and fearing his children were coming down with dust pneumonia, Jim Emmett joined the **exodus**. His grandfather had started for the Northwest over the Oregon Trail in 1849, but he had stayed in the Dakotas instead. Richard Neuberger, a prominent author of the time, observed a number of these Dust Bowl pilgrims. His description of the Emmett family is a touching word picture of hard times:

*Jim headed the radiator cap of the automobile into the West. A thin roll of ten-dollar bills was tucked in his*

Families from the Dust Bowl states of the Great Plains packed up and drove to California, Oregon, and Washington to work on farms and in cities. *Photo by Dorothea Lange*

Sometimes cars broke down. Migrants hitched rides to the promise of a better life in the West.
*Photo by Dorothea Lange*

*purse—the proceeds of the sale of his livestock. Martha sat at Jim's side in the front seat, holding the youngest child on her lap. The other three children shared the **dilapidated** [back seat] with pillows, books, pots, dishes, jars of preserves and pickles, irons, baskets and other articles of household equipment. From a trailer jolting along behind protruded bedsprings, chairs, tables, lamps.*

By 1940, more than 400,000 migrants had followed Jim Emmett to the Northwest. But not every migrant found the Promised Land. Many were able to make only a bare **subsistence** living by working as fruit and vegetable pickers.

This army of **transient** workers moved into the Yakima, Willamette, and Snake River Valleys during the harvest seasons. Living in crowded, unsanitary shack camps, these people received little attention until 1939. That year, a federal government program provided housing and medical clinics for migrant workers in the Northwest.

# Roosevelt's New Deal

The depression got worse in 1932. It was a presidential election year and the Democrats chose Franklin D. Roosevelt, governor of New York, as their candidate. Northwesterners were unsure of Roosevelt's views, but they were anxious for a change. FDR, as he was called, won the election. He pledged himself and his party to a "New Deal" for the American people.

President Roosevelt viewed the Pacific Northwest, with its small population and abundant natural resources, as a "last frontier" of undeveloped places. He wanted people to use forests and rivers wisely. He was also willing to use federal money to help them.

Political cartoons give insight into the past. The one above shows the viewpoint of Hoover supporters who wanted him to be reelected. The cartoon on the right depicts a Republican version of what FDR promised if he were elected.

## Civilian Conservation Corps

FDR and Congress created New Deal programs to put people back to work. The most popular New Deal **conservation** effort was the Civilian Conservation Corps (CCC). Young men from every part of the nation were stationed in more than 200 camps throughout the Northwest. They earned from $30 to $45 a month, and received good food, education, and discipline—the CCC camps were commanded by army officers.

Young men worked on soil conservation projects, provided labor at fish hatcheries and wildlife refuges, and planted millions of trees on public lands. They also fought forest fires.

An Indian division of the CCC, with headquarters in Spokane, worked on Indian reservations. They built trails, roads, and forest fire lookout towers.

## Work for Everyone

In addition to conservation projects, there were hundreds of smaller construction jobs funded by the New Deal. These provided much needed employment. Workers built highways, bridges, school buildings, libraries, post offices, parks, and sewer and water systems.

Another New Deal program was the Works Progress Administration (WPA). The WPA hired musicians, writers, historians, and artists. Old newspaper articles were catalogued and old diaries were published. Histories of cities and states were written and published. Public buildings received a facelift. New art murals were painted on the walls of libraries and government buildings.

*The creation of Olympic National Park in 1938 was a major New Deal project.*

Young men in the CCC worked to help support their families back home. They wore uniforms and lived and ate in army tents.

# A NEW DAM ON THE

The right and left sides of the dam near completion, with the spillway under construction in 1939.

The Pacific Northwest soon found itself on the receiving end of a lot of New Deal money to develop the region's waterpower. President Roosevelt thought large-scale public works projects such as Grand Coulee Dam would provide immediate jobs for many of the **destitute** Dust Bowl migrants.

In 1942, journalists described the dam:

- "It will contain enough concrete to build a highway from Philadelphia to Seattle and back."
- "Enough water will flow through the dam each year to provide New York City's drinking water for a hundred years."
- "A surprising feature is the number of young men employed at Grand Coulee. I noticed dozens of tall lads wearing football sweaters from nearby universities."
- "The work is dangerous and scarcely a day passes without someone's being injured. 54 men have already been killed."

When construction on the dam began, the town of Grand Coulee sprang up from the desert.

The boomtown of Grand Coulee was described by journalist Richard Neuberger:

*Grand Coulee sprawls over the uplands above the great dam like a torn and ragged carpet. . . . Shacks and cabins dot the hills as unevenly as marbles rolled on a rug. . . . Over the desert plateau a veritable caravan rolled in. From trucks, wagons, and trailers protruded barber chairs and hand-printing presses. Cooks dreamed of making fortunes out of hamburgers and custard pie and beer. Real-estate agents envisioned lucrative returns on the sale of lots. Ministers thought of men to reform spiritually and morally. . . . "*

– from *Our Promised Land*

# COLUMBIA RIVER

Seven thousand men from all over the Pacific Northwest found jobs on the giant construction project.

President Roosevelt (standing on the right) and his wife Eleanor (in the car) toured the site of the Grand Coulee Dam. He addressed a crowd of 25,000 people.

## Songs Promote Electricity

The Bonneville Power Administration (BPA), under the direction of James D. Ross, made low-cost power available to public utility districts and encouraged the districts to take over private companies.

The BPA began a vigorous advertising campaign to promote a wider use of electricity. Famed folk singer Woody Guthrie was hired for one month. His job was to compose the music for a promotional film about the Columbia River projects. "Roll on, Columbia" became popular. It was made Washington's official folk song in 1987. Guthrie also wrote the well-known song "This Land is Your Land."

### Roll On, Columbia

Roll on, Columbia, roll on,
Roll on, Columbia, roll on.
Your power is turning the darkness to dawn,
Roll on, Columbia, roll on.
And far up the river is Grand Coulee Dam,
The mightiest thing ever built by man,
To run the great factories and water the land,
It's roll on, Columbia, roll on.

At the dam site, a metal sculpture of Woody Guthrie and two young friends shows Woody singing one of his Columbia River ballads.
*Photo by Mike Green*

# The End of the Great Depression

By 1939, the worst of the Great Depression was over. Slowly, businesses opened up again. People were working and starting to buy goods. Unemployment was still high, but many people were working. They could afford to buy more meat and other food so farmers made more money. Industry and trade in the Pacific Northwest spread to new U.S. and global markets.

## ACTIVITY

### What Did It Cost?

Compare these costs to costs today. To find today's food costs, take a trip to the grocery store. For the cost of houses, look at newspaper ads. (The classified ads from your local newspaper are probably on the Internet.) Write your answers on a separate sheet of paper.

Remember that today's workers earn a lot more money than workers during the Great Depression. A standard wage then was less than 50 cents an hour for labor.

### Costs in Spokane During the 1930s

| | |
|---|---:|
| Admission to the Empress Theater | $ .10 |
| Bread, loaf | .10 |
| Beef roast, per pound | .10 |
| Prime rib, per pound | .15 |
| Shampoo | .35 |
| Toilet paper, 6 rolls | .20 |
| Lady's dress | 5.00 |
| House for rent, 4 bedrooms, per month | 20.00 |
| House for sale, 4 bedrooms | 1,475.00 |

# Native Americans Get a New Deal

Indian populations reached their lowest level in the early 1900s. Poor diets and poor living conditions contributed to high death rates, especially among children. A new wave of diseases—tuberculosis, pneumonia, and influenza—ravaged the reservations. Alcoholism was also a big problem.

A Columbia University anthropologist, John Collier, was appointed to lead the Bureau of Indian Affairs. Collier believed the whole concept of the Dawes Act—giving land to individual Indian people—had been a mistake. He said that tribal organization was the only form of society Indians understood and that it should have been preserved. The tribe upheld the social, moral, and spiritual values of the group.

The Indian Reorganization Act repealed the Dawes Act and encouraged the formation of tribal governments. Tribes would again have common land and would promote Indian languages, arts, crafts, and ceremonies.

# Union Quarrels

Once again, workers wanted more. For the first time, federal laws were passed that gave workers the right to organize unions and bargain. Both the American Federation of Labor (AFL) and a new rival, the Congress of Industrial Organizations (CIO), fought management and each other in a series of bitter strikes. Thousands of workers in Washington joined unions and started getting better wages and working conditions.

The AFL Teamster's Union fought repeated battles with the CIO's **longshoremen** and **warehousemen** unions over who should represent workers.

Longshoremen loaded and unloaded ships. It was hard work and the men worked long hours. Warehousemen worked in huge warehouses where goods were stored until they could be transported to other places. The warehouses were freezing cold in winter and very hot in summer.

Strikes paralyzed industries. "Goon Squads"—groups of paid thugs—were on both sides of the AFL-CIO dispute. Baseball bats and cargo hooks were often used as weapons when the two groups met at dockside warehouses.

Lumber mills, breweries, and warehouses were centers of conflict. Newspaper articles took sides. Washington became one of the most unionized states in the nation.

# Another World War

The American economy was improving and the worst of the Great Depression was over, but there was trouble in other parts of the world. Adolf Hitler, dictator of Germany, believed that the Germans were a *superior* race. Hitler set out to conquer Europe and to cleanse it of what he called *inferior* peoples—especially Jewish people.

Hitler sent millions of Jews to concentration camps, where over six million were put to death in the gas chambers or died from starvation. This mass murder of the Jews is called the Holocaust.

When Hitler's army and air force conquered Poland, England and France declared war. They were called the Allied Powers, or the Allies. Later, Russia was attacked by Germany and joined the Allies. Italy and Japan joined Germany. A second World War had begun.

Once again, Americans were *adamant* that the United States stay out of the European war. President Roosevelt sent ships and supplies to help the Allies, and he warned Americans that someday they might have to fight Hitler.

## Surprise Attack on Pearl Harbor

Sunday morning, December 7, 1941, was a beautiful one at Pearl Harbor, Hawaii. The morning sun shone over the many U.S.

Washington men fought in Europe and in islands of the Pacific.

Navy ships tied up at the docks. Suddenly the skies darkened as wave after wave of Japanese fighter planes dropped bombs on U.S. ships.

The next day, President Roosevelt asked Congress to declare war on Japan. The United States joined the Allies and entered World War II.

## Through the Eyes of Children

**W**hat was it like to be a child during the Second World War? There were air raid drills, newsreels, recycling of metal and rubber, and restrictions on food. Children had fun playing soldier or playing nurse. They also felt fear. Washington children lived with the widespread belief that the Japanese, who had bombed Pearl Harbor, would soon bomb west coast cities.

The death of a father or older brother was the most devastating event for children. But the loss of a friend's father or brother, marked by a gold star in a front window, affected the entire neighborhood.

Schoolyards, vacant lots, and backyards echoed with the sounds of children fighting the war in their own way. One Spokane resident remembers his wartime childhood:

*We played war games constantly. We built dugout forts in vacant lots and covered them with boards and dirt. They became command centers from which we launched attacks on similar forts in other neighborhoods. The object was to destroy the enemy's fort when the other children had been called in for dinner or something. . . . We got the younger kids or girls to be the enemy or prisoners of war. Sometimes girls played nurses.*

*Even though we didn't have television we were totally absorbed by the war. As soon as school was out, we raced home to listen to our favorite radio programs.* Superman, The Shadow, *and* The Green Hornet *all had patriotic wartime themes.* Captain Midnight *was always chasing Nazi spies. [In the* Captain Midnight *oath, the children pledged, "to save my country from the dire peril it faces or perish in the attempt."]*

*Popular war songs were also on the radio and we sang them at school. We sang "Remember Pearl Harbor," "Coming in on a Wing and a Prayer," "Praise the Lord and Pass the Ammunition," and "White Cliffs of Dover."*

*I was only ten when the war ended, so my memory of rationing and shortages is a bit fuzzy, though I do remember that bubble gum became impossible to find.*

In 1942, these children collected junk for the war effort. Rubber and metal were needed to make planes, ships, and tanks.

# World War II and an Economic Boom

Worldd War II ended what was left of the Great Depression. War brought horror; it also brought economic prosperity. Suddenly, there were war-related jobs for everyone.

Because the Northwest was located close to the Pacific war zone, the region became a center for the shipment of military personnel and equipment. The ocean shoreline meant the region could once again become a large ship-building center.

Hydroelectric power from Bonneville and Grand Coulee Dams on the Columbia River played a vital role in wartime production. The great amount of cheap power produced from the dams boosted industrial development.

## Aluminum

Aluminum production became the region's great new war industry. Five huge aluminum manufacturing plants were constructed. These plants were enormous consumers of electrical energy. Giant mills were built at Spokane, Longview, and Tacoma. The mills shaped aluminum into a variety of forms. Much of the metal was sent in rolled sheets to the Boeing Company in Seattle. There it was used to build airplanes.

## Shipbuilding

Henry J. Kaiser, an aggressive business-man, became the world's greatest ship-builder. Nearly 100,000 people worked in the Kaiser yards in the Portland-Vancouver region. From 1941 until the end of the war, Kaiser built fifty "baby flattop" aircraft carriers and several hundred merchant ships. Kaiser used fast, simplified methods of welding. He used steel from his own plants in California and Utah. Kaiser pro-

## Boeing's War Planes

Just in case enemy planes flew over the area, Boeing's plant was disguised to look like a residential neighborhood. Using paint and wire, buildings were made to look like homes with trees in the yards.

At the peak of production, the Seattle plant produced sixteen B-17s every day. The B-17 was the main weapon in the air war against Germany. At its Renton plant, Boeing began work on the larger B-29. The B-29 "superfortress" was the most advanced bomber of its time. It was used in the air war against Japan. By mid-1945, six new B-29s rolled out of the plant every day.

Boeing employed 50,000 people by the end of the war. Nearly half of them were women.

By the end of the war, Boeing had built nearly seven thousand B-17s and more than one thousand B-29s. Boeing sales were ten times the income of all other Seattle industries combined.

The final Boeing B-17 was decorated with names of missions flown by other planes during the war.

duced more ships than any other company in the country. Warships were built at ship-yards in Seattle, Tacoma, Bremerton, and Bellingham, too.

It seemed the state's natural resource economy based on farms, fish, and lumber had changed overnight to an economy based on aluminum, airplanes, and ships.

*Kaiser was the same man who had organized the companies that built Grand Coulee Dam.*

# Hanford and the Atom Bomb

In September 1939, President Roosevelt received a letter signed by the Jewish scientist Albert Einstein, warning him that Hitler's Germany might be the first country to make an atom bomb. Roosevelt started the secret Manhattan Project to develop the atom bomb for Americans.

Directed by General Leslie Groves, a former University of Washington student, the Manhattan Project built one of its research facilities at a place called Hanford. Located in a remote section of eastern Washington, the site had obvious advantages. Its location ensured both security and public safety from possible radiation.

Hanford produced plutonium used for bombs. The plant's **reactors**—machines that create nuclear energy—required a huge amount of electric power and vast amounts of fresh water for cooling. The location was perfect—Grand Coulee Dam was ready to provide the power and the Columbia River had the water.

Hanford

During the war, local newspapers agreed to a voluntary **censorship** of news about Hanford. They did not want to let the world know U.S. secrets.

A "mystery city" of houses, cafeterias, and other buildings for 51,000 men and women and train loads of equipment disappeared behind the project's fences. In nearby Richland, the tiny town was being expanded to house the administration center and a complete city for 15,000 more people. Most of the workers did not know the end product of their work.

It was not until the dropping of atomic bombs on Japan ended the war that the world discovered the secrets of Hanford. The hydroelectric power of the Columbia River had combined with science to produce the atom bomb.

Women provided a tremendous workforce after the men left for war. Iona Murphy became a welder and made parts for ships.

# Social Change

The social impact of the war on the state of Washington was enormous. This was particularly true of the Puget Sound region. The war transformed Seattle into an industrial center and brought a large number of migrants from every part of the country.

Seattle's African American population, for example, increased from 3,700 in 1940 to 30,000 by the end of the war in 1945. White people resented the influx of newcomers, and racial discrimination became part of daily life for the black residents.

Members of the Women's Army Corps parade in Seattle during World War II.

Signs that said "We cater to white trade only" appeared throughout the city.

The demand for housing turned renovated chicken coops, garages, and empty service stations into apartments. Some families lived in tents. Other people lived in the backseats of cars.

## Hispanics

The war was also a turning point in Hispanic migration to Washington. After men went overseas to fight, there were not enough workers on the farms. Growers in the Yakima Valley became so desperate for help that one farm advertised for 5,000 workers.

The government's answer was the Bracero Program. Braceros were Mexican men allowed to work in the United States as temporary farm laborers. Thousands were employed in the Northwest. The program encouraged the migration of another Hispanic group. Chicanos—Americans of Mexican descent—began moving into the state from the Southwest in significant numbers. Whole families made the journey from Texas and other states to work in Washington fields and orchards.

# Relocation of Japanese Americans

The surprise attack on Pearl Harbor produced an irrational, almost hysterical, fear of Japanese invasion. Some people thought that Japanese Americans might give aid to Japan or secretly try to

Japanese children left friends and pets behind and went with their families to relocation camps. The people organized their own schools, clubs, and other entertainment at the camps.

destroy American companies. Without any evidence to support their decision, government leaders decided to classify anyone of Japanese ancestry as a security risk.

On March 2, 1942, all persons of Japanese descent living on the West Coast were given relocation orders. Many lost their property or were forced to sell at low prices. They were removed from coastal areas, including Washington. Most of the Japanese in Oregon and Washington were sent to the Minidoka Relocation Center in the Idaho desert. Minidoka was the temporary home to 10,000 people, most of whom were second and third generation Japanese American citizens of the United States. They spent the war surrounded by barbed wire and armed guards.

## WHAT DO YOU THINK?

**America was fighting Japan, Germany, and Italy during the war. Why do you think German Americans and Italian Americans were not relocated?**

## ACTIVITY

### Primary Source Documents

*Every Japanese American family received a copy of the evacuation order like the one on the next page. Some of the text reads:*

All persons of Japanese ancestry, both alien and non-alien, will be evacuated from the above area by 12 o'clock noon, Friday, May 1, 1942.

No Japanese person living in the above area will be permitted to change residence after 12 o'clock noon, Friday, April 24, 1942, without obtaining special permission from the representative of the Commanding general.

The Civil Control Station is equipped to assist the Japanese population affected by this evacuation in the following ways:
1. Give advice and instructions on the evacuation.
2. Provide services with respect to the management, leasing, sale, storage or other disposition of most kinds of property, such as real estate, business and professional equipment, household goods, boats, automobiles and livestock.
3. Provide temporary residence elsewhere for all Japanese in family groups.
4. Transport persons and a limited amount of clothing and equipment to their new residence.

Evacuees must carry with them, on departure for the Assembly Center, the following property:
a. Bedding and linens (no mattress) for each member of the family
b. Toilet articles for each member of the family
c. Extra clothing for each member of the family
d. Knives, forks, spoons, plates, bowls, and cups for each member of the family

**Discuss with your class how you would have felt if:**

1. You had been a teenager of Japanese descent during the war and your family had received the notice to relocate. What changes in your life would you immediately have had to make?

2. You were the close friend of a Japanese American who had to leave.

3. You were a government official in charge of providing housing, food, and work for thousands of Japanese Americans in a relocation camp.

WESTERN DEFENSE COMMAND AND FOURTH ARMY
WARTIME CIVIL CONTROL ADMINISTRATION
Presidio of San Francisco, California
April 24, 1942

# INSTRUCTIONS
## TO ALL PERSONS OF
# JAPANESE
## ANCESTRY
### Living in the Following Area:

All of those portions of the Counties of Contra Costa and Alameda, State of California, within the boundary beginning at Carquinez Strait; thence southerly on U. S. Highway No. 40 to its intersection with California State Highway No. 1, at or near Hercules; thence easterly on said Highway No. 4 to its intersection with California State Highway No. 21; thence southerly on said Highway No. 21 to its intersection with California State Highway No. 24, at Walnut Creek; thence westerly on said Highway No. 21 to the southerly limits of the City of Berkeley; thence following the said southerly city limits to San Francisco Bay; thence northerly and following the shore line of San Francisco Bay, through San Pablo Strait, and San Pablo Bay, to the point of beginning.

Pursuant to the provisions of Civilian Exclusion Order No. 19, this Headquarters, dated April 24, 1942, all persons of Japanese ancestry, both alien and non-alien, will be evacuated from the above area by 12 o'clock noon, P. W. T., Friday, May 1, 1942.

No Japanese person living in the above area will be permitted to change residence after 12 o'clock noon, P. W. T., Friday, April 24, 1942, without obtaining special permission from the representative of the Commanding General, Northern California Sector, at the Civil Control Station located at:

2345 Channing Way, Berkeley, California.

Such permits will only be granted for the purpose of uniting members of a family, or in cases of grave emergency.

The Civil Control Station is equipped to assist the Japanese population affected by this evacuation in the following ways:

1. Give advice and instructions on the evacuation.
2. Provide services with respect to the management, leasing, sale, storage or other disposition of most kinds of property, such as real estate, business and professional equipment, household goods, boats, automobiles and livestock.
3. Provide temporary residence elsewhere for all Japanese in family groups.
4. Transport persons and a limited amount of clothing and equipment to their new residence.

**The Following Instructions Must Be Observed:**

1. A responsible member of each family, preferably the head of the family, or the person in whose name most of the property is held, and each individual living alone, will report to the Civil Control Station to receive further instructions. This must be done between 8:00 A. M. and 5:00 P. M. on Saturday, April 25, 1942, or between 8:00 A. M. and 5:00 P. M. on Sunday, April 26, 1942.

2. Evacuees must carry with them on departure for the Assembly Center, the following property:
   (a) Bedding and linens (no mattress) for each member of the family;
   (b) Toilet articles for each member of the family;
   (c) Extra clothing for each member of the family;
   (d) Sufficient knives, forks, spoons, plates, bowls and cups for each member of the family;
   (e) Essential personal effects for each member of the family.

   All items carried will be securely packaged, tied and plainly marked with the name of the owner and numbered in accordance with instructions obtained at the Civil Control Station. The size and number of packages is limited to that which can be carried by the individual or family group.

3. No pets of any kind will be permitted.

4. The United States Government through its agencies will provide for the storage at the sole risk of the owner of the more substantial household items, such as iceboxes, washing machines, pianos and other heavy furniture. Cooking utensils and other small items will be accepted for storage if crated, packed and plainly marked with the name and address of the owner. Only one name and address will be used by a given family.

5. Each family, and individual living alone, will be furnished transportation to the Assembly Center or will be authorized to travel by private automobile in a supervised group. All instructions pertaining to the movement will be obtained at the Civil Control Station.

**Go to the Civil Control Station between the hours of 8:00 A. M. and 5:00 P. M.,
Saturday, April 25, 1942, or between the hours of 8:00 A. M. and 5:00 P. M.,
Sunday, April 26, 1942, to receive further instructions.**

SEE CIVILIAN EXCLUSION ORDER NO. 19.

J. L. DeWITT
Lieutenant General, U. S. Army
Commanding

## Making Amends

**M**any years after the war ended and the Japanese were freed from the camps, the U.S. Court of Appeals reversed the relocation wartime order. The next year, Congress apologized and provided $20,000 compensation to every Japanese American who had been relocated.

This victory owed much to the perseverance of Gordon Hirabayashi, a University of Washington student who, in 1942, was convicted of failing to follow the relocation order. It was his appeal of that conviction that finally forced the courts and Congress to turn around one of the worst violations of civil rights in American history.

# The War Ends

**I**n April of 1945, Washington people were stunned to learn that President Roosevelt had died from a stroke. Businesses closed. Theaters emptied. Traffic slowed to a halt. For three days and nights, radio stations aired only news broadcasts and religious music.

Less than a month later, Germany surrendered, ending the war in Europe. People celebrated in the streets. Sons, brothers, and husbands were coming home. The war in the Pacific, however, was still raging. Leaders in the United States had to make a terrible decision. Should they invade Japan, which might cost a million American casualties and even more deaths to the Japanese? Or should they use their new weapon—the atomic bomb?

When the bomb was dropped on Hiroshima, Japan, it completely destroyed the city in one terrible explosion. A few days later, another bomb devastated Nagasaki. It was a terrible tragedy for the Japanese people. The war with Japan was over.

Three months after the peace treaty was signed in Europe, Japan surrendered. Once again, there was celebrating all over America and the Pacific Northwest. The war was over.

## ACTIVITY

### Research and Perform

Choose an event from this chapter and research it in library books, library microfilm copies of newspapers from the time period, encyclopedias, or on the Internet. Then choose one of the following ways to present what you learned:

- Write a short skit and perform it with a group of friends.
- Interview people who lived during the time. Compare experiences of those from different races and genders.
- Copy articles from microfilmed newspapers and organize them in a scrapbook.
- Gather information from and about your relatives who lived during the time period. Are there any letters, photographs or souvenirs from their lives?
- Prepare a program of World War II music for a class presentation.

## CHAPTER 9 REVIEW

1. When was the Great Depression?
2. List at least three ways the Great Depression was hard on Washington residents.
3. "Hoovervilles" were named after which U.S. president, and why?
4. What caused the Dust Bowl in the Great Plains?
5. Why did Dust Bowl migrants come to Washington? What kinds of work did many of them find here?
6. Which president of the United States started the New Deal?
7. Name at least three ways the New Deal helped Washington.
8. What kinds of work did the men in the CCC do? Who paid them?
9. Building dams on the Columbia River was part of the New Deal. List at least three ways building the dams benefited people of the Pacific Northwest.
10. Why was "Roll On, Columbia" written? Who wrote it?
11. What national park in Washington was created as part of the New Deal?
12. What act of Congress again encouraged the formation and power of tribal governments?
13. What happened to cause the United States to enter World War II?
14. Which industries were boosted by the war?
15. Why was the Hanford site chosen for plutonium production? What secret weapon was eventually produced?
16. How did the war affect children?
17. What were two ways the war transformed the social structure of the Seattle region?
18. During the war, what people were forced to move to relocation camps in other states?

## GEOGRAPHY TIE-IN

- Write a paragraph about how geography shaped Washington's wartime experience.
- On a world map, locate all of the countries involved in WWII. Which was the farthest from Washington? Which country was closest?

# Cold War and

The Dalles (Celilo Falls) was a popular fishing place in the 1950s, as it had been for centuries. In 1957 the site was buried by water from the Dalles Dam.

**1946** The Cold War begins.

**1949** Soviets test atomic bomb.

**1950** Northgate Shopping Center opens in Seattle.

**TIMELINE** 1945 — 1949 — 1953

**1945** World War II ends. Baby Boom begins.

**1950** ······· **1953**
Korean War

**1952** Columbia Basin Project sends irrigation water to farms.

# Civil Rights

**956** Interstate
eeways are started
ross America.

**1963** Wing Luke is the first
Asian American elected to
public office in Washington.

John F. Kennedy
is killed in Texas.

**1964** Civil
Rights Act
outlaws
discrimination
in public
places.

**1968** Martin
Luther King
Jr. is killed in
Tennessee.

**1972**
Washington passes
Equal Rights
Amendment to the
state constitution.

**1957**

**1961**

**1965**

**1969**

**1973**

**1957** Russians
launch *Sputnik*,
the first satellite.

**1962** Seattle
World's Fair

**1966** Civil Rights Act
outlaws discrimination
in housing.

**1969** America's
*Apollo 11* astronauts
land on the moon.

**1960s–1973** Vietnam War

## Post-War Washington

When World War II ended, people everywhere breathed a sigh of relief. The news on the radio would no longer contain stories of evil and death, and the days of *rationing* were over. The country celebrated, then eagerly returned to normal life.

Washington residents were grateful that the war was over, but they were worried about what lay ahead. Plants that manufactured chemicals, aluminum, steel, tanks, airplanes, and many other products slowed down. In 1944, shipyards had employed 150,000 people. Boeing Airplane Company had employed nearly 50,000 people the same year. Would thousands of workers lose their jobs now that the war was over?

*Farms changed, too. Many farm families moved to town. Other farmers bought more land so farms got bigger in size.*

### WHAT DO YOU THINK?

**A popular saying at the time was, "When Boeing sneezes, Seattle catches cold." What did that mean? How important are good jobs to a community?**

Life in the 1950s meant life in the suburbs. The suburbs grew so large that many became cities.

## Soldiers Come Home

Most soldiers had joined the war right out of high school, and they needed job training. The federal government passed the G.I. Bill to assist former soldiers as they settled into *civilian* life. Part of the bill provided money for college tuition. Many veterans took the opportunity and were the first in their family to attend college.

### The Sawdust Empire

The G.I. Bill also helped war veterans buy houses. This sparked a building boom across the nation. Families were able to get mortgage loans with no *down payment*. There had been little building during the war because the entire nation's resources had gone to the war effort. Once the war was over, however, the demand for housing created a rush for timber.

The timber industry in the Pacific Northwest boomed for two decades after the war ended. There continued to be thousands of jobs in logging and sawmills. Loggers used large equipment such as bulldozers and logging trucks to haul enough trees to fill the demand.

## Families in the Suburbs

Suddenly, women who had worked in factories during the war were no longer needed. Some of the jobs were gone, and in other cases the jobs were given to returning soldiers. Most people thought of the women's jobs as temporary wartime jobs anyway. Women returned to their families. So many babies were born that there was a "baby boom." Today, the "baby boomers" are grown and have children and grandchildren of their own.

Families with young children wanted to have homes of their own. That meant a move to the **suburbs.** Suburbs are places where many homes are built together outside a city center. Schools, parks, and shopping centers were often built in the suburbs, too. People bought homes instead of renting an apartment in town.

Living in the suburbs meant new ways of shopping. The Northgate Shopping Center opened north of Seattle. It was the first shopping center in the world and was described as a small town because it had over 100 shops, a hospital, and a movie theater all in one place.

Within a few years, suburbs ran together and entire cities such as Redmond, Bellevue, and Lynnwood had been created. By the 1950s, two-thirds of Washington's families lived in the suburbs. The other third still lived on farms or in small rural towns.

# A Cold War and a Space Race

Communist Russia had been an ally of the United States during the war. Afterwards, however, each country feared an attack from the other. Both countries built huge military and defense systems. The Cold War had begun.

Cold War fears included worrying that members of the Communist Party might take over the U.S. government. People suspected of being Communists were fired from jobs as teachers or government workers. They were rarely given a chance to defend themselves.

In 1957, a little over a decade after the end of World War II, Americans were shocked to learn the Soviet Union had launched the world's first satellite. Called *Sputnik,* it made Americans aware that they were no longer leading the way in space. By this time, the United States and the Soviet Union had become bitter rivals.

In America's schools, more science and math courses were required. American students were to be the nation's "secret weapon." Within a few years, the U.S. space program had caught up and *surpassed* the

Soviets. We had satellites gathering photos and information in space. The U.S. even sent astronauts to walk on the moon.

Once again, war—even a cold war where there was no actual fighting—provided jobs. Aircraft factories and shipyards continued to build planes and ships in case of a Soviet attack. Thousands of workers were able to find good jobs working at Boeing's aircraft plants.

## Atomic Weapons

Hanford had been part of the development of the atomic bomb during World War II. During the Cold War, nuclear fuel for atomic weapons was produced at the Hanford site.

Richland was proud to be the location for federal research and called itself the "Atomic City." The high school sports team was called the "Bombers," and a mushroom cloud was the school's emblem.

The Soviets exploded their first atomic bomb in 1949. Immediately the U.S. was terrified that the Soviets might send airplanes to bomb the West Coast. People in Washington State talked about being a good target because of the large Boeing plant and the Hanford nuclear site. Towns held civil defense drills and practiced how to *evacuate* buildings and streets in case of a bomb attack.

Boeing built long-range B-47 bombers and Minuteman missles that could hit a target 6,000 miles away.

*The color red was a symbol of the Communist Party, so anyone suspected of being a Communist was called a Red. People who sympathized with Communists were called "Pink."*

The entire city of Spokane practiced an evacuation drill. It was the first city in the nation to do so. Other cities had plans, too, but most people realized it would be impossible to escape if a bomb hit a city.

As part of the process of producing nuclear material for bombs, and in various experiments, large amounts of **radioactive** material were released into the air and water. A high number of people who lived down-wind of Hanford, called "downwinders," later got cancer. They blamed the nuclear tests.

## LINKING THE PAST TO THE PRESENT

**For many years after the war, chemical and nuclear wastes were poured onto the ground. Radioactive materials got into the air and into the Columbia River, too.**

**Today, the government is very concerned about contamination at the Hanford site. The federal Department of Energy is cleaning up the toxic wastes. Clean-up work provides many jobs as the soil and radioactive waste are removed and stored safely. Radioactive waste from other areas, even foreign countries, is now stored at Hanford.**

## Seattle World's Fair

The Space Needle, now an emblem for downtown Seattle, was built for the World's Fair in 1962. The Space Needle was a symbol of the nation's space program, which was pushing hard to get a man on the moon before the Soviets did.

The World's Fair was a chance to show what the future might bring in science and technology. A huge science exhibit stressed more science education for American students. The monorail was an example of future transportation. It still operates in downtown Seattle.

Seattle's Space Needle is a familiar sight. It represented science, space exploration, and the future at the World's Fair in 1962. *Photo by Chuck Pefley*

# Transportation

Post-war prosperity meant many people had good jobs and could afford automobiles. Families who had moved to the suburbs preferred driving their own cars to work instead of riding city buses. The roads, however, were narrow, and driving was slow. Traveling across town took a long time because drivers had to stop at every corner traffic light.

The U.S. government began building a national network of superhighways called freeways. They made it easier to travel across the country quickly. President Dwight Eisenhower had seen such highways in Germany during the war. He knew they would make it easier to evacuate cities if a Cold War attack ever came.

The Interstate Highway System linked Washington State to the rest of the nation.

Interstate freeways linked cities and suburbs to other states. *Photo by Doug Wilson*

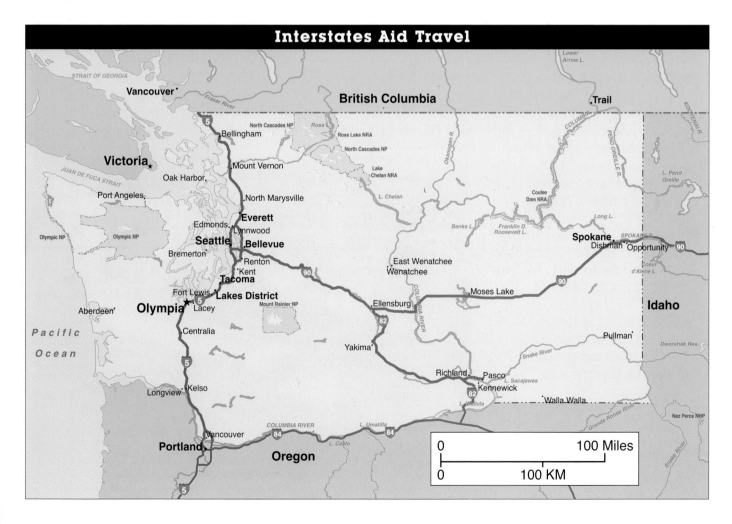

## Interstates Aid Travel

The new freeways let travelers zoom right past towns and cities without getting off the freeway. Interstate 84 along the Columbia River was useful to people driving across Washington's southern border. Interstate 90 connected the eastern part of the state to the Puget Sound region. Interstate 5 ran from Canada to Mexico. Today, all of the interstates near Seattle, Tacoma, and Everett are very congested.

## ACTIVITY

### Miles and Miles of Freeways

Work in teams to figure out how many miles of Interstate highways were built in Washington. Divide the class into three teams, one for each Interstate: I-5, I-90, and I-82.

Each team must look at a Washington State road map and estimate which freeway has the most miles and which has the least within the state's borders. Then the teams should use the map scale to measure the miles of their interstate. When finished, compare and see how close the teams came to their guesses.

## Damming the Rivers

In the depression years before World War II, dams were built to create jobs and provide electricity. After the war, dam building increased, and over a dozen dams were built on the Columbia and Snake Rivers. Dams provided well-paid construction jobs in eastern Washington for over twenty years.

Eventually, the dams controlled the Columbia River. The water became *placid* enough for towboats to move barges between

## Trucking Companies

Kenworth Truck Company was formed in Seattle in the 1920s. In 1933 the first diesel engines were built into trucks, making transportation more economical because diesel fuel was one-third the price of gasoline. Kenworth trucks were sent to the Pacific war zone during World War II. They were used as tow trucks to retrieve damaged tanks, sometimes under Japanese fire. Later, Kenworth trucks helped build the Alaskan oil pipeline.

The trucking industry grew quickly once the Interstate Highway System was in place, making it quicker and easier to transport goods by road than by rail. Today, Kenworth trucks are built in factories around the world, but the main factory is still in Seattle.

Trucks and planes were Washington's contribution to faster transportation. This is a Boeing 247 and a Kenworth gasoline truck in 1937.

the Pacific Ocean and the Snake River. Clarkston became a "seaport" where barges were loaded with logs, wood pulp, and wheat to be exported to foreign countries.

## The Columbia Basin Project

The dams of the Columbia Basin Project created seventy-five reservoirs, produced electricity, and provided irrigation water for farming. Cheap electricity brought new industries to Washington. There were jobs for many workers. Richland, Pasco, and Kennewick grew quickly.

The waters held by the Grand Coulee Dam were used to irrigate *semiarid* land in central Washington, turning a desert wasteland into a lush farming area. Sugar beets, potatoes, apples, cherries, grapes, and other crops could be easily

grown in the sandy soil with irrigation water. Towns like Moses Lake and Othello grew quickly as people moved in to begin farming.

The dams did not come without sacrifice, however. Lake Roosevelt flooded eleven towns. The people who had lived in the towns had to find another place to live. Native Americans lost access to Kettle Falls, an ancient fishing spot. Migrating salmon could no longer return to the upper parts of the Columbia River because Grand Coulee Dam was too high for fish ladders.

Wheat is an important dryland crop in Washington.
*Photo by Chuck Pefley*

## Larger Farms

The Columbia Basin Project was planned to create 20,000 new farms. When it was completed, there were only 6,000 farms. Instead of creating farms for many farm families, the irrigation system created large profits for larger corporate farms. The new approach to farming is called ***agribusiness***.

The project eventually irrigated 550,000 acres of land. Alfalfa, grapes, asparagus, corn, onions, and potatoes were grown. The crops were picked, cleaned, and sorted. Then they were either shipped fresh to markets, canned, or frozen. Processing plants created jobs, but many were seasonal and employed workers only during the harvest.

## Agriculture Research

Chemical fertilizers were developed after World War II and resulted in larger harvests. Nitrogen fertilizer, the most common type used on wheat farms, was made by combining natural gas with air. The inexpensive fertilizer was spread by the ton on huge farms.

Agricultural research at Washington State University in Pullman resulted in plants that grew faster, repelled diseases, and matured at the same time, making harvesting by machine possible.

## Farm-in-a-Day

"**I**rrigation fever" swept the Columbia Basin when reservoir water reached the first farms. Electricity powered the pumps that pushed the water out into canals, ditches, and sprinkler systems.

Towns held festivals to celebrate. The people of Moses Lake held a "Farm-in-a-Day" program. Hundreds of people volunteered. In twenty-four hours, they built an entire farm—outbuildings, corrals, a house with furniture, and even newly-planted crops!

The Farm-in-a-Day was given away free to the "most worthy ***veteran***" of war. Donald Dunn, a veteran of World War II, had farmed in Kansas and been flooded out. He was chosen to receive the eighty-acre farm.

*"The community got together and built this guy a house and a barn and we leveled the land and set the sprinkler systems on it. We did that all in a 24-hour period."*
—Ed Ebel, Moses Lake

Family farms remained in some places like these in Kittitas Valley near Ellensburg. In other places, small farms were bought out by larger farming businesses. *Photo by Chuck Pefley*

*I*magine an onion being called "sweet." Walla Walla onions are famous for their mild flavor.

## ACTIVITY

### Graph the Farm

The Farm-in-a-Day was 80 acres. That was considered enough land to make a living for a married couple in 1952. That was raised to 960 acres in 1982. By the 1990s, there were several farms that each had over 2,000 acres.

Larger farms were more profitable because they brought in enough money to pay for the expensive machinery that did the work of many people. Corporations or landowners with large farms bought out their neighbors and became even larger.

Make a graph with the number of acres in a farm on one side, and the years in even increments on the other. Graph the facts in this activity to see how the size of farms grew.

## Kwik-Lok

Floyd Paxton, of Yakima, realized there was a need for a simple way to close plastic fruit and bread bags. The fruit-growing industry in the Yakima area was growing quickly, and much of the fruit was shipped to stores in plastic bags. At the grocery store, customers picked out their own fruit and put it into plastic bags.

Floyd, who had never completed high school, whittled a sample clip out of plastic. When he showed it to the executives at Pacific Fruit Company, they ordered a million. Other orders followed, and eventually bread bags were sealed with his Kwik-Loks, too. Floyd became wealthy, and now bread stays fresher longer.

# Korea—Another War

In 1950, North Korea invaded South Korea. Communist North Korea used Soviet tanks and planes. The United States and fifteen other nations sent troops to help South Korea defend itself. At first, Americans did not pay much attention to the war. Everyone felt the war would quickly end after four months of sporadic fighting. "Home by Christmas!" was the cry.

Eventually the three-year war ended with a stalemate. Of the 33,000 American men killed, 528 were from Washington. Thousands of soldiers from both countries still guard their common border.

## *Washington* PORTRAIT

## GERALD FOLEY

Gerald Foley had grown up in the Puget Sound area and played baseball whenever he could. He was drafted into the Korean War, and found himself stationed along the Yalu River one cold November. Soldiers were terrified as 120,000 Chinese soldiers swooped down on just 19,000 U.S. and Korean troops. It was the first battle between Chinese and American troops.

"We were just overrun," Foley said. A desperate hand-to-hand battle followed. Foley survived by using a shovel to fight off four enemy soldiers. He swung it like a baseball bat and saved himself.

# The Longest War— Vietnam

U.S. Marines blow up bunkers and tunnels in 1966.

In 1954, the U.S. became involved in a war in a far-off country in Southeast Asia. Few Americans even knew where to find Vietnam on a map then, but for the next twenty years, American troops were involved in events there. In the early 1960s, the war started in earnest. Thousands of soldiers trained at military bases in Washington. Washington's young men were drafted and joined other Americans in Vietnam.

The Vietnam War incited protests across the nation. Many people believed it was wrong to send troops to a nation where we had no reason to be involved. Others thought it was important to help fight Communism everywhere in the world. They knew millions of innocent civilians were being killed in Vietnam.

Protest marches and demonstrations against the war were held all over the United States. In Seattle, 500 people walked from the courthouse to where Westlake Plaza is now. One march in downtown Seattle filled the street with nearly 25,000 people.

Finally, after over ten years of fighting, the war ended. More than 58,000 Americans had been killed and between 2-3 million Vietnamese had died.

## After the War

Several large Washington industries had relied on government war contracts. Many residents depended on those manufacturing jobs to make a living. They built weapons, ships, and planes. After the war finally ended in 1973, war materials were no longer needed. Unemployment soared in the Puget Sound region.

## Asian Immigrants

A wave of immigrants fled the war zone to make their home in Washington State. About 30,000 came from Vietnam, 15,000 from Cambodia, and about 10,000 from Laos. Their lives were changed completely. They had to learn a new language and new ways. Many of their children have now graduated from college and have begun new lives here.

*Joe Martin protested the Vietnam War while he was a college student. "There was never any rational explanation for the war," he told a newspaper reporter. Martin now works as a social worker in Seattle, helping the homeless and poor.*

A Hmong refugee works in a garden in her new country. *Photo by Jan Thompson*

*Hanh Nguyen was a child in South Vietnam. She remembers her family trying fifteen times to escape by boat after the war ended. Her father was imprisoned each time. The government allowed them to leave in 1991. Today, she is a student at the University of Washington. "We do lose our identity—our language, our culture, ourselves—so we're trying to maintain that," she says.*

## Civil Rights

During the 1960s, racial problems erupted across the nation. African Americans challenged **segregation** by race in public places. Reverend Martin Luther King Jr., from Atlanta, Georgia, led peaceful protest marches, sit-ins, and boycotts. King and his wife Coretta visited Seattle to help efforts in Washington State.

In Washington, like in most other states, minorities were not allowed to sit with whites in movie theaters, were not welcome in most restaurants or hotels, and could not use public swimming pools.

Blacks could buy houses only in certain sections of cities, including in Seattle and Spokane. At the Bremerton Navy Base as well as the Hanford Nuclear Reservation, blacks and whites worked together but lived in separate areas.

A Spokane Valley real estate code of ethics said:

*A realtor should never introduce into a neighborhood any race . . . whose presence will [lower] property values in that neighborhood.*

Rules for an Ephrata subdivision said:

*No persons other than those of the Caucasian race shall ever occupy any building in this subdivision, except* **domestic servants** *. . . employed and living in the building occupied by said owner.*

### Civil Rights Murders

The civil rights turmoil erupted in a wave of assassinations of political leaders. President John Kennedy was shot in Dallas, Texas. Later his brother, Senator Robert Kennedy, a civil rights advocate and candidate for president, was assassinated. Malcolm X, an important African American leader who used violence to gain attention to inequality, was murdered. Reverend King was murdered in Memphis, Tennessee. Edwin Pratt, the director of the Seattle Urban League (a civil rights group) was shot when he opened his front door.

## A Multi-Cultural Washington

Over the next decades minority citizens in Washington became more involved in government. Many were elected to public office. Others were appointed to government leadership positions. Today, Washington is a very multi-cultural state. Ethnic groups and their heritage make the state a dynamic place to live.

### African Americans

During World War II many African Americans moved to the Puget Sound area to work in defense manufacturing plants. Many others were stationed at army or navy bases. When the war ended, many stayed on, becoming the largest racial minority in the state for many years.

Lucille Bankhead talked about growing up in Tacoma. "We'd have friends sleep over at our house, or we'd go to theirs. It didn't matter if you were black or white. We all got along. But we could not go to the movies and sit with our friends because we were colored. That's the way we lived."

*The U.S. Congress passed the Civil Rights Act of 1964 that prohibited any kind of discrimination in public places.*

*In 1965, the act eliminated the literacy test for voters.*

*In 1969, a new Civil Rights Act prohibited discrimination in the sale or rental of property.*

## Spokane's African American Attorney

Carl Maxey was the first black attorney in Spokane. He worked hard to end segregation in the city. Restaurants, hotels, and parks were segregated. The swimming pools were off-limits to blacks. Carl Maxey began filing lawsuits for black customers who were denied service in restaurants and stores. He challenged discrimination in court in the 1950s and 1960s.

## Asian Americans

Before World War II, many Japanese American families farmed in rural areas outside Seattle, Tacoma, and other cities. They grew fruits and vegetables and sold them to city dwellers.

After the war, the Japanese left the relocation camps and returned to their homes. Many found difficult conditions. They had been gone three years and much had changed. Often their property had been vandalized and strangers were living in their homes.

Some Asian Americans later entered politics. Wing Luke was elected to Seattle's City Council in 1963. The son of an immigrant laundryman, Luke was the first Chinese American elected to any office in the state. Luke died in a plane crash a few years later.

Over thirty years later, in 1996, Gary Locke, another man of Chinese heritage, was elected governor. Locke was the first Chinese American governor in the mainland United States. You will read more about him in another chapter.

Large numbers of immigrants from Southeast Asia fled to the United States during and after the Vietnam War. In 1960, two-thirds of Washington's Asian Americans had been born here. By 1980, two-thirds had been born in Asia. They had come as refugees of war.

Asian Americans grew most of Seattle's fresh fruits and vegetables before World War II. Here a woman shows off fresh strawberries at Seattle's Pike Place Market.

The Wing Luke Asian Museum in Seattle honors the first Asian American elected to public office in the Pacific Northwest. The museum displays Asian culture and art.

Evening classes in public schools gave classes in English to Hispanic immigrants.

## Hispanic Americans

Today the Hispanic population is the largest minority group in the state. What brought so many Hispanic immigrants? During World War II, thousands of Mexican Americans came to Washington to harvest crops. Many stayed and settled in the central part of the state.

By the 1970s, migrants were coming each year to harvest crops. Many of them settled here permanently. In Othello and other farming towns, Mexican Americans soon made up more than half of the population.

By the 1990s, Hispanic Americans were no longer working just on the farms. Many trained to become lawyers, physicians, and teachers. Others owned their own businesses.

Hispanic citizens worked for civil rights, too. Before the 1970s, Washington citizens had to prove they could read English before they were allowed to vote. A civil rights group, the Mexican American Federation, challenged voting restrictions in court and won. They also got assistance for voter registration. The effort resulted in more Hispanic voters.

# Women's Rights

In the 1970s, another group worked for equal rights. They were not a minority group; women made up over half the population.

In most jobs, women were paid less than men. There was a great separation of men's and women's jobs—men were doctors, and women were nurses. Men were business owners and women were secretaries. School principals were nearly always men. School sports teams were open only to boys. Women had a hard time getting loans or credit cards in their own names.

The national movement for women's rights was called *feminism,* or women's liberation. The women's goals were to gain equal legal status and equal opportunities.

## The Equal Rights Amendment

Across the nation, people worked to add an amendment to the U.S. Constitution that would guarantee that neither men nor women would be denied rights. The amendment was called the Equal Rights Amendment, or the ERA. It was eventually defeated, and did not go into effect.

In Washington State, however, the state legislature passed an Equal Rights Amendment to the state constitution. It then went to the voters and passed by a narrow margin.

Why was the ERA needed in Washington? Before 1972, some state jobs were for men only, and retirement ages for state jobs were different for men and women. Women had to retire earlier and received less retirement pay. After the amendment was added, over 100 Washington laws were changed, forcing equal treatment for men and women.

# Health Care

Washington was a pioneer in health care. The first HMO (health maintenance organization) in the nation was formed at the end of World War II in Seattle. Union members and farmers joined together to hire their own doctors. Four hundred families formed Group Health Cooperative of Puget Sound, and bought a clinic and hospital. Known today as Group Health, the idea has been widely copied across the nation. Members pay a monthly fee for health services from doctors who work in a company clinic.

The state has a medical school at the University of Washington in Seattle, where physicians are trained and researchers work on new treatments. The state's school for dentists is also at the University of Washington. Washington's animals are taken care of, too—the state has a school for veterinarians at Washington State University in Pullman.

## CHAPTER 10 REVIEW

1. What was a large concern of workers after the end of World War II?
2. What education benefit did veterans get from the G.I. Bill?
3. How did the G.I. Bill help create a "sawdust empire" in Washington?
4. What is a suburb?
5. How did the Cold War help Washington workers?
6. What is the largest problem at the Hanford site today?
7. What was the main attraction at the Seattle World's Fair in 1962?
8. How did the U.S. Congress help transportation between states?
9. How were Kenworth diesel trucks used?
10. What were two advantages and two disadvantages of building dams?
11. How did chemical fertilizers help farmers?
12. Why did the people of Moses Lake build a "Farm-in-a-Day" and give it away free?
13. What was the longest war ever fought by Americans?
14. What countries did many immigrants leave after the Vietnam War?
15. Describe two problems the Civil Rights Act of 1964 tried to solve.
16. List the three main ethnic groups who lived in Washington after World War II.
17. What is the largest ethnic group in Washington today?
18. What was the ERA? Which group did the ERA try to help?

## GEOGRAPHY TIE-IN

1. Make a list of all the natural resources used by businesses in this chapter. Research how the resources are used in today's economy.
2. Choose one of the businesses in this chapter and research the company to see what it is producing today and where in the world the products are used.

# Taking
## in

Spaceship Earth, as one man said, is entirely self-sufficient. All the natural resources are all there will ever be.
*Photo by NASA*

**TIMELINE**

**1970**
Environmental Protection Agency is established.

**1973**
Endangered Species Act

**1974**
*U.S. v. Washington* (Boldt Decision)

Spokane hosts Expo 74.

**1975**
Indian Self-Determination and Education Act

1970    1973    1976

# Our Place the World

# 11

**1980** Electric Power Planning and Conservation Act

**1985** Heavy metals pollution is identified in Lake Roosevelt.

**2000** Yakama tribe approves alcohol ban on reservation.

1980 — 1985 — 1990 — 1995 — 2000

**1981** Seattle chooses "Emerald City" as a new nickname.

**1988–1989** Canadian-American Free Trade Agreement

**1996** Flood causes severe heavy metals pollution in Idaho.

**1999** Battle in Seattle

**2001** Energy crisis strikes California and the Pacific Northwest.

## Environmental Crisis

In the 1800s, pioneers struggled across the Oregon Trail. The journey was exhausting as the travelers crossed immense prairies, climbed snow-capped mountain passes, and forded raging rivers. The travelers thought of nature as a ***formidable adversary***.

One century later, people were discovering that nature was not an enemy to be defeated, but a partner that was the source of all life. In the 1960s, astronauts said from outer space, "Earth looks isolated and very ***vulnerable.*** Life is sustained only by a thin protective atmosphere."

According to writer Arthur Clarke, "Spaceship Earth" travels through the heavens with an unknown destination. One thing, however, is clear. All the supplies available for the voyage are onboard. There will be no opportunity to replenish them. Starting in the 1960s and 1970s, people in Washington and elsewhere became aware of the damage that had been done to the environment.

It is clear that people in Washington and the rest of the world have to face the complex issues of how to both use and save natural resources. They will sometimes have to compromise what they want now for what is best for the future. They will have to cooperate so the earth's resources can be shared by all, both now and into the next century, and the next.

## Seattle's Urban Problems

In 1981, Seattle held a nickname contest to replace "Queen City." Promoters hoped to find a name that would lure tourists to the state's largest city. The winner was "Emerald City." It seemed perfect for a city where abundant rain helps green plants grow. The name also evoked images of that tantalizing city in *The Wizard of Oz*.

In 1999, however, satellite photos showed that Seattle's natural tree cover had declined 50 percent in twenty years. When viewed from space, Seattle looked more black than green. Asphalt and concrete had taken over.

Seattle's environmental record since the 1970s is mixed. Lake Washington, which had become polluted with raw human sewage,

*A study showed that only 7 percent of rainy Seattle was covered with plants, compared to 10 percent in Phoenix, the desert capital city of Arizona.*

Traffic congestion in Seattle continues to frustrate drivers.
*Photo by Bill Youngs*

was cleaned up. The largest problem, however, is still to be solved. The city continues to suffocate from traffic congestion.

Voters rejected funding for a **mass transit** commuter rail system in the 1970s. There is little room to build more freeways because Seattle is squeezed between Puget Sound and Lake Washington. A commuter ferry system offers some hope to commuters living north or south of the city or on the peninsula. For other drivers, however, there are few options except the current rush hour traffic jam.

Visitors still flock to visit the city's many attractions, but they feel the frustration of getting from place to place on crowded freeways. Traffic woes are the major topic of conversation and a main reason some people move out of town.

# Spokane and Expo 74

Spokane—the smallest city to ever host a world's fair—hosted Expo 74. The fair called attention to a wide range of environmental issues.

The entire community worked together to make Expo a success. Before construction, the site of the fair was an ugly complex of warehouses and railroad tracks along the Spokane River in the heart of the city. The railroad companies were persuaded to donate most of the land. When the fair had run its six-month course, the site was converted to a magnificent downtown park.

Expo's theme, "Progress Without Pollution," was appropriate for Spokane. It encouraged the city to stop using the Spokane River as an open sewer, which it had been doing for years. A modern sewage treatment plant was constructed in time for Expo.

A Spokane resident remembers the river in the 1940s and 1950s:

*I lived only a half mile from the river and my friends and I played and fished along its banks. We caught large suckers from the mouths of sewer discharge pipes. Sometimes we fished an area where a large spring entered and we would catch trout, though they would stink up the kitchen if you tried to cook them.*

Expo 74 drew 5 million visitors. It represented a turning point in Spokane's history. Ugly warehouses and railroad tracks were converted into a beautiful fair site and a magnificent downtown park.

A sign warns of heavy metals pollution on the Couer d'Alene River. What does it say about pregnant women? About children making mud pies? Where can children play safely?

Treated waste water is returned to the Spokane River from the city's efficient sewage treatment plant.

*Photo by Mike Green*

# Industrial Pollution

The **heavy metals** such as lead, zinc, cadmium, and arsenic from mining operations in Idaho's Coeur d'Alene region **leached** into **groundwater.** Then the dissolved metals made their way into Idaho rivers and lakes. They eventually flowed into the Spokane River.

The leaching of mine wastes through groundwater has increased by massive **clear-cuts** in the mountains. The clear-cuts are huge land areas, once covered by forests, that were left with no vegetation to slow water runoff.

In the 1970s, lead poisoning from a smelter in Idaho produced the highest lead levels in human blood ever recorded. Lead poisoning in children produces serious health problems, including mental retardation.

Large amounts of toxic metals leached from Idaho mine **tailings** and abandoned mines during a severe winter flooding in 1996. Efforts are underway to clean up the mining mess, but the task is enormous. Every day the South Fork of the Coeur d'Alene River carries a ton of dissolved heavy metals downstream. The Coeur d'Alene Indians, hoping to force a cleanup of the waterways, have sued eight mining companies, the Union Pacific Railroad, and the State of Idaho for polluting the water.

## Pollution at Grand Coulee

At first, no one noticed the growing pollution in Lake Roosevelt, the reservoir behind Grand Coulee Dam. Then a U.S. Fish and Wildlife study showed that fish collected at Grand Coulee had cadmium and lead levels among the highest in the nation.

The sources of the contamination were a British Columbia smelter and a paper mill. Both these companies dumped all their untreated waste directly into the Columbia River. The resulting bad publicity and political pressure led to dramatic improvements by the mid-1990s.

### LINKING THE PAST TO THE PRESENT

**In 2001, the Washington Department of Health warned that the Spokane River was the most PCB-polluted stream in the state. PCBs are chemicals from industrial sites such as the Kaiser Aluminum Plant. PCBs cause cancer. Fish from the river are a health threat to everyone who eats them, especially pregnant women.**

Hanford nuclear waste storage tanks are under construction. Double-wall steel storage tanks have been built to replace some of the leaking ones. Eventually, some of the wastes will be pumped out and contained in safe glass logs at a plant that has yet to be built. To get a sense of size, note the workers in the photo. *Photo courtesy of Columbia River Exhibition*

# Hanford's Nuclear Wastes

As bad as the upstream pollution is, there is nothing that compares with the problems found downstream on the Hanford Nuclear Reservation. Decades of producing plutonium for nuclear weapons left Hanford one of the most contaminated places on the face of the earth.

In the mid-1980s, a reporter with the *Spokesman-Review* began publishing articles about Hanford's radioactive releases into the atmosphere. The stories showed that the testing had released high levels of cancer-causing elements into the atmosphere in the 1940s and 1950s. The government had gone to great lengths to hide this from the public.

Finally, in 1989, state and federal agencies agreed to a plan for cleaning up stored radioactive waste. It would be the largest and most expensive public works project in American history, costing more than $200 billion over seventy years.

How could the mess be cleaned up? The first problem was to find out what had been dumped and where. More than 1,400 sites were identified. Over 440 billion gallons of radioactive and chemical waste had been poured into the soil. Some of the wastes had reached groundwater supplies and made their way toward the Columbia River. Strontium 90, tritium, and uranium—all known cancer-causing elements—were still seeping into the river in 2001.

Hanford

## Drought, Electricity, and Nuclear Power

In March, 2001, Governor Gary Locke declared a state-wide drought emergency. The lack of winter rain and snowfall, he warned, would produce the lowest summer stream flows in a century. What would this mean for the state?

• Hydroelectric power production would be sharply reduced if less water flowed through dams.
• Residents faced power blackouts.
• The cost of electricity would jump dramatically.
• The use of water would have to be curtailed.
• Salmon and steelhead runs would suffer.
• Western farm crops would suffer.

A shortage of electricity led to renewed interest in finishing one of the nuclear plants started in the 1970s and halted in the 1980s.

# Timber—a Dwindling Resource

Four large Pacific Northwest companies—Weyerhauser, Potlatch, Boise Cascade, and Plum Creek Timber—have rapidly harvested trees across Montana, Idaho, and Washington. Much of the logging was done on massive one-mile-square clear-cuts. Many of the raw logs were sold and exported to Japan. Local lumber mills were closing because of a shortage of logs to turn into lumber.

U.S. Interior Secretary Bruce Babbitt noted in 1993:

> *We have a dwindling supply of logs for mills in the Northwest, and at the same time you can go out to Port Angeles and see logs stacked to the sky, as far as the eye can see, destined for mills and jobs in Japan.*

Timber companies had been planting new forests for years, but the trees would not be ready for harvest for twenty-five years. Afraid of running out of trees on their own lands, timber companies started cutting logs in the federally-owned national forests. Environmental groups responded with anger.

Labeled "tree huggers," environmentalists tried to preserve the dwindling supply of old-growth forests, eliminate clear-cutting, and stop all unnecessary road building on public lands. Tempers flared. Some environmentalists fought by spiking trees. They hammered long metal spikes into trees so saws would be ruined when loggers tried to cut down trees.

The struggle over old-growth forests was a lesson in **ecology**. These forests were more than just stands of trees; they were complex **ecosystems**. They were filtering sponges for clean water and producers of fresh oxygen. No tree farm could match the importance to the environment of a mossy old-growth forest. When it was gone, like an extinct species, it was gone forever.

Logs await export from Longview to Japan and other places in 1991.
*Photo by Elizabeth Feryl*

## Fighting Back

The Inland Empire Public Lands Council is one of the most important environmental-action groups founded in response to the timber crises. The council publishes a monthly newsletter, *Transitions,* that features political cartoons and articles on environmental issues.

In this 1992 photo, massive clear-cutting of forests leaves bare land in the shadow of Mt. Rainier. *Photo by Trygve Steen*

## The Spotted Owl

A strange ally of environmentalists was the northern spotted owl. In 1990, the U.S. Fish and Wildlife Service ruled that the owl was a threatened species. Environmentalists tried to halt logging in forests where the owls lived. Annual timber harvests on the Olympic Peninsula dropped 85 percent.

As a result of protected spotted owl **habitats**, over cutting, log exports, and imports of lumber from Canada, 132 sawmills and plywood mills closed in just three years in the early 1990s. Logging was not just an industry in many logging communities—it was the only industry. Closing the mills threw thousands of workers out of work.

Bumper stickers on loggers' pickups said, "If It's Hootin, I'm Shootin" and "I like spotted owls—fried!"

Habitats for owls–or logs and jobs for people? That was a hot question in the Pacific Northwest.

John Osborn, a Spokane physician and environmental activist, founded the Lands Council in the late 1980s. An army of volunteers track timber company actions across the Pacific Northwest.
*Photo by Paul Chesley*

## Going Fishing

Biologists believe the Columbia River system once supported 16 million salmon and steelhead a year. Today, fewer than 1 million fish return from the ocean to spawn each year. About 90 percent of the fish begin life in hatcheries.

Biologists consider hatcheries to be partly to blame for the decline of wild fish. Why?

Hatchery fish cannot find their way to natural spawning grounds. Hatcheries can also introduce diseases into fish stocks. Without fish hatcheries, however, there would be a terrible shortage of fish in our rivers and lakes.

Spring chinook salmon are counted as they pass a viewing booth at McNary Dam, 2001. *Photo by Mike Green*

McNary Dam, like others on the lower Columbia and Snake Rivers, have fish ladders to help fish get back to their spawning grounds. *Photos by Mike Green*

Locks at McNary Dam aid ships in moving up and down the sharp elevations of the rivers. If dams were breached, there would not always be enough water behind the dam to fill the locks and ships might not be able to pass.

## Salmon or Electricity?

The Pacific Northwest salmon crisis is even more complex than timber management. Fish runs have declined dramatically because fish habitats have been severely damaged by pollution, careless logging and grazing, and dams.

In 1980, Congress passed the Northwest Power Act. It required that:

> *Fish and wildlife of the Columbia River Basin . . . be treated on a par with power needs and other purposes for which the . . . dams of the region were built.*

This means that there must be a balance between needs of fish and human needs for fish, water travel, and hydropower. What can be done to maintain a balance?

Fish ladders have been built on the sides of dams. They aid fish in going upstream to spawn. Water is spilled over the ladders to help salmon and steelhead make their way downstream. Some people, however, want to remove the dams altogether. Because dams slow down the natural water flow, they are responsible for higher water temperatures and higher nitrogen levels that kill fish. Dam turbines used to produce electricity kill thousands of fish swimming to the ocean.

Other people suggest that a good compromise is **breaching** of the four dams on the lower Snake River. Breaching would remove the earth-filled "wings" of the dams so water could flow past the center of the dam and fish migration could partly return to a natural state. Breaching would leave the expensive and important locks, spillways, and power plants intact. Later, the wings could be replaced.

How do dams affect commerce? Before dams were built, rivers were too shallow and fast for barge traffic. Dams, however, hold river water in long reservoirs. The amount of water leaving the dams is controlled. This puts people, instead of nature, in charge of river flow. Locks raise and lower ships as river elevation changes.

Today, barges going up and down the rivers are very important. They carry wheat and other agricultural products from eastern farms to western shipping ports.

Movie stars such as Marlon Brando (second in from the left) joined "fish-ins" in support of the Puget Sound tribes. At a fish-in, named after civil rights protest sit-ins, Native Americans and supporters fished illegally all day long. The fish-ins stopped when the Boldt Decision gave fishing rights back to Native Americans.

## LINKING THE PAST TO THE PRESENT

**During the electric power crisis of 2000–2001, power shortages in California and throughout the West sent electricity rates soaring. With power blackouts a reality, fewer people supported dam breaching because it would reduce the amount of electricity dams could produce.**

## Native American Fishing Rights

One of the most important court decisions in Washington's history was handed down in Tacoma by federal judge George Boldt in 1974. *U.S. vs. Washington,* or the Boldt Decision, has had an enormous impact on Native American rights, salmon management, and state politics. Citing the treaties signed in the mid-1800s, Judge Boldt ruled that "The Indians of Puget Sound are entitled to 50 percent of all salmon and steelhead that pass through the Indians' 'usual and accustomed' fishing sites."

Boldt's ruling restored off-reservation fishing sites to Native Americans. It gave them the right to harvest steelhead, as well as salmon, for food.

Before the Boldt Decision, Indians had been forced from their fishing sites off the reservations. This preserved the *lucrative* commercial fishing places for non-Indians. The state also had declared steelhead to be game fish (not food fish). This saved steelhead for sports fishermen.

Non-Indian fishermen were outraged by the decision. Bumper stickers appeared with "CAN JUDGE BOLDT – NOT SALMON!"

All the parties involved now work to restore larger fish populations. Nearly a third of the scientists working on salmon issues are Native Americans. Even the smallest tribes have their own scientists and lawyers, and many of them are Native Americans. It is common for half of a tribe's employees to work in natural resources.

## WHAT DO YOU THINK?

• **What are the arguments for and against honoring Indian treaties signed in the 1800s?**
• **What are the moral and legal issues involved?**

## The Toughest Indian

The following words were written and published by Sherman Alexie, a Spokane Indian:

*The Indians [I picked up hitchhiking] wore hope like a bright shirt. My father never taught me about hope. Instead, he continually told me that our salmon—our hope—would never come back.*

*All of us, Indian and white, are haunted by salmon. When I was a boy, I leaned over the edge of one dam or another—perhaps Little Falls or the great gray dragon known as the Grand Coulee—and watched the ghosts of the salmon rise from the water to the sky and become constellations.*

—from *The Toughest Indian in the World*, Atlantic Monthly Press, 2000

What mental image do you get from Alexie's writing? Can you identify with the feelings of hope and longing?

## The New Indian

The Makah people hunted whales until the 1920s, when commercial whaling **decimated** the whale population. Pacific gray whales were added to the endangered species list. They were removed from the list in 1994. Today, the gray whale population has recovered to the point that its present population—estimated at 27,000—is about as many as the ocean ecosystem can support.

Cape Flattery and Neah Bay

The following event happened in May 2000. It shows the high emotion of fishing rights issues.

*The Makah whale hunters paddled furiously, quickly closing the gap that separated them from the gray whale swimming slowly just beneath the surface. In the bow of the hand-crafted cedar canoe, the harpooner raised his lance for the strike. Standing next to the harpooner was a Makah man armed with a powerful .50 caliber rifle. His intention was to kill the whale after it was caught.*

*Circling the Indian canoe, a young activist from Greenpeace, an environmental protection group, tried to position her jet ski to interrupt the whalers. At the last minute, the whale dove out of sight. A U.S. Coast Guard boat, trying to keep the protesters away from the hunt, accidentally crashed into the jet ski and knocked its rider into the sea. Hovering above, a helicopter camera sent live footage of this bizarre scene to television stations.*

Two Makah Indian whalers stand triumphantly atop the carcass of a dead gray whale moments after helping tow it close to shore at Neah Bay, 1999. Makah treaty rights to hunt whales were negotiated over a century ago. *Photo courtesy AP/Wide World Photos*

## Rights and Sovereignty

The issue of Indian **sovereignty**—freedom from outside control—is particularly important in Washington, where there are thirty tribes. In Oregon, by comparison, there are only nine tribes.

Congress gave additional powers to Indian tribes when it passed the Indian Self-Determination and Education Assistance Act. In 2000, the Yakama Reservation adopted a ban on alcohol that threatened to shut down taverns and liquor stores inside the reservation.

The Yakamas consider alcohol abuse a serious problem for the tribe. The 80 percent rate of alcohol-related traffic deaths on the reservation is twice the statewide average. Infants born with fetal-alcohol syndrome—a disease that affects the mental and physical development of babies—is five times the national average.

Indian casinos advertise widely via television, newspapers, and billboards. They are jammed with customers seven days a week.
*Photos by Mike Green*

### WHAT DO YOU THINK?

**Some non-Indian residents are fighting the alcohol ban on the Yakama Reservation. More than 20,000 of the 25,000 people living on the reservation do not belong to the tribe. They want to be able to drink alcohol there. Taverns and restaurants want to sell alcohol to customers. What do you think about this use of tribal sovereignty?**

## The New Buffalo

Since Indian sovereignty means tribes on a reservation can make many of their own laws, some tribes run gambling casinos. This is against the law in other parts of the state.

The "new buffalo" is the term used for tribal gambling operations. Long ago, buffalo supplied the needs of Native Americans. Today, casinos are helping modern Native Americans by creating thousands of jobs.

Casinos, however, have provoked sharp criticism. Non-Indians point out that they do not have the same right to open casinos. Some Native Americans worry about the influence gambling will have on tribal youth.

So far, however, tribes believe the results of casinos are mostly good. Both the Spokane and Coeur d'Alene tribes have reduced unemployment and funded social programs. The Tulalips have used casino profits to build retirement homes for their elders. The small Kalispel tribe has opened a casino just west of Spokane. The Kalispels have suffered generations of extreme poverty and unemployment. Most tribal members believe the "new buffalo" has arrived.

Yakama Indian Reservation

# The Battle in Seattle

When the World Trade Organization (WTO) decided to meet in Seattle in 1999, city officials were pleased. The WTO is an international body that rules on trade disputes. This important meeting would generate revenue for businesses and publicity for Seattle. Seattle boasted of its export industries and its Pacific Rim connections.

Seattle also had a history of labor problems and environmental unrest. Activists from the United States and around the world planned to bring their concerns to Seattle. Local protesters joined them. The result was a huge demonstration. The angry words and the tactics of the protesters seemed a throwback to the days of the Seattle General Strike and the Wobbly Free Speech fights, and in some ways it was.

The protesters considered the WTO to be an organization of capitalist greed. Protesters said that the 135 member nations of the WTO are really promoting a corporate version of world trade that overlooks environmental concerns, labor issues, and human rights. And, they said, its secret meetings undermine democratic principles. They said rich nations are getting wealthier at the expense of poor nations.

About 40,000 protesters marched through the downtown region, completely disrupting the opening session of the meeting. Seattle police, aided by the National Guard, finally cleared the area. They used armored cars, officers on horses, tear gas, pepper spray, and rubber bullets. There were over 600 arrests and several million dollars in property damage and lost business.

Seattle mayor Paul Schell had been a civil rights and anti-war protester in the 1960s and 1970s. "I remember the sixties. I remember the protest marches," he said. "It hurts me deeply to be the mayor that called out the National Guard, but I had to protect my citizens."

The "Battle in Seattle" was front-page news around the world. For better or worse, Seattle would serve as a symbol of the promise and the peril of global trade for years to come.

A protester stands among flaming trash bins during protests in downtown Seattle. Demonstrators blocked streets and forced a delay in the opening ceremonies of the largest trade event ever staged in the United States.
*Photo by Peter Dejong, AP/World Wide Photos*

# Who Are We?

People, as well as goods, move around the globe. There is a wide diversity of people in the cities and on the farms today. Immigration, especially from Latin America and Asia, continues to grow.

Hispanics are still the state's largest minority, up 75 percent in ten years. Asian and Pacific Islanders were up 60 percent since the last census. The number of Native Americans increased 20 percent.

It is important to remember that cultural diversity has many faces, and that people cannot be grouped by a census report alone. In today's world, many people have a mixed racial heritage.

Here are some statements from Washington's minorities:

"When I was younger, it was annoying when people would just assume I was Mexican," said Efrain Olivares. "I am from Venezuela. Young people are very concerned with such things, but I don't mind so much anymore. I have a lot of Mexican friends, so I just let it go. My wife is from Guatemala. Our neighbors are from Puerto Rico. On the census, we are all Hispanic."

Moon Ji said, "People make similar assumptions about Asians, the majority of which are Chinese. But there are Japanese, Vietnamese, Koreans, Filipinos, Asian Indians, and others. I wish people would be more culturally sensitive. We are not all alike. We like to explain our culture to people, if they would ask."

It's important to remember people all over the world are more alike than they are different. Everyone needs friendship, education, and work, along with food and shelter.

## CHAPTER 11 REVIEW

1. What did Arthur Clark mean by the term "Spaceship Earth"?
2. What makes Seattle an example of environmental problems?
3. What was the main focus of Expo 74 in Spokane?
4. Where does pollution from heavy metals in the Spokane River come from?
5. What are the pollution problems on the Hanford Nuclear Reservation, and what is being done about them?
6. What are people for and against when it comes to protecting old-growth forests?
7. What are people trying to do to increase the supply of salmon? Why are some people against these methods?
8. Which Indian group is continuing to hunt whales, despite opposition from environmental groups?
9. What was the Boldt Decision, and why was it so controversial?
10. How has the concept of Indian sovereignty been strengthened since the 1970s?
11. Why has the "new buffalo" (Indian gambling casinos) been important to people on Indian reservations?
12. What was the Battle in Seattle?
13. According to the United States Census in 2000, which groups make up Washington's ethnic population? Which ethnic group is the largest?
14. Which group is the state's largest ethnic minority?

| Group | Percent |
|---|---|
| White | 82.0 |
| Hispanic | 7.5 |
| Asian | 5.5 |
| African American | 3.0 |
| American Indian | 1.5 |
| Other | 0.5 |
| Reporting two or more races: | 3.6 |

3   1.5   .5
5.5
7.5
82

Total population: 5,894,000
Source: 2000 U.S. Census Report

## ▶▶ WORDS TO UNDERSTAND

capital
capitalism
commodity
compound interest
cooperative
corporation
credit card
debit card
economics
entrepreneur
exports
free enterprise
goods
inflation
median
minimum wage
monopoly
partnership
philanthropy
proprietorship
retail
salary
services
shortage
supply and demand
surplus
wage

Aplets and Cotlets are candy invented and made in Washington. Candy is one of the products that provides jobs for the people of our state.
*Photo by Liberty Orchards*

# Making a Living in Washington

# Economic Systems

**E**conomics is the analysis of the production, distribution, and consumption of goods and services. In other words, it is making, selling, and buying.

Economics affects all of us. In a strong economy, people have jobs, earn money, save for the future, pay for a college education, and can buy things they need. In a poor economy, many people are out of work or earn such low wages that they cannot afford the basic things that make life enjoyable.

In the United States we have a **free enterprise**, or **capitalistic**, system. Anyone is free to start a business and make or sell goods. The owner can keep the business for years or sell it. The owner chooses whom to hire as employees and decides how much to pay them. All businesses have to follow government regulations and almost all businesses pay taxes, but the government does not own or run private businesses.

*D*o the adults in your family work to provide goods, services, or both?

*Capital is the tools, machines, and other products used to make new products that are sold. Capital is also money used to run a business. Different economic systems use capital in different ways.*

**Free Enterprise (Capitalism):** Private ownership and control of capital and business. Some government regulation and rules.

**Socialism:** Various forms of ownership and control by the government.

**Fascism:** All capital is privately owned, but controlled by the government.

**Communism:** All capital and means of production are owned and controlled by government.

# Goods and Services

**E**veryone needs basic things to survive—food, clothing, and shelter. Other things—such as certain brands of clothes, books, computers, sports equipment, televisions, CD players, musical instruments, and automobiles— are not necessities, but are probably important to your lifestyle. Whether they are "needs" or "wants," all these items are **goods** that are sold.

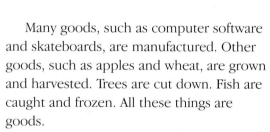

Many goods, such as computer software and skateboards, are manufactured. Other goods, such as apples and wheat, are grown and harvested. Trees are cut down. Fish are caught and frozen. All these things are goods.

We also need **services** from people who have skill and training. We need the services of nurses and doctors when we get hurt or sick. Teachers educate students, pilots fly business people on business trips, plumbers install pipes in homes, and computer programmers develop software. People pay other people for these services.

# The World of Business

A business is formed to make money. In order to make money, almost all businesses sell either goods or services, or both. There are three ways to form a business:

• A **proprietorship** has only one owner. It is owned by the person who does the work of either making products, like a cabinetmaker, or providing a service, like a dentist.

• A **partnership** is when two or more people create a business together. They share in the profits and losses. One partner can sell his or her share to

someone else. All partners are responsible for running the business and helping it succeed or fail.

• A **corporation** is when many people invest money to start a business. They hire a board of directors to manage the corporation's affairs. Corporations are a good way to organize a business when it needs large amounts of money to get started.

## Supply and Demand

When people have money to spend, the amount of goods and services available affects how much those things cost. We call this **supply and demand**.

## Supply and Demand on the Farm

The laws of supply and demand shape agriculture. When the market is good for a product, more people begin to grow it. As more people grow the same item, the price for it often drops because of the increased supply.

In the 1950s, for example, there were so many apples that prices fell. Why was there such an increase in the apple harvest? Many people planted orchards after World War II because new chemicals such as DDT had been developed to wipe out insects, which resulted in more fruit. The market had also changed—dried apples were not being exported to soldiers around the world.

Washington Boxed Apples
Produce of U.S.A.

Shipped by
J. D. HAMILTON FRUIT CO.
WENATCHEE, WASH.

CONTENTS 1 VOLUME BU.

Consumers bought a lot of the cheap apples, but there were still too many. Farmers began dumping them by the truckloads at the Chelan town dump. A story about the apple market in *Life Magazine* showed 5,000 railway cars dumping fruit into the Columbia River.

Then, in 1960, desperate apple growers formed a **cooperative** and purchased an apple juice factory. Tree Top, the new company, pioneered frozen fruit juice in 1963, when frozen foods were a new technology. Tree Top is still owned by the grower's cooperative of over 2,500 members. They market juice and dried apple products around the world.

If there is a lot of something on the market and few people buy it, we say there is a **surplus**. There is not much demand for the supply.

When there are many more buyers than the supply of something, there is a **shortage** of that product. There is a great demand for a small supply.

When there is a shortage of something people want, the price goes up. In 2001, for example, there was a shortage of gas and electricity. Prices increased drastically, but people still continued to drive to work, heat their homes, and run their electric clothes dryers. If they could afford it, many people chose to pay high bills rather than change their lifestyles. Other people, of course, could not afford the high rates and found ways to use less gas and electricity.

*The minimum wage in 2001 was $6.72 per hour.*

### Workers Are Part of Supply and Demand

Employers compete with each other to find workers. If thousands of teenagers want to cut lawns during summer vacation, they will probably all earn low wages. However, if most teenagers wanted to sell clothes in stores, the few who were willing to cut lawns could earn a lot of money.

Fast food stands, for example, are paying much more than they used to. So many people eat out that there is a need for many workers to run hamburger, chicken, and taco stands. The owners have to pay more to get good help.

### Paying Employees

Most businesses hire employees and pay them **wages** or **salaries**. A wage is figured by the hour. A salary is a set amount that is paid each month, no matter how many hours the employee works.

### The Minimum Wage

In Washington, the state **minimum wage** applies to all workers sixteen years of age or older. Younger workers must be paid 85 percent of the minimum wage. If you must work over forty hours a week, the employer has to pay one-and-one-half times

A dock worker at the Port of Seattle cannot be paid below the minimum wage. *Courtesy The Port of Seattle*

## WHAT DO YOU THINK?

**Do you remember reading about the children and teens who worked in factories, logging camps, and mines in the past? How have labor laws such as the minimum wage helped workers? Do you think the laws are good ones? What changes would you like to see made in labor laws?**

your regular wage for time you work past the forty hours.

Who sets the minimum wage? The federal government sets a minimum wage, but states may set their own as long as it does not go below the federal wage. Washington State voters passed a law that set the wage, to be adjusted by the rate of *inflation* every year. Farm workers, who usually receive low wages, must now be paid at least the minimum wage.

## Profit and Loss

Businesses try to make a profit. A profit is the amount of money left after expenses are paid. Expenses include paying workers, suppliers, rent, insurance, taxes, and other things. If a business doesn't have money left after expenses, it has a loss. Companies can't continue to lose money for long, or they will be out of business.

# Working around the State

Have jobs changed in the last 200 years? What education and training do workers need today? Who buys the products and services? This section will answer some of these questions.

## Food for the Nation

More than one-third of the state's land is used for agriculture. In the Puget Sound area, greenhouses and nurseries are built on tiny plots of land. The land west of the Cascade Mountains is used mostly for dairy cows and for growing fruits and vegetables. In the eastern part of the state, wheat farms are often several thousand acres in size. In the Columbia River Basin, farmers grow irrigated nut, peach, apricot, cherry, and apple orchards as well as potatoes, corn, hops, and grapes.

Cattle, pigs, poultry, and milk production are also important to our economy. Farm

Many food preparation workers will be needed in the coming years. Where will the workers fall on the pay scale?

animals are raised in different regions, just as crops are. Dairies and poultry farms are common on the west side of the state. Sheep are raised in the southeast. Cattle ranches are most common in central and eastern regions where livestock graze in the mountains and river valleys.

## The Fishing Industry

Washington's coastline and many rivers make fishing a major source of income. Fishing crews work on the lower Columbia River, the waters of Puget Sound, and off the coast as far as Alaska. Salmon, albacore, herring, halibut, rockfish, cod, flounder, crabs, and ocean perch are caught and sold.

Fish farming, called aquaculture, is also becoming more common. Fish farms along the coastline raise salmon, oysters, and other seafood.

## The Logging Industry

Washington is second in the nation for lumber production. The forests are made up of Douglas firs, ponderosa pines, and hemlocks. Most logging operations and sawmills are located between Puget Sound and the Columbia River. Trees used to be cut just for lumber, but now they are also

*Washington State leads the nation in the number of apples grown. We are second in the nation for potatoes, third for winter wheat, and fourth for barley.*

used to make pulp for paper and cardboard.

In the 1990s, many smaller sawmills went out of business because the supply of trees was limited. When sawmills closed, thousands of jobs disappeared. Towns in timber areas experienced great economic difficulties.

## Manufacturing

Our most important manufacturing industry is aircraft, but companies also build boats, trucks, and other equipment. Aluminum plants, such as Kaiser Aluminum in Spokane, create aluminum used to make airplane parts and soft drink cans.

Many industries came to the state because of the large supply of hydroelectric power. Most industries are near Seattle and Tacoma because of close access to rail lines, seaports, and a large supply of workers.

Food processing plants are important in Washington, too. Flour mills operate in Spokane, Seattle, Tacoma, and Vancouver. Cleaning, sorting, canning, and freezing fruits and vegetables are important jobs. Workers and machines make apples into apple juice and grapes into juice and wine. Dairy products such as milk, cheese, butter, and ice cream are made and sold, too.

The Boeing Company airplane manufacturing plant in Everett covers almost 100 acres. About seventy-four football fields would fit inside the building. Inside, workers assemble jets such as the 747. It takes about eleven months to build an airplane. How much does a 747 cost? Prices start at $165 million.

## That's Electric!

Washington's dam system provides hydroelectric power that is sold to California and other states. That power is sent across the land through heavy-duty power lines.

The dams provide most of the electrical power, but coal-fired electric plants produce 11 percent of the electricity. A single nuclear plant at Hanford produces 7 percent of the state's electric supply.

## The Computer Industry

The computer software industry plays a big role in Washington's economy. Most computer-related businesses are located in the Seattle area. Microsoft Corporation, in Redmond, is the world's leading software manufacturer for personal computers. In 2000, Microsoft sold about $20 billion of software. The company has plants in sixty countries and employs 32,000 people around the world.

## The Largest Employers

In 2001, the companies who hired the most workers in Washington were (in order):

- Boeing Company (Everett, Auburn, Renton)
- University of Washington (Seattle)
- Microsoft Corporation (Redmond)
- Seattle-Tacoma International Airport (Seattle)
- Boeing Defense & Space Group (Kent)
- Washington State University (Pullman)
- South Seattle Community College (Seattle)
- Virginia Mason Hospital (Seattle)
- Mary Bridge Children's Health Center (Tacoma)
- Tacoma General Hospital (Tacoma)
- Fairchild Air Force Base (Airway Heights)

Notice that three schools and a military base are on the list. They are government institutions that employ thousands of people who provide services. They are supported partly by tax money and do not have to make a profit.

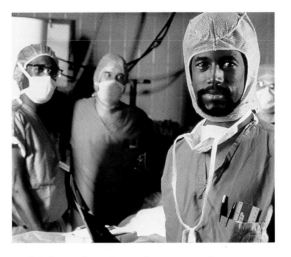

Doctors go to college a minimum of eight to ten years. Surgeons study even longer. They are at the top of the pay scale, although some businessmen earn more.

## Which Jobs Pay the Most?

Sometimes jobs that need the most workers do not pay the highest salaries. While there are lots of jobs for **retail** salespeople, for example, the wages are low. That's because the jobs selling in stores require little education or training. Jobs that require the most education nearly always pay the highest salaries.

**Here are the highest-paying occupations in Washington State (in order):**

Dentists
Physicians and Surgeons
Podiatrists (foot doctors)
Optometrists (eye doctors)
Lawyers
Engineering Department Managers
Mathematics Department Managers
Natural Sciences Managers
Chemical Engineers
Dental Hygienists
Pharmacists
Actuaries (work with insurance)
Firefighters
School Administrators
Police Department Supervisors
Computer Engineers
Elevator Installers
Factory Managers
Real Estate Brokers
Electric Power Managers

(From Washington Employment Security Department, Labor Market and Economic Analysis Branch, 2000)

*The median (middle) household income in Washington state in 1998 was $47,400.*

*The per capita (per person, or per worker) income was $28,700.*

*The median household income includes all working adults who live in the home. Why is household income larger than per capita income?*

## ACTIVITY

### Jobs for Everyone

Today's economy and job market change constantly. The occupations on the chart are expected to have the most new job openings in Washington before 2006.

1. Which occupation will need the most workers?
2. Which jobs require the most education?
3. Which jobs will probably pay the highest salaries?
4. Jobs in logging, mining, and fishing are not listed in this group. Why do you think the number of jobs in those fields is not growing? Look at the list of exports on page 201 and you'll see that lumber products and fish are major exports, but machines have replaced many jobs in these industries.

| JOB | NEW OPENINGS EACH YEAR |
|---|---|
| Salespersons | 5,500 |
| Cashiers | 4,000 |
| Teachers (high school and elementary) | 3,000 |
| Waiters and Waitresses | 2,700 |
| Managers and Executives | 2,500 |
| General Office Clerks | 2,500 |
| Food Preparation Workers | 1,900 |
| Supervisors/Managers | 1,700 |
| Child Care Workers | 1,600 |
| Registered Nurses | 1,300 |
| Information Clerks | 1,300 |
| Computer Engineers | 1,300 |
| Systems Analysts (data processing) | 1,300 |

### A Great Job

**What do workers want from a job?**

- ✔ Steady work without layoffs
- ✔ Fair wages
- ✔ Health insurance
- ✔ Paid sick days, vacations, and holidays
- ✔ Safety in the workplace
- ✔ Appreciation for good work

**What do employers want from workers? They want employees who are:**

- ✔ On time
- ✔ Willing to work
- ✔ Careful
- ✔ Trained to do the job
- ✔ Able to get along with other workers
- ✔ Able to keep customers satisfied

# The Global Market

Ever since the early days when sea otter furs were taken by ship to Chinese markets, Washington's location on the Pacific Rim has been a big advantage in overseas trade. The value of Washington *exports* is higher than any other state. One in every four state jobs depends on international trade.

International trade has always been an important feature of the economy. In earlier times, furs, lumber, canned salmon, wheat, and fruit were exported to distant markets. During the end of the twentieth century, a global market became a reality. Every *commodity*, product, and service is now produced and sold around the world. Computers and the Internet have linked the entire globe in a web of information, trade, and finance.

While trade with Canada has increased because of the Canadian-American Free Trade Agreement, most of the new business has been with Asia, especially Taiwan, China, and Japan.

Boeing airplanes still lead Washington's exports, but computer software, electronics, medicines, aluminum, frozen french fries, and wines are added to the traditional exports of lumber, wheat, fruit, and fish. More than half of the region's wheat crop is exported, with most going into Asian countries.

However, the global market can be brutal. Washington's Red Delicious apples once commanded a high price overseas. Then newer, tastier varieties such as Fuji, Braeburn, and Gala became more popular. Furthermore, labor costs in Chile and China were much lower. Apples from these countries could be sold at a lower price than apples grown in Washington.

China is now the world's leading apple producer. This competition has hurt Chelan and Okanogan Counties, where orchard owners are planting more popular apples. Many growers are planting sweet cherries instead of apples.

*A commodity is any useful thing that is bought or sold. Products of agriculture, mining, or manufacturing are commodities.*

## Washington Exports

| Major Trading Partners (in order of total value) | Top Exports (in order of total sales) |
|---|---|
| Japan | Aircraft/Spacecraft/Parts |
| United Kingdom | Computers/Industrial machinery |
| Canada | Electric machinery/Sound/TV |
| Germany | Cereals |
| South Korea | Medical/Surgical equipment/Photo |
| China | Oil seeds/Grain/Fruit |
| Netherlands | Wood (logs, boards, plywood, chips) |
| Taiwan | Paper |
| Spain | Fish/Crustaceans |
| France | Mineral Fuel/Oil |
| Sweden | Fruit/Nuts/Citrus fruit |
| Turkey | Inorganic chemicals |
| Saudi Arabia | Prepared vegetables/Fruit/Nuts |
| Australia | Vehicles and parts (cars/tractors) |
| | Meat |
| | Aluminum and articles |
| | Toys/Games/Sports equipment |
| | Plastics |

(from Office of Trade and Economic Development, 2001)

1. Which three countries receive the most goods from Washington?

2. What are the top three exported products from Washington?

3. How many times do plant products appear on the list?

4. How many times do products made of metal appear on the list?

5. Which products are probably the most high-tech?

# ENTREPRENEURS

An **entrepreneur** is a person who has a business idea, finds enough capital (money) to start the business and keep it running, organizes the business, hires employees, and takes the risk of entering the market. On this page are some of Washington's creative and hard-working entrepreneurs. Do you recognize any of them?

## Debbie Mumm

Debbie Mumm is a Spokane artist who draws designs used on T-shirts, cookie jars, dishes, calendars, rubber stamps, and fabric. She started by selling books of her own quilt designs. Her company, called Mumm's the Word, employs forty people in Spokane. Over $90 million of her products sold in 2000.

As a young girl, Debbie enjoyed art. She learned drawing, painting, cartooning, and calligraphy. After high school, she studied art at college. Debbie's advice to entrepreneurs: "Start small, find a niche, and promote yourself."

DEBBIE MUMM® | Success

A typical business leadership manual doesn't say anything about the CEO buying movie tickets for the employees, springing for a monthly all-staff lunch out, or inviting the whole crew home for eggnog and homemade cookies. Debbie Mumm isn't your typical CEO.

The CEO and Creative Director at Mumm's The Words regularly puts tubs of licorice in the break room, keeps employee morale high on her priority list, and has been known to strap on a guitar during a staff Christmas caroling night. In return, the highly talented workforce gives Debbie and the company the abilities that have secured Mumm's The Word's position atop the world's quilt and design market.

does best—creating wonderful designs, following each design from concept to final production, and making sure each product fits her vision and high standards of quality.

This formula has worked well for Debbie all of her life, beginning with her childhood when she remembers putting all of her creative energy into a small handmade village which she carefully unpacked each Christmas and set in the same spot in her family's Seattle home. As the years went by, she added accessories to this holiday display, like a tiny sleigh pulled by even smaller reindeer.

"I've always enjoyed art–I love making things and working with my hands," she said.

*"I've always enjoyed art~*
*I love making things and working with my hands."*

Her parents, Richard and Ardis Kvare, encouraged Debbie's creativity, and they praised her early efforts at drawing, cartooning, painting, and calligraphy.

Her story could be lifted from a textbook for success. Start small, find a niche, and promote yourself. Study the market and connect with everyone from the manufacturer to the consumer. Then, throw in all the things Debbie

## Eddie Bauer

Eddie Bauer began selling sporting goods in Seattle in the 1920s. At first, he sold mostly tennis and golf equipment, but his business really grew when he began including fishing tackle and hunting gear. Bauer enjoyed sports and used his experience to help customers choose the best equipment.

In this photograph, taken outside his store in downtown Seattle, Eddie Bauer shows off his fishing tackle and a catch of steelhead trout. Later, he included outdoor clothing, opened other stores, and became a national success.

## Armen Tertsagian and Mark Balaban

Aplets and Cotlets are candy that were created in 1918 by two young men. Armen Tertsagian and Mark Balaban had both emigrated from Armenia. They met each other in Seattle and decided to start a business. First they tried a yogurt factory, but few people had heard of yogurt then.

The men moved to Cashmere, where they bought an apple orchard. Fresh apples were not selling for good prices at the time, so they dried apples to sell. Their company, called Northwest Evaporating, was a good idea because it supplied dried apples to soldiers fighting in World War I.

The men finally decided to use surplus apples to make *rahat locoum*, a popular candy they had enjoyed as children. They called the candy Aplets. Then they created Cotlets from apricots. Today Aplets and Cotlets are sold around the world.

## Harry Brown and J.C. Haley

In 1914, when World War I was beginning in Europe, two young men in Tacoma got an idea for a candy bar they named the Mount Tacoma Bar. They sold the mounds of chocolate in boxes printed with Mount Tacoma on the front. Then Seattle residents began calling the mountain Mount Rainier instead of Mount Tacoma. So in 1923, the men changed the name of their candy bar to just plain Mountain Bar. Machines can now make 592 Mountain Bars per minute, complete with a cherry in the middle!

They're only ugly until you taste them!

Brown and Haley continued experimenting with different recipes until they came up with a log-shaped candy bar coated with chocolate and almonds. They called it Almond Roca.

## Gary Larson

Gary Larson is a world-famous cartoonist. He was born in Tacoma and now lives in Seattle. His clever comics, known as "The Far Side," have been published in more than seventeen languages in 2000 newspapers worldwide. Thirty-one million copies of his books have been sold. His animal cartoons are printed on calendars, mugs, and T-shirts. Larson is now retired, but his cartoons live on.

Where did Gary Larson get his ideas? As a child, he loved to draw, but did not study art. He was a science student at Washington State University when he began publishing cartoons.

Larson's offbeat humor has made him wealthy, and it also earned him the honor of having a species of biting lice and a butterfly named after him!

## Bill Gates

Bill Gates is probably Washington's most famous citizen. His father was a Seattle attorney, and his mother was a schoolteacher. He started programming computers when he was thirteen years old.

In college, Bill met other young men who shared his interest in computers. They created software for home computers and started a company called Microsoft. Windows became an important part of their programs. The company has made Bill Gates the world's wealthiest man.

Finally, the company had such an impact on the Windows computer software that a federal anti-monopoly lawsuit accused the company of being a monopoly. A *monopoly* is when a company has exclusive ownership or rights to a certain kind of business.

Bill and Melinda Gates and their children live in the Puget Sound area. The Gates family are *philanthropists* —wealthy people who give money to others. The Gates Foundation gives millions to support health and learning in poor countries. It also gives college scholarships and develops housing for homeless families.

# The Mighty Dollar

Today, we have a free enterprise economy, but it wasn't always so. American Indians used the barter system to exchange items they had for ones they wanted. People living on the coast gathered small shells and traded strings of them to people living on the plateau for food, skins, moccasins, or tools.

When fur traders arrived, they wanted to buy furs, not shells, so furs became valuable. A beaver skin, called a plew, was used like money. Metal pots and tools, guns, horses, and even slaves were worth a certain number of plews.

Chinese immigrants worked long hours with smelly salmon for very little pay. They often sent part of their money back home to their families.

Traders sometimes used Spanish coins. Later, after gold was discovered in the West, a pinch of gold was called one measure and was used to buy things. Once towns were established, banks printed paper money called bank notes. The holder of a note could come in and exchange it for silver or gold, or use it as money to buy things. The notes were not always reliable, however, because banks sometimes closed or failed to honor the notes.

After a time, state governments printed money, but people in other states sometimes did not trust its worth. The federal government printed paper money and made coins that could be used across the country and around the world. In an effort to get people to trust the value of paper money, an equal value of gold or silver was held in a safe place, but this is not true today.

## WHAT DO YOU THINK?

**Why did people want to use paper money or coins instead of bartering for goods? How do we trade our time and goods for what we want today? What makes our paper money and coins valuable?**

### A Dollar Saved

Saving money is as important as earning it. In the early days, people saved money in fruit jars, under the mattress, or in a hole out in the yard. Today, banks are convenient and safe places to keep savings. Bank savings up to $100,000 are insured by the federal government. That means if the bank fails, the federal government will give you back your savings.

### Cash, Checks, Cards

Today, personal checks, backed up by money deposited in a bank or credit union, are an easy way to pay for things. **Debit cards** can also be used to subtract money from your bank account as you make purchases. **Credit cards**, on the other hand, are a way to postpone paying for things you buy. They add up charges that you pay off in monthly payments. Credit card companies charge for the service of lending you money by adding interest to each month's bill.

## Interest

Banks pay you a small amount of money, called interest, on the money you put into a savings account. You can also buy a certificate of deposit, called a CD, that will earn interest at a higher rate than a savings account. If you purchase a CD, however, you agree to keep the money in the bank for a certain number of months or years—usually at least five years. Some banks also pay interest on money in a checking account.

When you put money into a savings account, a CD, or a checking account, the money doesn't just stay there with your name on it. The bank uses your money to make loans to other people. Those people pay interest on the money they borrow. They pay a lot higher rate of interest than the bank is paying you on your savings. This is one way banks make money to stay in business.

## Why Save?

You can use your savings as a down payment for expensive items. Automobiles, for instance, can be purchased by making monthly payments. If you save enough money to pay half the cost of a car before you buy it, you will only have to borrow enough money for the other half of the cost. You will save thousands of dollars in interest.

## Inflation

It doesn't take a financial expert to realize that the prices of many things have gone up over the years. Inflation is the rate at which prices for everything, from a loaf of bread to a new car, increase over time.

For most of this century, the rate of inflation has averaged about 3% per year. There are some exceptions, thank goodness. Electronic items such as calculators, VCRs, CD players, and laptop computers have gone way down in price because the manufacturers learned better ways to make them.

## The Stock Market

To guard against inflation, people who are serious about seeing their money grow often invest in the stock market. There are no guarantees in any one year, and you may actually lose all your money, but people who invest over many years have received an average of 10% earnings.

*To decrease the amount of interest you pay, borrow less, get the lowest interest rate you can, and pay off the loan as fast as you can.*

## Compound Interest

When credit card companies or banks loan money, they charge **compound interest**. It adds up much faster than interest that is figured as a percent of the total only once. How does compound interest work?

If you are being paid compound interest, every time an interest payment is added to your account—once a day or once a month—it stays there, making the total higher. The next time interest is figured, you get a percentage of the higher amount. Compound interest grows rapidly if the percentage of interest is high enough and if it is added often.

Compound interest works against you if you are the one paying. If you owe money on credit cards, for instance, or are paying off a car loan, you are paying compound interest. By law, banks have to tell you how much total interest you will end up paying on a loan.

Credit cards, however, just keep compounding interest until the loan is paid. The less you pay each month, the longer you are paying interest on the total balance. If you take a long time to repay the loan, you could end up paying more in interest than you borrowed in the first place.

There are many computer programs that can help you figure compound interest, or you can ask a bank for a schedule that lists payments and interest rates.

*"If you will live today like most people won't, you can live in the future like most people can't."*

*How does this saying apply to saving, avoiding debt, and investing?*

Even young workers should start thinking of ways to save and avoid paying interest on credit purchases. *Photo by John Ivanko*

## ACTIVITY

### Save or Spend?

**Save for larger items.** Abby earns money babysitting and mowing lawns. She spends her money quickly on CDs, fast food, and jewelry. Abby's friend Sarah also earns money. She works at a hamburger stand after school. She spends half of her money on clothes and activities with friends, and puts the other half in the bank. She is saving for a car.

**Save to avoid paying interest.** When Sarah first started saving at the bank, she was very disappointed in the low amount of interest her money earned. She was earning about 2.6% interest, but inflation, at 3%, was eating that up. Sarah's parents, however, encouraged her to keep saving. They showed her how much money she would save by not having to borrow money for the car.

### Interest Earned and Paid

**YOU EARN**

| | |
|---|---|
| Savings Accounts at a Bank | 2% to 2.6% |
| CD Certificates at a Bank | 4% to 5% |

**YOU PAY**

| | |
|---|---|
| Credit Cards | 13% to 21% |
| Bank or Credit Union Loans | 9% to 13% |

### How Does It Grow?

Savings Account Starting with $1,000 at 2.6% Interest
(Multiply times 5 if you need $5000 in five years)

| | Ending Balance |
|---|---|
| 1 year | $1,026.25 |
| 2 years | $1,053.20 |
| 3 years | $1,080.85 |
| 4 years | $1,109.23 |
| 5 years | $1,138.35 |

### Debt of $5,000 at 18% Interest

| Length of Loan | Interest Paid | Principal Paid |
|---|---|---|
| 1 year | $845.89 | $677.75 |
| 2 years | $713.31 | $810.33 |
| 3 years | $554.80 | $968.84 |
| 4 years | $365.28 | $1,158.36 |
| 5 years | $138.66 | $1,384.72 |
| **Total paid:** | **$2,617.94** | **$5,000.00** |

Be wise! Beware of credit cards that have very low interest rates for a few months. When the rate goes up, you probably won't even notice. And, if you are a day late in making a payment, you will pay a large late fee—often as much as $30 or more.

Borrowing carefully is justified in some cases. Very few people can save enough for all their college tuition or a new home. But study debt and interest to make wise decisions. If you do borrow, pay off the debt as quickly as you can. Making double and triple payments can save you thousands of dollars.

## CHAPTER 12 REVIEW

1. Give three examples of goods. Give three examples of services that people do to earn money.

2. Describe the free enterprise system.

3. Describe the three ways to form a business—proprietorship, partnership, and corporation.

4. When there is a lot of something, the price usually goes _____. When there is not much of something people want, the price usually goes _____. This is called _____ ____ _____.

5. The lowest wage an employer can pay an employee per hour is called the _____ wage.

6. Name two of Washington's largest employers.

7. Name two Washington entrepreneurs and the companies they started or the products they sell.

8. List three of Washington's industries and what they produce. Example: the logging industry produces paper, boards, plywood, etc.

9. In a global market, what three foreign countries do the most trade with Washington?

10. List five of Washington's top exports.

11. Which three occupations will probably need the most workers by 2006?

12. List five occupations that will probably earn the highest salaries.

13. What system did early American Indians use to exchange what they had for what they wanted? What do we use today to get what we want?

14. What is the difference between a debit card and a credit card?

15. What does the FDIC do for people who save money in a bank?

16. What kind of interest works against you if you borrow money?

17. How can you decrease the amount of interest you pay?

18. What are the advantages of saving money?

## GEOGRAPHY TIE-IN

Only two of Washington's largest companies are outside the Puget Sound region. (See the list on page 199.) Why do you think this is so? Use what you have learned about Washington's major population center (to supply labor and education), the availability of water (rivers and sea-ports), location on the Pacific Rim, and natural resources to draw conclusions about why companies do business in the Puget Sound region.

**THE TIME**
# 1945–1974

**WORDS TO
UNDERSTAND**

absentee ballot
bill
checks and balances
electors
executive branch
federal government
initiative
judicial branch
legislative branch
legislators
lobbyist
political party
precinct
primary election
municipal
referendum
repeal
representatives
veto

# Our State Government

Lawmakers meet
in Olympia.
*Photo by Jeffrey High*

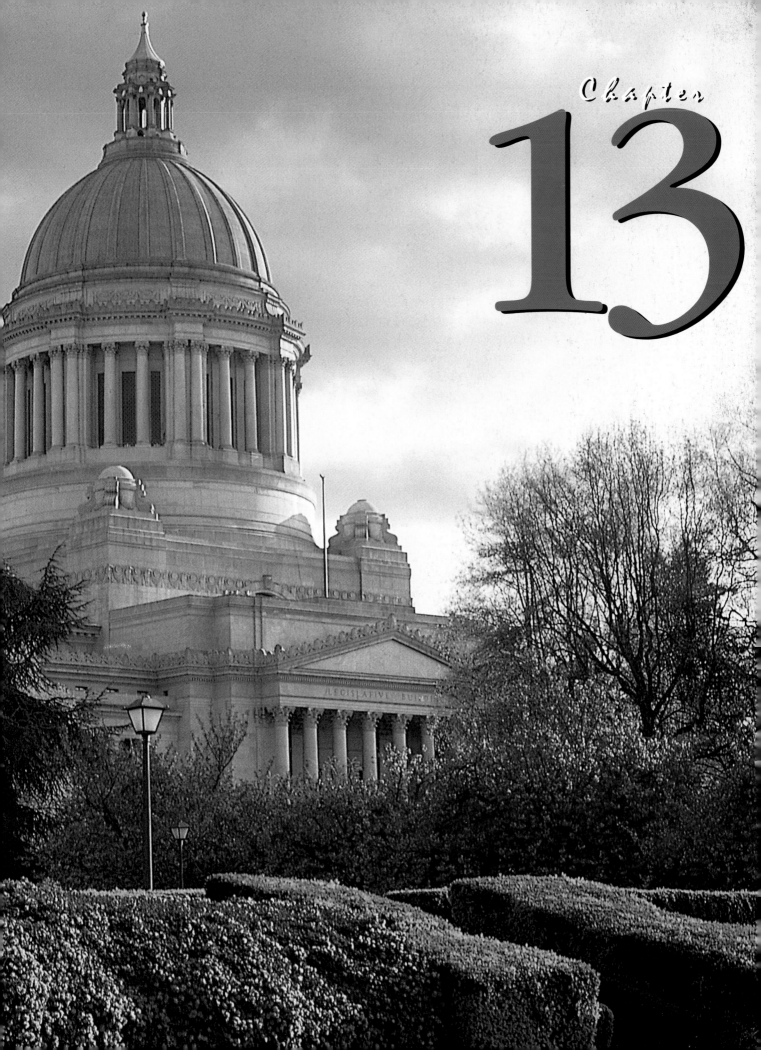

Chapter

13

## People Need Rules and Laws

Whenever people live in groups, they need rules or laws. Families have rules about honesty, respect, housework, homework, and when to be home at night. American Indians had tribal rules. As early settlers traveled to the Pacific Northwest, they followed rules aboard ship or rules set by the wagon train master. Rules help things go smoothly—laws protect people and their rights. Rules and laws reflect what is important to people in a community.

In Washington and all other states, there are several levels of government. The **federal government** makes laws that apply to everyone in the country. Other laws are made at the state level. Rules, called ordinances, are made locally at the county and city levels. We must live by the laws of all the levels of government.

The story goes that George Washington, shown in the center of this painting, did not want to leave his home and family to make the trip to Philadelphia to write the Constitution. James Madison implored him to give of his wisdom, and Washington arrived to lead the convention.

*Painting colored by North Wind*

## Governing the United States

Back in 1787, several years before Robert Gray explored the coast of Washington by ship, fifty-five men met in Philadelphia, Pennsylvania, and began the difficult task of writing a constitution for the United States of America. James Madison, from Virginia, came to be known as the Father of the Constitution because he had studied ancient governments of the world and designed most of the plan for the new government. Other famous men at the convention were George Washington and Benjamin Franklin.

The Constitution was written to limit the powers of government so the people would never have to live under the kinds of tyranny they had seen in European countries. The Constitution is still, after over 200 years, the foundation of our government.

## We the People

*We, the people of the United States, in order to form a more perfect Union, establish justice, insure domestic tranquility, provide for the common defense, promote the general welfare, and secure the blessings of liberty to ourselves and our posterity, do ordain and establish this Constitution for the United States of America.*

–Preamble to the Constitution, 1787

When the Constitution was written, most American men were farmers or merchants. Most women worked at home and on the family farms. Few men and women had much education. Today, over 200 years later, most Americans live in urban areas, work at thousands of kinds of jobs that nearly always include computers, and are educated in public and private schools. In spite of the many changes in the country, the Constitution remains a source of pride and the basis of a government for a free people.

## Changing the Constitution

One year after the Constitution was ratified, Congress added ten important amendments called the Bill of Rights. The men remembered the words of the Declaration of Independence:

*We hold these truths to be self-evident— That all men are created equal; that they are endowed by their Creator with certain unalienable rights; that among these are life, liberty, and the pursuit of happiness.*

The men wanted a guarantee that their new government could never take away their rights. You may be familiar with some of these amendments to the U.S. Constitution:

## Amendments 1-10. Bill of Rights (1791)

These amendments include freedom of religion, speech, and the press. Other freedoms are the right to assemble, to bear arms, the right to a speedy public trial, and

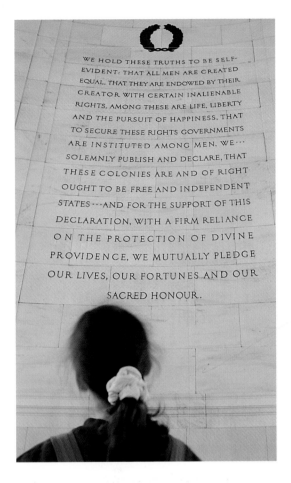

WE HOLD THESE TRUTHS TO BE SELF-EVIDENT: THAT ALL MEN ARE CREATED EQUAL, THAT THEY ARE ENDOWED BY THEIR CREATOR WITH CERTAIN INALIENABLE RIGHTS, AMONG THESE ARE LIFE, LIBERTY AND THE PURSUIT OF HAPPINESS, THAT TO SECURE THESE RIGHTS GOVERNMENTS ARE INSTITUTED AMONG MEN. WE··· SOLEMNLY PUBLISH AND DECLARE, THAT THESE COLONIES ARE AND OF RIGHT OUGHT TO BE FREE AND INDEPENDENT STATES···AND FOR THE SUPPORT OF THIS DECLARATION, WITH A FIRM RELIANCE ON THE PROTECTION OF DIVINE PROVIDENCE, WE MUTUALLY PLEDGE OUR LIVES, OUR FORTUNES AND OUR SACRED HONOUR.

Thomas Jefferson wrote the Declaration of Independence that stated the belief that certain rights were given to men by their Creator, not by government. James Madison later wrote the Bill of Rights.
*Photo by Scott Barrow*

a trial by jury. These amendments are very important to our way of life in America.

The Tenth Amendment is very important. It states that the government has only the specific powers given to it by the Constitution. All other powers remain with the states or the people.

Over the years, people have tried to pass laws that would take away the freedoms granted by the Bill of Rights. The judges of state courts and the Supreme Court of the United States interpret laws as constitutional or unconstitutional. If a law is declared unconstitutional, that law cannot stand.

Study these amendments to see how they have affected your life or the lives of your ancestors:

## Amendment 13. Slavery Abolished (1865)

## Amendment 14. Civil Rights (1868)

Citizenship became a right of anyone born in the United States, including former slaves. It prohibits states from limiting the

---

**Government by the People**

**Democracy:** rule by the majority

**Republic:** citizens elect representatives to make laws

**Federal:** government shared by national, state, and local governments

---

**Forms of World Government**

**Democracy:** rule by the majority

**Monarchy:** rule by a single person

**Oligarchy:** rule by a few (the elite)

rights of citizens. The Supreme Court later outlawed segregation in public schools on the basis of this statement, saying everyone, regardless of race, must have an equal opportunity for education.

### Amendment 15. The Vote (1870)

This amendment insured black males the right to vote. Soon, however, some states made requirements that voters must pass a reading test and pay fees to vote. The laws were unconstitutional and kept most blacks and many other men from voting.

### Amendment 16. Income Tax (1913)

Congress can pass and collect income taxes. Today, income taxes are the federal government's greatest source of revenue.

### Amendment 17. Election of Senators (1913)

Senators would be elected by the voters.

Prior to this, state legislators chose senators to send to Washington, D.C.

### Amendment 18. Prohibition (1919)

This amendment banned people from making, selling, or transporting liquor. It was later *repealed*, or revoked.

### Amendment 19. Women's Suffrage (1920)

Forty years after the first suffrage bill was sent to Congress, women finally won the privilege of voting.

### Amendment 21. Repeal of Prohibition (1933)

This amendment repealed the Eighteenth Amendment and made the making and selling of liquor legal once again.

### Amendment 26. Eighteen-Year-Old Vote (1971)

Before this amendment, states set the voting age. Almost all states had set the voting age at twenty-one.

## The Amendment that Died

Since an amendment will affect millions of people all over the country, a change has to be considered very carefully. An amendment must be approved by Congress and then by three-fourths of the state legislatures. In over 200 years, only twenty-seven amendments have been added to the United States Constitution.

The Equal Rights Amendment, or the ERA, is the most famous amendment proposal. It stated in part: "Equality of rights . . . shall not be denied . . . by the United States or by any state on account of sex."

In 1972, the U.S. Congress passed the amendment, but by 1982, after thousands of demonstrations, TV discussions, and feverish campaigning on both sides, the amendment was still three states short of the required number to approve and so it did not pass.

Many states, however, including Washington, added amendments to their own constitutions that prohibited employers and other agencies from discriminating against either men or women solely on the

basis of sex. No longer could a company pay a man more than a woman for the same job. No longer could state agencies restrict jobs only to men. Positions had to be open to both sexes. Jobs, payment, and privileges had to be based on ability and not gender.

These women worked to get the vote for women in 1902. In 1920, the 19th Amendment made it possible for all women who were citizens to vote. Later, in the 1970s and 1980s, women worked to get the ERA passed, but did not succeed.

# Your Voice in Congress

The Constitution outlines a plan for three divisions, or branches, of government. Each branch has its own powers. Each branch of government also limits the power of the other two. The power of government is divided so that no single branch can become too powerful. This balance of power is a system of **checks and balances.**

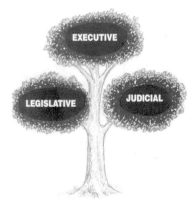

Three branches of government

## The three branches of the national government are:

- **Legislative** (also called Congress, which is made up of two houses—the Senate and the House of Representatives)
- **Executive** (a president, vice president, cabinet, and many agencies)
- **Judicial** (the Supreme Court and lower courts)

Article 1 of the Constitution describes the legislative branch of government:

*All legislative powers herein granted shall be vested in a Congress of the United States, which shall consist of a Senate and House of Representatives.*

It is impossible for all citizens to be experts on the law, and it is impossible for all citizens to attend Congress and vote for laws in person, so the Constitution set up a plan where **representatives** are elected by the people. Then the representatives vote on behalf of the group who elected them.

Voters in each of the fifty states elect two representatives to be part of the U.S. Senate in Washington, D.C. This means that many densely populated states have the same vote as those with fewer people. In the Senate, Washington State gets the same amount of votes as California, Texas, and New York—states that have the largest populations in the country.

The number of people elected to the U.S. House of Representatives, however, is based on population. That means that California, Texas, and New York have many representatives, while the least-populated states have only one. In 2002, Washington had nine representatives. If our population changes a lot, that number may change.

**Representatives to Washington, D.C.**

CONGRESS

| Senate | House |
| --- | --- |
| 2 senators | 9 representatives |

---

**SOME STATE POPULATIONS**
(from largest to smallest)

Each of these states sends two senators to Congress.

| | |
| --- | --- |
| California | 33,872,000 |
| Texas | 20,852,000 |
| New York | 18,976,000 |
| Washington | 5,894,000 |
| Oregon | 3,421,000 |
| Idaho | 1,294,000 |
| Alaska | 626,900 |
| Vermont | 608,800 |
| Wyoming | 494,000 |

Source: U.S. Census, 2000, rounded to nearest thousand

---

## Voting Districts

How does Washington choose its congressmen? The state is divided into regions called districts. The people in each district vote for one representative. Everyone in the state, however, votes for the two senators.

Our representatives travel to Washington, D.C., and serve on a variety of important committees in Congress. Serving on committees allows our representatives to enact federal programs and laws that affect the people in Washington State.

## The Electoral System

The president of the United States heads the Executive Branch. People in all the states vote for the president, but the president is not elected by a direct vote of the people. Instead, the Constitution set up an electoral system to vote for the president.

> *"Each state shall appoint . . . a number of electors, equal to the number of Senators and Representatives . . ."*
> —Article 2, Section 1, U.S. Constitution

Washington's eleven electoral votes all go to one candidate. This means that if sixty out of each hundred Washington citizens voted for Mr. Blue, and forty out of each hundred voted for Mrs. Red, all of Washington's electoral college votes would go to Mr. Blue, and none would go to Mrs. Red.

In fact, electors are not legally bound to vote for anyone. They can choose who to vote for, but they nearly always cast their vote for the person who got the majority of state votes.

## The Judicial Branch

The U.S. Supreme Court is the highest court in the land. The nine judges determine if laws made by Congress are constitutional. Did the Constitution really mean that all people should be treated equally, for instance? Did this mean that African Americans and women could attend any public university? These are some of the hard decisions the court has had to make.

The Supreme Court also hears appeals from people who don't think lower state courts handled their cases properly.

# WILLIAM O. DOUGLAS

William O. Douglas became the only justice of the U.S. Supreme Court from the Pacific Northwest. His father was a minister who brought his wife and young children to eastern Washington, where he died shortly after arriving. Young William grew up in Yakima. He was determined to fight his lameness from polio, so he took long, slow, painful hikes.

Douglas grew up and became a high school teacher in Yakima, but quit to attend law school in New York. He hitchhiked east, hopping freight trains, and arrived in New York with six cents.

After graduating from law school, Douglas held several important positions in government. He worked closely with President Franklin D. Roosevelt, who appointed Douglas to the Supreme Court, where he served longer than any other justice in history.

In addition to Douglas's reverence for law, he loved the land of the Pacific Northwest. Today, there is a large wilderness area named after him.

Douglas served as U.S. Supreme Court justice from 1939 to 1975—the longest time in history.

# Washington's State Government

Before Washington could become a state in 1889, its leaders had to write a constitution and have it approved by the voters. The state constitution followed the national Constitution in many ways. Like the national Constitution, our state constitution includes the three branches of government.

# The Legislative Branch

The state legislature is patterned after the national Congress, but it makes laws only for the state of Washington. Like the national Congress, the state legislature is made up of two parts: the Senate and the House of Representatives.

The state is divided into forty-nine districts of about equal population. Each district sends one senator and two representatives to the state legislature in Olympia. Because the legislature is not in session all year, many of the members have other jobs. *Legislators* are paid a salary for their work as representatives of the people.

• The legislature meets in January each year and stays for sixty days or longer.
• The governor can call special sessions.

### The legislature oversees:

• **Taxes:** determines what to tax and how much the tax will be.
• **Spending:** decides what the state will spend tax money on.
• **Regulations and Policies:** passes laws to protect and govern citizens; regulates state licenses.
• **State Government:** sets rules for branches of government.
• **Local Governments:** gives authority to counties and towns.
• **State Constitution:** makes sure the rights and responsibilities of the state constitution are observed; amends the constitution.

## Committees

The work of the legislature is done in committees. Both political parties appoint members to serve on various committees. All legislators serve on more than one committee.

Committees review proposed laws before they are sent to the rest of the House or Senate for a vote.

Government offices are located in the capital cities of both the state and the nation.

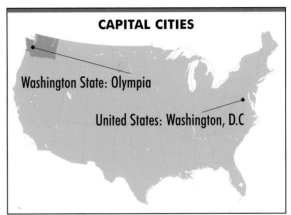

**CAPITAL CITIES**

Washington State: Olympia

United States: Washington, D.C

The state legislature started meeting in the capitol in Olympia in the first part of the twentieth century.

## Lobbyist

*Lobbyists* work for large companies, environmental groups, and others. Groups that want certain bills to pass or not pass pay lobbyists; other lobbyists are volunteers. A lobbyist contacts legislators to give advice and information about the bill.

A lobbyist is often the only person who works full time to understand the issues presented in the bill and so can be a great source of information.

Lobbyists, for instance, work for and against tax breaks for private schools, regulating trade, protecting wild animals and public lands, and making lands and water available to industries and farmers.

# Political Parties

A *political party* is a group of people who have a lot of the same ideas about government. Most people in Washington and the rest of the United States belong to either the Democratic Party or the Republican Party. There are also third parties, such as the Socialist Party, Libertarian Party, Green Party, and Reform Party. Some citizens run for office or vote as Independents. They do not belong to any party.

Political parties work and raise money to get members of their party elected to office.

---

*The following guidelines are some beliefs of the two main parties. Remember that there are always many different beliefs within a party.*

## Democrats

- Government should be wisely used to improve life for all.
- Public education is a high priority and should be fully funded.
- Civil rights should be protected regardless of color, gender, or sexual orientation.
- Pro Choice (the mother should be able to choose whether or not to have an abortion).
- The environment is fragile and should be protected.
- Unions have the right to strike.
- The state has a responsibility to assist the poor, children, and the elderly.
- Health care should be available to everyone regardless of income.

## Republicans

- Government has grown too large and should be downsized.
- Public education is a priority, but private and home schools also have a role.
- Government should not legislate personal responsibility.
- Pro Life (no abortions except in certain cases regarding health of the mother).
- Environmental decisions should be balanced against economic impact.
- Strong businesses provide good jobs, so businesses should be protected.
- The wealthy should not be penalized for making good choices and making money.
- Health care should be available, but it is not a right and is best handled by the private sector.

---

## Which Party?

Washington citizens voted mostly for Republicans between 1900 and 1930. Then, from 1940 to 1990, they elected mostly Democrats to Congress, but still voted for Republicans for govenors. Voters said they made their decisions on issues, not party membership.

## WHAT DO YOU THINK?

- Can a political party whose members share many of the same ideas be more effective than individuals working alone?
- Do you think it is a good idea to vote for a party, or to find out about the candidates on an individual basis?

## How an Idea Becomes a Law

**H**undreds of new **bills** are presented during every state legislative session. The idea for a bill can come from nearly anywhere—citizens, businesses, clubs, organizations, cities, legislative committees, or the governor. Only legislators can introduce a bill to the legislature, however. Once a bill is written up properly, it is introduced to either the House or Senate and assigned to one of the committees.

The committee reviews a proposed bill. If it is approved, the bill moves on to a hearing, where any interested person may testify for or against it. When the hearing is finished, amendments may be added to the bill. Or, a committee can let a bill "die" and not take any more action on it.

If the committee sends a bill on, it goes to the Rules Committee and gets on the calendar to be discussed on a certain day. Senators or representatives debate the bill and then vote. If they pass it,

the bill is reviewed once more by the Rules Committee, then given a final vote. Once it has passed, it is passed on to the other house.

After both houses have passed the same bill, it goes to the governor. Citizens can contact the governor to voice their opinion at this point. If the governor signs it, it becomes law. If the governor does nothing, it becomes law in five to ten days. If the governor **vetoes** it, it dies.

However, if the legislature wants to pass the law in spite of the governor's veto, a two-thirds vote by both houses can override the veto and the bill becomes a law. This is one of the checks and balances of power—neither the executive nor the legislative branch can make a law alone.

The process of turning an idea into a law is long, but it happens a lot. In the 2000 legislative session, over 1,500 bills were introduced. From those bills, 348 bills were passed in Washington State.

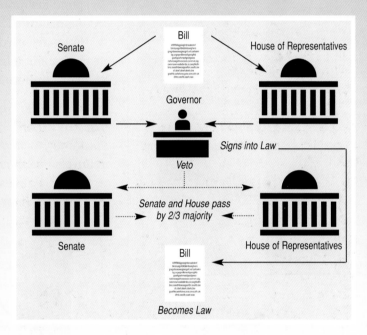

### What Can Citizens Do?

#### A lot! Citizens can:

• Give ideas for laws to their legislators. Many ideas for bills start this way.

• Attend a public hearing on the day the bill is debated, or "heard." It is a good idea to bring as many people as possible to the meeting. They may get to talk to legislators about their experiences.

• Call the governor's office to give an opinion on signing or vetoing a bill.

### Initiative and Referendum

Our state constitution has been amended over seventy-five times. The most important amendments allow for **initiative** and **referendum**. They were added to the constitution in 1912.

An initiative is a powerful way for voters to get new laws passed by submitting signed petitions to the legislature.

The power of referendum allows voters to approve or reject laws already passed by the legislature. Voters do this by submitting signed petitions and then voting on the laws in a general election.

## SOME LEGISLATORS IN 2002

Representative Don Cox, Republican

Representative Velma Veloria, Democrat

Senator Jeralita Costa, Democrat

Senator Paul Shin, Republican

### IN THE PAST

Gladys Kirk served six terms in the House of Representatives, from 1961 until 1973.

Peggie Joan Maxie was also elected to six terms in the House. She served from 1971 to 1983.

### Teenagers in the Legislature?

You might think about applying to serve as a page in the state legislature. Pages help legislators and staff with tasks while the legislature is in session. Student pages work for one week and are paid. Pages must:

*Have a grade point average of C+ or better*
*Get parent/guardian's permission*
*Get school's permission*
*Be sponsored by a Senator*
*Be between 14 and 17 years old*

To request an application or find out more, contact the Secretary of the Senate's office at P.O. Box 40482, Olympia, WA 98504-0482, or check out www.leg.wa.gov/senate/sadm/senpage.htm

# Executive Branch

The executive branch is responsible for carrying out the laws. Officers can be a member of any political party no matter what party the governor belongs to.

**Governor:** executes and enforces the laws and manages state government. The governor:

- hires a staff of hundreds of people.
- presents the legislature with the "State of the State"—a report of how the state is doing and how the governor wants to spend tax money.
- commands the Washington State National Guard.
- can submit bills to the legislature.
- signs bills into law.

Washington's governor has a power many other states do not allow. Our governor may veto an entire bill, or use a "line-item veto" to single sections.

Dixie Lee Ray, a marine biologist, was Washington's first female governor and one of the first female governors in the nation. She was elected in 1976.

**Lieutenant Governor:** serves as president of the state Senate; replaces the governor if he or she is unable to finish a term; acts in place of the governor if the governor is out of the state.

**Secretary of State:** runs state elections; registers corporations; maintains archives and records.

**Treasurer:** is in charge of the state's finances.

**Auditor:** prepares financial information.

**Attorney General:** acts as the chief attorney for the state; gives legal advice to members of the executive branch.

**Superintendent of Public Instruction:** oversees public schools, state education standards, and funding for education.

**Commissioner of Public Lands:** heads the Department of Natural Resources; manages state-owned lands, forests, and water.

**Insurance Commissioner:** regulates insurance companies; serves as the state fire marshal, setting safety standards and investigating fires.

## Judicial Branch

The legislators make the laws, but it is up to the judicial branch—the courts—to determine exactly what the laws mean. How many times have you heard on the news that a law was judged unconstitutional? That means that judges decided a law took away the rights that are guaranteed in the U.S. Constitution and its Bill of Rights or in the Washington State constitution.

The highest court in Washington is the state Supreme Court. It is made up of nine judges, each elected by state voters. Candidates run for election without being sponsored by any political party.

Below the Supreme Court are other courts. They include the court of appeals, superior court, justice-of-the-peace courts, and *municipal* (city) courts.

How are judges paid? Judges are not paid from fees and fines, as some people think. Their salaries come from taxes each citizen pays.

# GARY LOCKE

**G**ary Locke was elected as Washington's governor in 1996, making him the first Chinese-American governor in U.S. history.

Until he was six years old, Gary lived in a public housing project in Seattle. He played with other children whose fathers had served in WWII. The family of five children was poor, but they all worked hard and studied to get an education. As he grew up, Gary worked in his father's grocery store, became an Eagle Scout, and graduated from high school. Then he graduated from Yale and got a law degree from Boston University.

Locke worked as a deputy prosecutor in King County and then was elected to the state House of Representatives.

As governor, Locke pushed to hire more school teachers to reduce class size, improved struggling schools, and created the Washington Reading Corps to help students learn to read. He also signed into law a welfare reform bill that reduced the number of families on welfare. He helped create more jobs by giving tax relief to businesses.

Governor Locke and his wife Mona are the parents of a son and a daughter.

# Local Government

Besides federal and state government, we also have governments that are closer to home. We live under the laws of all levels of government. Each level includes the three branches of government.

## Counties

Washington is divided into thirty-nine counties. One town in each county is the county seat where the county government is located. Each county is run by three county commissioners. They are elected to four-year terms. Washington's two largest counties—King and Pierce—are ruled by a council.

## City Governments

Washington has about 270 municipal governments. Each is governed by one of the following:

- Mayor and city council
- City manager and city council
- Commissioners

The city council acts as a legislative branch and the mayor acts as the chief executive.

Both counties and cities make rules called ordinances. They also collect tax money and spend it on services.

City governments usually provide services only to people living in the city. They may provide police and fire protection, water, sewage, streets, libraries, and hospital services.

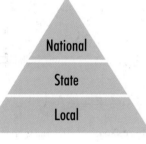

## LEVELS OF GOVERNMENT

| Branch | National | State | Local: County | Local: City |
|---|---|---|---|---|
| Legislative | Congress | State Legislature | Commission | City Council |
| Executive | President | Governor | Commissioners | Mayor or City Manager |
| Judicial | Federal Courts | State Courts | County Courts | Traffic Court, Others |

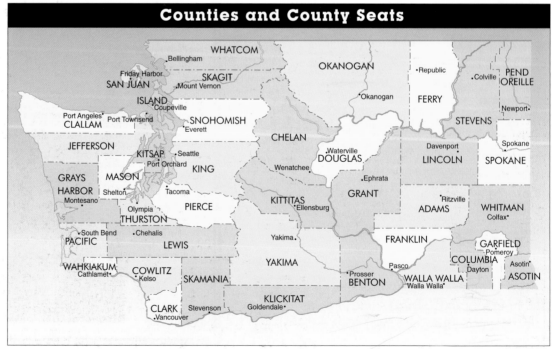

**Counties and County Seats**

# Government Services

Today, national, state, and local governments do more than make laws and enforce them. They do more than tax people. Governments have established many agencies that regulate many activities of the citizens and provide services.

State and local governments collect taxes to establish and pay for public education, roads, police and fire protection, libraries, public health services, job services, welfare support, and many other services.

Washington State helps the unemployed, disadvantaged children, the elderly, disabled people, and the mentally ill get cash for food, clothing, and shelter. However, adults in good health who receive assistance from the state are required to seek jobs through the state's Work First program. Work First provides job training and counseling to help people find jobs.

Vocational Rehabilitation is a state agency that helps handicapped and disabled people train for and find jobs.

The Employment Security Department helps all people find jobs through Job Service. The office matches workers and employers. It also provides money to help workers who have been laid off to cover expenses until they find a new job.

Firefighters are trained and paid with tax dollars. In 2001, wildfires burned thousands of acres of beautiful forests. Firefighters came from many states to help local firefighters control the blazes.

Roads and freeways are paid for with tax dollars. They are built and maintained by local, state, and national government agencies.

---

## ACTIVITY

### The Role of Government

The authors of the U.S. Constitution gave the national government power to provide only a few limited services that the Constitution calls powers. Here are some of them:

**Section:**

**8.1. Taxation.** The Congress shall have power to lay and collect taxes . . .

**8.2. Credit.** To borrow money on the credit of the United States.

**8.3. Commerce.** To regulate commerce with foreign nations, and among the several states, and with the Indian tribes.

**8.5. Money.** To coin money, regulate the value thereof . . . and fix the standard of weights and measures.

**8.7. Post Office.** To establish post offices and post roads [toll roads].

**8.11. War.** To declare war . . .

**8.12 Armed Forces.** To raise and support armies.

**8.13. Navy.** To provide and maintain a navy.

Many other services are provided by your local and state governments. Do you agree or disagree with the government providing these services? Do you agree or disagree with paying taxes to support the services? Would you prefer that private companies provide the services and charge for them? Would you like to see more or less services by the government? Why or why not?

# Education

Public schools are also a government service. Tax dollars are used to pay for school buildings, teacher's salaries, and textbooks. If you attend a private school, your parents pay a fee for your education.

Since state and local tax money is used to pay for public education, the state legislature can require school districts to do certain things. In 2000, Washington's legislature gave new guidelines that stated that students must attend 180 days of classes each school year. They must meet standards in core subjects—reading, writing, science, social studies, communication, mathematics, health and fitness.

## Local School Districts

The voters of each school district elect members of the school board. The boards adopt policies to fit local needs, make decisions about teachers and school staff, set learning standards, and help choose teaching materials.

## ACTIVITY

### Higher Education

Washington students can study a wide variety of subjects after high school graduation. The state has five universities, one state college, and twenty-seven two-year colleges. Other schools teach subjects such as auto mechanics, welding, carpentry, secretarial work, and other subjects designed to help people make a living. There are colleges for future dentists, doctors, and nurses.

Match each college and university with the town where it is located. Research the schools, colleges, and universities in your city. What do they charge for tuition? What degrees can you get there, and in what subjects? Is student housing available? How do you apply for scholarships?

| | |
|---|---|
| University of Washington | Pullman |
| Washington State University | Olympia |
| Eastern Washington University | Bellingham |
| Western Washington University | Seattle |
| Central Washington University | Cheney |
| Evergreen State College | Ellensburg |

Dave Allen celebrates after graduating from Western Washington University, 2001.

# The Power of the Vote

Voting is a very important privilege of the American people. Our state and national constitutions guarantee that all adult citizens can help create and operate their government. How do we do that? By voting for representatives and leaders.

Public servants usually want to represent the ideas of the people who elected them. If they don't, they may be replaced at the next election.

## Registering

At least a month before you can vote for the first time, or after you move, you must register to vote. This is so people can't vote over and over again in different places in the same election.

Ask others in your family or your neighborhood where and when to register, or find a form in your phone book in the government section. In many places, you can register where you apply for a driver's license. You will need proof that you are at least eighteen years old and will have to give your address. When you register, you will be told what ***precinct*** (voting region) you live in and where to vote.

## Voting

When you vote, your name will be checked on a list of registered voters. Then you will receive a ballot. You can ask for help if you don't understand how to vote, cannot read the ballot for any reason, or have a disability that prevents you from voting in the voting booth.

If you cannot go to the polling place to vote, you can request an ***absentee ballot***, and vote by mail before the election is held.

It is important for citizens to vote when elections are held. It is even more important that they know as much as possible about the political parties, the candidates,

and any amendments or initiatives they will be voting on. There is always a lot of information in newspapers around voting time.

## Primary Elections

Before the general election, a ***primary election*** is held to decide who will be on the ballot from each political party. Each political party can only sponsor one candidate. If three or more Republicans, for instance, wanted to run for governor, the voters would vote in a primary election. The Republican candidate who got the most votes in that election would run in the general election.

*Before you are old enough to vote, you can post signs or pass out flyers. You can remind adults to vote.*

## American Responsibilities

**Along with rights and privileges come responsibilities.**

- You have the privilege of voting at age eighteen, so you should study the issues before you vote.
- You have the right to freedom of religion, so you have the responsibility to respect the right of others to belong to a different religion, or no religion at all.
- You have the right to free speech, but you have the responsibility to speak respectfully and kindly to others, and to listen to their point of view without ridicule.
- You have the right to a jury in court, so when you are old enough, you will have the responsibility to serve on a jury.

What other privileges and responsibilities do you have?

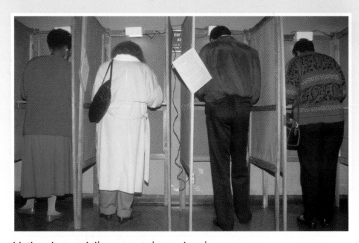

Voting is a privilege we take seriously.

## CHAPTER 13 REVIEW

1. What are the three levels of government in the United States today?

2. Who is called the Father of the Constitution?

3. "We, the people of the United States . . ." is the beginning of what important government document?

4. Define: republic, federal.

5. Define: democracy, monarchy, oligarchy.

6. Why was the Bill of Rights added to the U.S. Constitution?

7. Which amendment abolished slavery? Which amendment gave women the right to vote?

8. Name the three branches of government and give an example of each branch.

9. In the United States, the voters elect _____ to vote for laws.

10. How many senators does each state send to the U.S. Congress?

11. Who elects the president of the United States?

12. What is the highest court in the nation?

13. The capital city of Washington State is _____.

14. Which month does the state legislature start meeting each year?

15. Most of the work of the legislature is done in groups called _____.

16. What can citizens do with the "initiative"?

17. Name two duties of the governor of the state.

18. Courts are part of which branch of government?

19. The governor of Washington State is _____.

20. Name the two largest political parties.

21. Define what local government is and two of the services it provides.

22. Where does the money used to pay for public education come from?

## GEOGRAPHY TIE-IN

Look at a map of the United States and locate Washington, D.C. (between Maryland and Virginia). If you were elected as a senator or a representative from Washington State to go to Washington, D.C. to help make laws for the nation, how far would you have to travel?

If you traveled by airplane, what states, large mountain ranges, and large rivers might you fly over? What direction would you travel? What ocean would you leave behind in the West? What ocean would you be close to in the East? What kinds of landforms would you see across the country? What natural features? What features have been changed by people?

## The Branches of Government

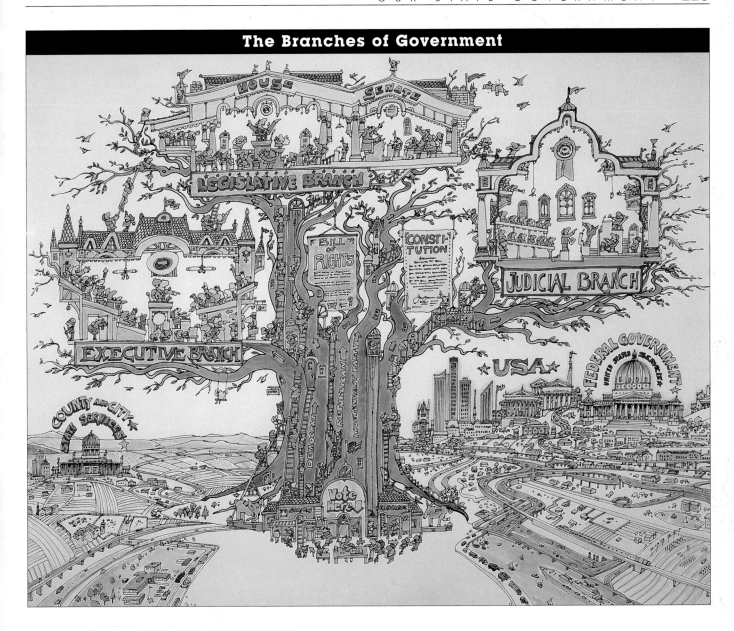

## ACTIVITY

### It's Your Government!

Remember, all **levels of government**—national, state, and local—have three **branches of government**—legislative, executive, and judicial.

This means that laws are made in the legislatures of both Washington State and Washington, D.C. It means that a president is head of the executive branch of the United States, and a governor is head of the executive branch of a state. There are courts at all levels.

Look at the drawing above.

1. Find the two documents that are the basis for our government today.
2. Find the symbols of the political parties.
3. Find the people voting for representatives who will vote in the legislature.
4. Find the two houses in the legislative branch. Remember, both houses must pass all bills. Who must sign them before they become law?
5. Find the people going from one branch to the other to get billls passed.
6. Find the jury and the judge in the judicial branch.

# Glossary

The definitions for words are as they are used in the chapters.

**abolitionist**: a person who tried to end the practice of slavery

**abrasive**: smoothing out a rough surface

**absentee ballot**: a ballot that can be mailed in

**adamant**: having a strong opinion

**adversary**: someone who is against someone else; an opponent

**affluence**: having a lot of money

**aghast**: struck with amazement or horror; shocked

**agribusiness**: the business of making money by growing crops and raising animals

**amendment**: an addition or change to a constitution

**animism**: a belief that both living and non-living things have spirits

**aquifer**: a layer of rock that holds water

**ardent**: with much feeling

**arid**: very dry

**barter**: to trade without the use of money

**basalt**: gray or black fine-grained igneous rock; cooled lava rock

**bill**: a written idea for a law submitted to the legislature

**bounty**: money paid to a person for killing certain animals

**breach**: to make a gap or break, such as in the walls of a dam

**cache**: a large supply hidden from view

**capital**: money and goods needed to start a business

**capitalism**: an economic system where land and businesses are owned and run by citizens, not the government

**capitalist**: a person of wealth; a person who supports private ownership of land and business

**cataracts**: large waterfalls over steep cliffs

**Caucasian**: of European ancestry; non-Indian and non-African

**censorship**: the action of examining publications for objectionable statements

**checks and balances**: a system that limits the power of any one branch of government

**civilian**: not in the military

**clear-cut**: a place where all of the trees have been cut down

**coerce**: to force

**commercial**: having to do with selling

**commodity**: any useful thing that is bought or sold; products of agriculture, mining, or manufacturing

**communism**: a system where land and businesses are owned and run by the government

**compound interest**: interest that is figured on both the original amount of the loan plus accrued interest

**compromise**: an agreement where both sides give up part of what they want to solve a conflict

**condensed milk**: milk from which part of the water has been removed; canned milk

**confluence**: the flowing together of two or more streams

**conservation**: a careful preservation and protection of something, especially land and natural resources

**conspiracy**: a plot or secret agreement to do an unlawful or wrongful act

**continental drift**: the theory that the earth's continents were one land mass and then drifted apart

**cooperative**: an organization owned and operated for the benefit of those using its services

**coroner**: a person who investigates unusual deaths

**corporation**: a group of people authorized by law to invest money to start or run a business

**coulee**: a dry streambed; a small shallow ravine

**credit card**: a card that authorizes purchases on credit and accumulates interest

**debit card**: a card where the cost of purchases will be subtracted from a bank balance without incurring interest

**decade**: a period of ten years

**decimate**: to kill a large number of the population

**decompose**: to decay or rot

**deficient**: not having enough

**degradation**: the decline or ruin of

**delude**: to mislead or trick someone

**deluge**: a heavy rain

**dentalium shells**: long thin seashells worn as jewelry and used for trade by Native Americans

**derogatory**: uncomplimentary; belittling

**desecrate**: to treat with lack of respect

**destitute**: having almost no means of financial support; without the necessities of life

**dilapidated**: run down, shabby, or out of repair

**domestic arts**: skills relating to housework; cleaning, cooking, sewing

**domestic servant**: a person who does housework

**dormant**: temporarily inactive

**down payment**: the money given at the time a loan is arranged

**ecology**: the study of the interrelation of animals and plants with their environment

**economics**: the making, buying, and selling of goods and services

**ecosystem**: a community of living things that interact and depend on each other

**electors**: people selected to vote (for president)

**elusive**: hidden from view

**entrepreneur**: a person who starts and runs a business

**erratic**: a huge boulder carried long distances by a glacier

**evacuate**: to leave

**executive branch**: the branch of government that carries out the laws

**exodus**: a mass departure

**exploit**: to use to an unfair advantage

**exports**: goods shipped out for sale

**fastidious**: having high standards

**fault lines**: breaks in the earth's crust, with displacement of earth and rock on one side

**federal government**: the level of government for all the United States

**feminism**: having to do with women's issues and rights

**finite**: having definite limits

**fissure**: a long crack in the earth's crust

**fjord**: a narrow inlet of the sea between steep cliffs

**forensic anthropologist**: a person who determines the cause of death of ancient humans

**formidable**: causing fear or dread

**fraud**: deceit, especially to get someone to part with something of value

**free enterprise**: an economic system where citizens own and control most production, buying, and selling

**geography**: the study of the earth and the location and activities of the people, plants, and animals living on it

**geologic time**: the long time period of the earth's history as defined by scientists

**geologist**: a scientist who studies rock and land formations to learn the history of the earth

**goods**: items that are made, bought, and sold

**grade** (roads): to smooth out the ground to make a road

**groundwater**: water that is naturally in the ground

**habitat**: the place where a plant or animal lives

**headwaters**: where a river starts

**heavy metals**: lead, zinc, cadmium, and arsenic

**hinterland**: land isolated from other places by distance and access

**human characteristics**: land features made by people

**humane**: having compassion or consideration

**hydroelectric**: relating to electricity produced by water-powered generators

**igneous rock**: rock that came from the interior of the earth as lava

**immortal**: exempt from death; living forever

**immunity**: resistance to disease

**incense**: to make very upset and angry

**industrial arts**: skills relating to industry; carpentry and the use of machines

**inferior**: of lower quality or importance

**infirmary**: a place where the sick are taken care of

**inflation**: a rise in the general price level of goods and services

**initiative**: a process by which citizens can write a bill and get it on the ballot for the voters to pass or defeat

**insatiable**: not able to get enough

**irony**: a result or outcome opposite of what was expected

**judicial branch**: the branch of government that interprets the law and determines punishment

**Kanaka**: a Hawaiian man

**lahar**: huge mudflow filled of volcanic debris, rock, and water

**leach**: to seep or pass down through the soil

**legislative branch**: the branch of government that makes the laws

**legislators**: members of Congress; men and women who are elected to make laws

**libel**: a statement that defames or ruins another person's character

**lobbyist**: a person who studies issues and works to get legislators to vote for or against bills

**loess**: soil believed to be mainly deposited by wind

**longshoremen**: workers who load and unload ships

**lucrative**: producing wealth

**mass transit**: buses, trains, or subway systems that move large numbers of people at a time

**median**: the middle

**menial**: requiring little skill

**migrant**: a person who moves regularly to find work, especially in agriculture

**minimum wage**: the lowest amount of money a business can pay an employee

**molten**: melted by high heat, as in liquid rock

**monopoly**: when one company has exclusive ownership and control of a type of product

**motley**: a mixture of different or unusual people

**municipal**: of the city

**negotiate**: to talk to another person or group to settle a matter

**Paleo-Indians**: the first people who lived on the American continents

**partnership**: when two or more people own a business

**per capita**: per person

**philanthropy**: the generous giving of money to worthy causes

**physical features**: the natural landforms and characteristics of a place

**placid**: calm, smooth

**political party**: a group of people who have similar ideas about government

**porcelain**: the material ceramic dishes are made from

**potlatch**: a large celebration of feasting and gifts held to celebrate a special event

**precinct**: a voting region

**primary election**: the first election held to narrow down the list of candidates

**proprietorship**: when one person owns a business

**protohistoric**: when there was a drastic change in the lifestyle of the American Indians

**radical**: drastic, extreme

**radioactive**: having nuclear properties

**ransom**: money paid to get back someone who has been kidnapped

**ration**: a small supply given on a regular basis

**reactor**: a machine that produces nuclear energy

**recall**: to remove a person from public office

**reclamation project**: a large project, such as the building of a dam, whose purpose is to make better use of the land

**referendum**: a process by which legislative bills are put on the public ballot

**relief** (art): where a design is above the background

**repatriate**: to return artifacts to the place of origin

**repeal**: to cancel (a law) by official authority

**representative**: a person elected to make laws for the whole group

**resurrect**: to rejoin the spirit and the body

**retail**: having to do with selling in stores

**retaliate**: to fight back

**revenue**: money brought in from a sale

**sabotage**: the destruction of property or materials

**salary**: a set amount of money paid by the week or month

**sanitation**: relating to health, cleanliness, disposal of human waste

**sedimentary** rock: rock formed from

sand, soil, rocks, and shells

**segregation**: the separation of people, usually based on race or gender

**semiarid**: partly dry or dry much of the time

**services**: in economics, work people do to earn money

**shaman**: a Native American spiritual leader who healed the sick

**shortage**: when there is more demand than the supply of goods

**sovereignty**: self-rule; freedom from external control

**spawn**: to produce and deposit large numbers of eggs

**spoils**: goods taken from an enemy of war

**strait**: a narrow passageway of water that connects two large bodies of water

**subsidy**: money or land given by the government

**subsistence**: barely supporting life

**suburb**: a place where people live outside the city

**suffrage**: the right to vote

**superior**: of higher quality or importance

**supply and demand**: when both the amount of goods available and the number of buyers affect the price

**suppress**: to put down or to stop

**surpass**: to go beyond or go farther

**surplus**: goods left over after the demand is met

**suspend**: to cause to stop temporarily

**tailings**: what is left over after metals are separated from earth or rock

**tectonics**: a branch of geology concerned with the crust of the earth and its folds and faults

**temperate**: not extremely hot or cold

**transient**: a person who stays in a place briefly; a person who travels in search of work

**tributaries**: smaller streams and rivers that flow into a river

**tule**: bulrushes used by Native Americans to make mats and houses

**vengeance**: punishment for an injury or offense

**veteran**: a person who has fought in war

**veto**: to officially turn down or reject a bill to stop it from becoming a law

**vigilante**: a person who takes it upon himself to punish others

**voyageur**: a man who transported furs by canoe

**vulnerable**: easily harmed

**wage**: money paid to an employee by the hour

**warehousemen**: workers in a warehouse

**weir**: a type of fence across a stream that aids in catching fish

**witness tree**: a tree carved with lot numbers indicating that property was claimed

# Credits

## MAPS
Knudsen, Scott
Rasmussen, Gary (hand-drawn maps)

## ART
British Library, London  58
Clymer, John  82 r
Esposito, Robert  (Panorama Designs)
    8 c, 56-57
Harper's Weekly  90
Rasmussen, Gary  2-3 b, 9
Russell, Charles  67
Sohon, Gustavus  93

## PHOTOGRAPHS
Allen, Donna  222
American Heritage Center  139
American Museum of Natural History
    45 b
Amon Carter Museum, Fort Worth  67
Arizona Historical Society  136
Associated Press AP  188, 190
Axtell  100, 101
Barrow, Scott  211
Boeing  198
Buffalo Bill Historical Center  82 r
California Historical Library, San
    Francisco  92 t, 106 b, 114
Carlson, Laurie Winn  78
Center for Pacific Northwest Studies
    105 l
Cheney Cowles Museum/Eastern
    Washington State Historical Society,
    Spokane  49 all, 50, 71, 110, 130,
    131, 140, 150 all, 151 all, 161, 162-
    163
Chesley, Paul  185
Chicago Historical Society  112
Columbia River Exhibition  183
Conboy, Larry  53
Curtis, Asahel  30, 106 t, 115
Curtis, Edward  96, 121, 122
Dartmouth College Library, Rauner
    Special Collections  63
Della Piana, Leandro  83
Denver Public Library  79 t
Discovery Channel Pictures  221 t
Feryl, Elizabeth  184
Fort Vancouver  70 c

Green, Mike  9, 15 b, 31 t,  41 all, 48 b,
    127 b, 142, 151 b,  182 all, 186 all,
    189 all
High, Jeffrey  208-209

Hopkinson, Glen  74-75, 81
Illinois State Historical Society,
    Springfield  80, 91, 92 b
Ivanko, John  206
Jacobsen, Karen  28 l
Kiver, Eugene  12 b, 27 all
Kleinknecht, Gary  32
Lange, Dorothea  148 all
Liberty Orchards  192-193, 203 l, 203 b,
Library of Congress  66 c,
Lincoln County Historical Society  126,
    127,
Los Angeles Dept. of Water and Power
    111 b
MacNulty, Barbara  15 t
McKinney, Bill  31 c
Microsoft  203 r
Mumm's the Word  202
Murray, Barbara  16 r, 19 t r, 31 b, 113
Museum of History and Industry,
    Seattle  61 t, 95 b, 96, 99 t, 99 l, 100
    t, 101 all, 103 all, 104, 105 t, 106 t,
    124, 128-129, 137, 146, 157, 168,
    175, 187
NASA  178-179
National Archives  172
North Central Washington Museum
    117 b
Northwest Museum of Arts and
    Culture/Eastern Washington State
    Historical Society, Spokane  142,
    181
Northwind  210
Office of the Governor  219
Ohio Historical Society  153, 212
Oregon Historical Society  45 t, 48 c,
    51, 52 t, 52 b, 64 l, 64 b, 66 t, 69 b,
    70 t, 72 c, 77 all, 79 b, 88-89, 93 l, 97
    all, 102 all, 120 b, 155, 156, 204
Oltersdorf, Jim  20 l
Pefley, Chuck  2-3, 13 all, 17 b, 18, 21,
    166 b, 169, 171
Sammis, E.M.  95, 99 l
Smith, Lori  29
Spokane Public Library  117 c
*Spokesman-Review*  120 t
Steen, Trygve  185 t
Stevens, Otto  16 l, 16 b
Stradling, Dale  33 l
Taylor, F.E.  102 b
Thompson, Jan  173
Till, Tom  front cover  9, 22-23, 26,
    36-37, 43
Timberline Press, Portland  33
*Tri-City Herald*  38
University of Arizona Library  158
University of Oregon  118

University of Utah Libraries  174
University of Washington Libraries 132,
    133, 138, 141
Walter, Sunny  4 l, 4 b, 8 t, 12 b, 19 b r
Washington State Historical Society at
    Tacoma  44, 46, 55, 86, 100 c, 108-
    109, 115, 117 t, 119, 121, 122, 144-
    145
Whitman Mission National Monument
    78
Wilse, Anders  103 b
Wilson, Doug  28 b
Wing Luke Asian Museum  175
Yakima Valley Museum  21
Youngs, Bill  180

All photos not listed are from the personal collection of the publisher.